Volume 3

Train the Trainer Guide

Training Programs

A Compilation of Basic Workplace
Learning Programs

Info-
line

An Info-line Collection

ASTD

*Linking People,
Learning & Performance*

Info-line is a series of "how-to" reference tools; each issue is a concisely written, practical guidebook that provides in-depth coverage of a single topic vital to training and HRD job performance. *Info-line* is available by subscription and single copy purchase.

ISBN: 1-56286-280-4
Library of Congress Catalog Card No. 00-110773

Printed in the United States of America.

Volume 3   Train the Trainer Guide

Training Programs
A Compilation of Basic Workplace Learning Programs

Editor
Cat Sharpe Russo

Contributing Editor
Ann Bruen

Production
Kathleen Schaner

Introduction

Dear Readers,

Today, workplace learning and performance is experiencing a ground swell of activity. Propelled by emerging technology and ever-increasing demands on productivity and process reengineering, management at all levels in all organizations is calling on the training department to come up with answers. Whether it is called training, performance improvement, workplace learning, or on-the-job education, the way individuals learn and the steps trainers use to put learning into place remain grounded in solid principles of adult learning, presentation skills, curriculum design, evaluation, and technology.

Since its inception in 1984, *Info-line* has provided readers with a quick, useful means of acquiring new information and applying that information on the job. Many people use *Info-line* as a tool for new trainers, to bring them up to speed without spending too much time studying "the books"—*self-directed learning* before the term was ever popular. The fact that the training profession sees new entrants every day is one of the reasons *Info-line* has been so successful. Because practitioners seem to enter, leave, and reenter the field frequently, *Info-line*'s founding mission of being "the training reference tool" with a long shelf life has become a self-fulfilling prophecy.

Realizing that many of our issues needed updating, we undertook a four-year project to revise a substantial number of our oldies, but goodies. At the same time, we made a concerted effort to publish new topics that reflected feedback from our reader surveys. Combining more than 75 revised titles with 60 new issues, we have now put together a comprehensive *Train the Trainer Guide*, which is divided into five volumes. Beginning with the foundations for training, each volume focuses on a specific area that not only helps novice practitioners acquire new knowledge but also serves as a handy reference tool for seasoned practitioners.

Here is how we devised the volumes:

Volume 1: Foundations & Delivery. Containing everything you need to get started as a trainer, this collection pays special attention to learning and training styles, good learning environments, facilities set-up, and presentation skills.

Volume 2: Instructional Design & Implementation. After reading this volume, you will have an essential understanding of instructional design and how to develop a training curriculum. As an introduction, you can learn project management and budgeting skills, vital to any curriculum developer.

Volume 3: Training Programs. Here are programs you can implement. Selected from our most popular issues, the contents of this volume will get you started with facilitation and workshop skills. Using this foundation, you then can move on to presenting programs based on these titles: orientation, mentoring, succession planning, change management, and much more.

Volume 4: Measurement & Evaluation. The best way to quantify the results of your training is to measure and evaluate those results. Here is an all-inclusive volume that details how to collect data from numerous sources, including benchmarking, focus groups, paper evaluations, and so forth. Then you will have all the methods available for calculating your return-on-investment as well as special evaluation practices.

Volume 5: Applying Technology to Learning. Emerging technology, especially e-learning, is having a major impact on training and the delivery of training. This collection gives you the best learning technologies and e-learning concepts for training applications.

Whether you are using an individual volume by itself or as part of the complete set, I hope you find these books a useful addition to the *Info-line* series of collections.

Sincerely,

Cat Sharpe Russo
Editor

How to Facilitate

How to Facilitate

Editorial Staff for 9406

Editor
Barbara Darraugh

Consultant
Don Aaron Carr

Revised 1999

Editor
Cat Sharpe

Contributing Editor
Ann Bruen

Production Design
Anne Morgan

Getting Teams to Work

The EXITS Publishing Company was experiencing difficulties in maintaining inventory on the rapidly increasing sales of a popular how-to book series. The organization wrote, published, marketed, and filled orders, handling all aspects in-house. As a result, this product required input and actions from many different units in the organization:

- customer service
- fulfillment
- editing and design
- product management
- accounting
- computer services

Although product sales were growing, the product manager frequently heard complaints about the handling of the product from the other area managers. Customer service and fulfillment often ran out of stock and became frustrated when clients ordered an unavailable issue. Accounting had difficulties with the computer reports it received. And the product manager often had to intervene in the process to soothe ruffled feathers and order emergency restocking of the product.

After several years, the organization instituted total quality management and decided to form a quality team to address what was considered to be an inventory problem. Through its total quality management mechanism, the organization brought together managers in each of the departments to discuss the problem. Each of the managers—Sara from customer service, Dan from fulfillment, Paula from accounting, Tom from computer services, and George, the product manager—were very enthusiastic about finally having a forum in which to address a problem that affected them all and that they had been unable to solve individually. They were hopeful that with the tools taught to them during their quality training, easy solutions to their problems would be found quickly and simply. They happily scheduled their first meeting.

At the first meeting, Dan told Sara that she needed to keep better track of orders, that too often his staff received back orders on items in stock and orders for items that weren't in stock. Sara refused to be accountable, noting that the responsibility for reordering rested with George. An argument broke out between Sara and George, who said he couldn't keep track of the inventory, since he received reports from her sporadically and always too late to help. Sara then attacked Tom, saying the computer generated the late or inaccurate reports.

Tom noted the "garbage in, garbage out" theory of data processing. Paula attacked the computer reports and Tom's handling of them. Sara left the meeting feeling she had been personally attacked, and Tom refused to discuss the computer output further. The two-hour meeting lasted only an hour. No progress had been made, and some fence-mending needed to occur before the managers met again.

Several months later, with no easy solutions in hand, the "team" dreaded each weekly meeting. They had only agreed that nothing had been accomplished, and all felt that the meetings were a waste of time. Territory that had been covered in the first meeting was re-covered endlessly, with each individual protecting his or her own turf. The team members distrusted each other and often attacked one another personally. The group was floundering, and inventory was still out of control.

Unfortunately, this team will continue to meet, possibly for many more months, until one of the members leaves for a different organization and the team dissolves. In the meantime, the team members' interactions outside of the team room have also deteriorated. All in all, this is not what management expected when it instituted the total quality management program and formed the team to look at the problem.

The disastrous effects could have been avoided had management provided the team with a qualified facilitator. The facilitator would have been able to defuse the personality issues, coach the team on the proper tools to use to examine the problem and provide solutions, and conduct refresher or minicourses on the quality tools. This issue of *Info-line* will outline the facilitator's role and his or her necessary skills.

Facilitators and Their Roles

Facilitators are usually individuals who assist teams in their meetings, to enhance the process—how the team works and comes to decisions. Generally, the facilitator is not involved in the process or task being examined: He or she is not a stakeholder and may begin team involvement knowing nothing about what is being discussed. Good facilitators ensure that teams don't get bogged down in personality or process issues and that every individual within the group is heard.

Don Aaron Carr, a consultant who specializes in team training, asserts that a good facilitator possesses "an attitude and philosophy that confirms a position of respect and admiration. Therefore, good facilitators display a high tolerance for ambiguity and conflict, patience and persistence."

Facilitators have a responsibility to both the team and the organization to support the team and integrate it into the organization's mainstream. Carr defines the facilitator's role as the following:

- coaching the team in process, roles, procedures, policies, and goals

- attending team meetings on an as-needed basis to provide feedback to the team leader and members

- acting as a regular consultant to the team leader

- monitoring team dynamics, diagnosing problems, and making appropriate interventions

- promoting the team concept

These roles contrast with those of the team leader, Carr says, noting that team leaders have the following roles:

- plan meeting agendas and conduct the meeting

- ensure through facilitation techniques that all members are involved in the team

- communicate with management about the team's progress

- consult with the facilitator on team issues

Since these two roles may overlap, the facilitator and the leader may negotiate which roles they want to play. A leader, for example, may want the facilitator to be present at every meeting to ensure that all team members participate if the leader feels uncomfortable in this team maintenance role. Or the leader may ask the facilitator to run or train the team in the processes involved in idea generation or decision making.

David Quinlivan-Hall and Peter Renner stress the use of a neutral facilitator who guides the group through its process stages. A neutral facilitator helps team leaders prepare the meeting and takes over the process. In this way, he or she allows the team leader to participate in the program.

Quinlivan-Hall and Renner list the following tasks facing facilitators:

Managing the Process

This includes the following:

- striving for consensus
- keeping members on task
- following the agenda
- focusing on problem solving
- controlling the flow of contributions
- rewarding and motivating group members

Acting as a Resource

This task includes:

- advising on problem-solving methods

- providing on-the-spot training in group-process techniques

- protecting group members from personal attacks

Remaining Neutral

This includes the following:

- keeping emotionally uninvolved

- keeping out of the spotlight

- becoming invisible when the group is facilitating itself

- keeping silent on content issues

Skills Required

The facilitator's role, while rather broad, is crucial to the success of the team. A good facilitator basically checks his or her personal concerns and causes at the door. Glenn Varney, president of Management Advisory Associates in Bowling Green, Ohio, suggests that facilitators should have the following skills:

■ *Listening*
The facilitator needs to be able to listen actively and hear what every team member is saying. "A day spent facilitating is as tiring as a day spent chopping wood," Quinlivan-Hall and Renner note. (For more on listening skills, see *Info-line* No. 8806, "Listening to Learn; Learning to Listen.")

■ *Questioning*
The facilitator should be skilled at asking questions. Good questions are open ended and stimulate discussion.

■ *Sharing*
The facilitator should be able to share his or her feelings and create an atmosphere in which team members are willing to share their feelings and opinions.

■ *Problem Solving*
Facilitators should be skilled at applying group problem-solving techniques. Group problem solving follows this process:

- defining the problem
- determining the cause
- considering alternatives
- weighing the alternatives
- selecting the best alternative
- implementing the solution
- evaluating the results

■ *Resolving Conflict*
Conflict among team members should not be suppressed. Indeed, it should be expected and dealt with constructively. This includes barring personal attacks. (For more information on conflict resolution, see *Info-line* No. 8909, "Coming to Agreement: How to Resolve Conflict.")

■ *Using a Participative Style*
The facilitator should be able to encourage all team members to participate in the meetings.

■ *Accepting Others*
The facilitator should maintain an open mind and not criticize the ideas and suggestions of the team members.

■ *Empathizing*
The facilitator should be able to "walk a mile in another's shoes" to understand the team members' feelings, and he or she should be able to express these feelings.

■ *Leading*
The facilitator must be able to keep the members focused and the discussion on target.

See the self-assessment instrument on the next page to assist facilitators in evaluating their skill levels.

Skill Inventory Self-Assessment Instrument

Glenn Varney provides the following inventory of team and interpersonal management skills to help you determine your strengths and weaknesses and chart your progress.

To What Extent Do You Need to Improve...

	1 (very little)	2	3 (somewhat)	4	5 (very much)

Relationships With Peers and Supervisors

	1	2	3	4	5
1. Competing with my peers.	☐	☐	☐	☐	☐
2. Being open with my seniors.	☐	☐	☐	☐	☐
3. Feeling inferior to colleagues.	☐	☐	☐	☐	☐
4. Standing up for myself.	☐	☐	☐	☐	☐
5. Building open relationships.	☐	☐	☐	☐	☐
6. Following policy guidelines.	☐	☐	☐	☐	☐
7. Questioning policy guidelines.	☐	☐	☐	☐	☐

Team Dynamics

	1	2	3	4	5
8. Knowing other team members as individuals.	☐	☐	☐	☐	☐
9. Meeting sufficiently often.	☐	☐	☐	☐	☐
10. Supporting open expression of views.	☐	☐	☐	☐	☐
11. Setting high standards.	☐	☐	☐	☐	☐
12. Punishing behavior that deviates from the team norm.	☐	☐	☐	☐	☐
13. Clarifying aims and objectives.	☐	☐	☐	☐	☐
14. Giving information and views.	☐	☐	☐	☐	☐
15. Using status to influence decisions of the team.	☐	☐	☐	☐	☐
16. Delegating to reduce workload.	☐	☐	☐	☐	☐

Relationships With Team Members

	1	2	3	4	5
17. Helping others identify problems.	☐	☐	☐	☐	☐
18. Practicing counseling skills.	☐	☐	☐	☐	☐
19. Being distant with some people.	☐	☐	☐	☐	☐
20. Intervening when things go wrong.	☐	☐	☐	☐	☐
21. Being strong when reprimanding.	☐	☐	☐	☐	☐
22. Giving energy to others.	☐	☐	☐	☐	☐
23. Clarifying individuals' objectives.	☐	☐	☐	☐	☐
24. Supporting others in difficulty.	☐	☐	☐	☐	☐
25. Bringing problems out.	☐	☐	☐	☐	☐
26. Supporting risk taking.	☐	☐	☐	☐	☐
27. Being open in assessment of others.	☐	☐	☐	☐	☐

Relationships With Employees

	1	2	3	4	5
28. Being known as a person by employees.	☐	☐	☐	☐	☐
29. Being available to employees.	☐	☐	☐	☐	☐
30. Knowing how people feel.	☐	☐	☐	☐	☐
31. Acting to resolve conflicts.	☐	☐	☐	☐	☐

To What Extent Do You Need to Improve...	1 (very little)	2	3 (somewhat)	4	5 (very much)

Relationships With Employees (*continued*)

	1	2	3	4	5
32. Emphasizing communication.	☐	☐	☐	☐	☐
33. Passing information quickly.	☐	☐	☐	☐	☐
34. Emphasizing personal status.	☐	☐	☐	☐	☐
35. Bypassing management structure when communicating.	☐	☐	☐	☐	☐

Working in Groups

	1	2	3	4	5
36. Using a systematic approach.	☐	☐	☐	☐	☐
37. Developing others' skills.	☐	☐	☐	☐	☐
38. Being prompt.	☐	☐	☐	☐	☐
39. Using time efficiently.	☐	☐	☐	☐	☐
40. Listening actively.	☐	☐	☐	☐	☐
41. Openly expressing views.	☐	☐	☐	☐	☐
42. Dominating others.	☐	☐	☐	☐	☐
43. Maintaining good group climate.	☐	☐	☐	☐	☐
44. Dealing constructively with disruptive behaviors.	☐	☐	☐	☐	☐
45. Building informal contacts.	☐	☐	☐	☐	☐
46. Disparaging other groups.	☐	☐	☐	☐	☐
47. Sharing objectives with other groups.	☐	☐	☐	☐	☐
48. Identifying mutual communication needs.	☐	☐	☐	☐	☐
49. Arranging intergroup social events.	☐	☐	☐	☐	☐
50. Acting to resolve conflicts.	☐	☐	☐	☐	☐

Helping Others Improve

	1	2	3	4	5
51. Making time for counseling.	☐	☐	☐	☐	☐
52. Identifying the group's training needs.	☐	☐	☐	☐	☐
53. Setting coaching assignments.	☐	☐	☐	☐	☐
54. Allocating time and money for training.	☐	☐	☐	☐	☐
55. Giving feedback to others.	☐	☐	☐	☐	☐
56. Sharing parts of the job for others' development.	☐	☐	☐	☐	☐

Self-Development

	1	2	3	4	5
57. Setting aside time to think.	☐	☐	☐	☐	☐
58. Visiting other organizations.	☐	☐	☐	☐	☐
59. Discussing principles and values.	☐	☐	☐	☐	☐
60. Taking on new challenges.	☐	☐	☐	☐	☐
61. Attending training events.	☐	☐	☐	☐	☐
62. Knowing when and how to use specialists.	☐	☐	☐	☐	☐

Participant Guidelines

Don Aaron Carr presents the following guidelines for effective team facilitation:

● Contract with the team on your roles and responsibilities up front.

● Don't take on the team's work (for example, recording or scribing).

● Intervene to satisfy the team's needs, not your own desire to be heard.

● Give team members time to correct problems themselves before intervening.

● Once you've said your piece, be quiet.

● Do more asking than telling.

● Facilitate the leader so the leader can facilitate the team.

● Don't repeat feedback the team has already discussed.

● Be willing to take risks.

● Be willing to be wrong.

©1994 by Don Aaron Carr.
Used with permission.

Appropriate Interventions

The word *intervention,* Carr says, is derived from a Latin word meaning to "interfere with the affairs of others." This is a good description of the kinds of actions facilitators are charged with taking. The facilitator, Carr notes, "performs an intervention whenever he or she decides to shift from that of a passive observer to that of an active participant or change agent."

Most frequently, interventions are focused on process, not on individuals or content. Carr maintains that there are four different types of interventions:

1. Interventions that cause the team to examine its dynamics and improve its performance.

2. Interventions that encourage member participation.

3. Interventions that encourage problem solving and decision making.

4. Interventions that ensure compliance with procedures, policies, ground rules, and requirements that define the process within the organization.

Active interventions alter the flow of events. They may quicken the development of the team, change the course of the discussion, increase the team's energy, or help the team become more aware of how it is functioning.

The facilitator should not intervene unless there is a reason for it—the intervention should alter what the team is doing or make available some additional information. Facilitators should intervene when the team wanders off track, when two team members are in conflict, when an individual isn't participating or is angry, or when the leader becomes autocratic.

Interventions, Carr continues, are made at four points in group process: before the meeting, during the meeting, at the end of the meeting with the team, and at a postmeeting coaching session with the leader. Timing an intervention depends on both the facilitator's style and the needs of the situation. Situational considerations include:

■ *Felt Need*

If the team is floundering and experiencing discomfort with its inability to move forward, the team may ask the facilitator to take some immediate action. If a felt need doesn't exist, Carr recommends not intervening, because the intervention might disrupt the group process. Carr also recommends that facilitators follow the "five-minute rule": Wait five minutes before intervening to see if the team corrects itself.

■ *Danger*

If an interaction occurs during a team meeting that would be difficult to repair later, the facilitator may intervene immediately—for example, if the team leader puts down a team member and the team shows no signs of addressing the interaction.

■ *Impact*

An immediate intervention has the greatest impact, but it may have to be repeated several times before the team begins to self-monitor. But beware of intervening every few minutes.

■ *Repeats*

If the facilitator intervenes with the same comment several times and the team doesn't act on it, the facilitator should mention the problem in a coaching session with the team leader.

How to Intervene

Knowing how to intervene in a group's process is key to the facilitator's success. David Quinlivan-Hall and Peter Renner in *In Search of Solutions* present 25 facilitator interventions and some guidance on when to use them. A few samples follow:

Describe process obstacles. If nothing is happening, the facilitator can describe the next step and perhaps encourage the contributions of several group members.

Encourage participation. The facilitator, Quinlivan-Hall and Renner note, should "establish a participative climate at the start of the meeting and maintain it throughout."

Stages and Phases

The work objective of an effective facilitator is to put himself or herself out of a job. It is easier to reach this end if the facilitator knows the stage of group development the team happens to be in. J. William Pfeiffer and Arlette C. Ballew have made several suggestions for the appropriate level of intervention in the various phases of group growth:

■ *Forming*

This is the "polite" phase. The facilitator's approach may be highly directive, instructing the group on what is to be done and how to do it. The facilitator intervenes by structuring getting-acquainted exercises, reviewing agenda items, and exploring similarities among members. During the later part of this phase, facilitators offer the group members the opportunity to set their own standards and identify each individual's reason for belonging to the team. Their task should be clarified, and the group members should be committed to it.

■ *Storming*

This is the "power" stage: who has it, who wants it, and who is doing what to get it. The facilitator's job in this stage is to create a common language and manage conflict: "Too little control can allow chaos, while suppression of all conflict can lead to apathy," Pfeiffer and Ballew point out. The facilitator engages in relationship-building activities, such as support, praise, encouragement, and simply paying attention.

■ *Norming*

This is the "positive" stage. The group comes together and works as a team. The team becomes self-monitoring. The facilitator can help the group share ideas, monitor or lead group problem-solving and decision-making tools, and provide feedback. Depending on the team, the facilitator may now become a consultant, attending only when the team feels his or her presence is needed, or working to blend in with the group.

■ *Performing*

This is the "proficient" stage. The facilitator turns over responsibility for decisions and implementation to the group and engages in both low-task and low-maintenance behaviors. He or she becomes "invisible."

■ *Adjourning*

This is the final phase. The team accomplishes its goal and disbands. The facilitator may help the team celebrate its success, debrief it on what worked and what did not, and help group members let go.

Roles Members Play

Team members can take on behaviors that hinder the group process. The following chart identifies several of these behaviors, explains why team members may behave that way, and tells what you can do about it.

Roles	Why It Happens	What to Do
Heckler	Probably good natured most of the time but is distracted by job or personal problems.	• Keep your temper under control. • Honestly agree with one idea, then move on to something else. • Toss a misstatement of fact to the group to turn down. • Talk privately with the person as a last resort to determine what is bothering him or her.
Rambler	One idea leads to another and takes this person miles away from the original point.	• When there is a pause for breath, thank him or her, refocus attention, and move on. • In a friendly manner, indicate that "We are a little off the subject." • As a last resort, use your meeting timetable. Glance at your watch and say, "Time is limited."
Ready Answer	Really wants to help, but makes it difficult by keeping others from participating.	• Cut it off tactfully by questioning others. Suggest that "we put others to work." • Ask this person to summarize. It keeps him or her attentive and capitalizes on his or her enthusiasm.
Conversationalist	Side chatter is usually personal in nature but may be related to the topic.	• Call by name and ask an easy question. • Call by name, restate the last opinion expressed, and ask his or her opinion of it. • Include in the discussion.
Personality Problems	Two or more individuals clash, dividing your people into factions and endangering the success of the meeting.	• Maximize points of agreement; minimize disagreements. Draw attention to the objective at hand. • Pose a direct question to an uninvolved member on the topic. • As a last resort, frankly state that personalities should be left out of the discussion.
Wrong Track	Brings up ideas that are obviously incorrect.	• Say, "That's one way of looking at it," and tactfully make any corrections. • Say, "I see your point, but can we reconcile that with our current situation?" • Handle tactfully since you will be contradicting him or her. Remember, all members of the group will hear how you respond to each individual, and you can encourage or discourage further participation.

Roles	Why It Happens	What to Do
Quiet One	Bored	Gain interest by asking for opinion.
	Indifferent	Question the person next to him or her. Then, ask the quiet one to comment on the view expressed.
	Timid	Compliment this person the first time he or she contributes. Be sincere.
	Superior	Indicate respect for this person's experience, then ask for ideas.
Bungler	Lacks the ability to put good ideas into proper order; has ideas, but can't convey them and needs help.	Don't call attention to the problem. Say, "Let me see if we are saying the same thing." Then, repeat the idea more clearly.
Mule	Can't or won't see the other side; supports own viewpoint no matter what.	• Ask other members of the group to comment on the ideas. They will straighten him or her out. • Remind him or her that time is short, and suggest that he or she accept the group consensus presently. Indicate your willingness to talk with him or her later. Then, follow up.
Talker	Highly motivated	Slow this person down with some difficult questions.
	Show-off	Say, "That's an interesting point. Now, let's see what the rest think of it."
	Well informed	Draw upon his or her knowledge, but relay to the group.
	Just plain talkative	In general, for all overly talkative folks, let the group take care of them as much as possible.
Griper	Has a pet peeve, gripes for the sake of complaining, or has a legitimate complaint.	• Point out that the objective at hand is to operate as efficiently and cooperatively as possible under the present circumstances. • Indicate that you will discuss his or her personal problem privately at a later date. • Have another member of the group respond to his or her complaint.

Use body language. Facilitators can sit away from the table to indicate noninvolvement or move to the table when intervening in the process. "Moving closer to someone who is 'under fire' from the group gives this person support," they claim, while "moving close to a noisy, disruptive person usually results in a quieting down."

Discourage personal attacks. The facilitator may need to remind individuals of one of the first tenets of team building: "Examine the process, not the person." If one group member begins to attack another, the facilitator needs to step in to refocus the discussion on the issue.

Suggest a process. The facilitator should be able to instruct or run certain processes, such as idea generating and decision making, in order to move the group along.

Encourage equal participation. Facilitators need to observe the group to notice who is talking and who is being quiet. The trick is to draw out the wallflowers and shut up those who monopolize the conversation, without offending either.

Suggest a break. Taking a spontaneous break can end a deadlock or simply reenergize the group. Refreshment breaks are common, but others work just as well, including a "seventh-inning stretch," moving to small groups for several minutes, taking a five-minute "joke break," or bringing in a guest speaker.

Summarize. If the group has presented many alternatives, and those alternatives have generated much discussion, the group may get lost. Summarizing the problem and several of the alternatives may help the group refocus and keep moving.

Have the group manage the process. During the group's maturity, the facilitator may appropriately turn some of his or her duties over to the group. This indicates both trust and respect for the team and its interactions.

Debrief the group. A debriefing requires all team members to look at what is happening. It should be done at the end of the meeting and may be useful at natural breaks in the meeting agenda. Facilitators may take several approaches:

Objective: What happened here?

Reflective: How do you feel about what happened?

Interpretive: What did you learn from what happened?

Decision making: What do you want to do with this information for the next time?

Search for common threads. If the group is wandering, the facilitator may stop the meeting and ask for members to search for what the solutions or problem definitions have in common. "With the common elements identified," Quinlivan-Hall and Renner assert, "focus is achieved for the next steps."

Present a straw man. During a break, the facilitator may develop, or suggest that someone else develop, a draft problem description or solution—the straw man. Encourage the team to criticize the plan, attack it, and pull it apart. "Only by picking it apart, adding to, and changing it, will the group develop ownership of it," the authors say.

Act stupid. Team members who are uninvolved may not understand what is happening or what someone else is saying, but may not, for many reasons, want to volunteer their ignorance. The facilitator may help these individuals by asking for clarification of issues, problems, terminology, or anything else that may get in the way of consensus later in the process. Remember, Columbo always got his criminal.

Get specific. Similar to acting stupid, getting specific can clear up hard-to-grasp issues, problems, and solutions.

The Power of Observation

All interventions have one thing in common: The facilitator has provided the proper feedback and timed the intervention to alter what the group is doing somehow. This means that the facilitator has paid careful attention to what the group as a unit is doing, as well as the interactions between individual team members.

The key tool in observing the group is listening. Listening shows interest in the individual speaking and respect for the other person's experience. According to Carr, there are three types of effective listening:

1. Passive listening, where one has no interaction with the speaker, such as listening to the radio or a cassette.

2. Attentive listening, where one has some interaction with the speaker, such as listening for content to lectures in class or taking notes in a meeting.

3. Active listening, where one has a high level of interaction with the speaker, listening for content, meaning, and feelings.

Facilitators listen actively throughout the meeting. They observe who talks and for how long, whom individuals look at when they talk, who supports whom, any challenges to group leadership, nonverbal communication, side conversations, and nonparticipation. They watch for individual reactions to what is being said in order to provide coaching. Facilitators may ask questions, restate what has been said, summarize positions, or reflect a speaker's feelings. They may also keep track of the different roles team members play.

Many facilitators find it helpful to develop a chart to "keep score" of the team members' different behaviors. Although these are helpful, the facilitator should get the team's permission to use it, especially in the early stages when team members may not trust each other completely. If the facilitator springs the results on the team at the end of

the meeting, team members may feel spied on and resent the tracking. A sample form with more detailed instructions is shown in the sidebar on the next page.

The chart attempts to quantify the contributions of team members in two broad areas: task and maintenance. Task functions facilitate the group in selecting, defining, and solving a common problem; maintenance functions alter or maintain the way in which group members interact. The chart also records any antigroup roles adopted by team members. Facilitators may want to chart the following behaviors:

Task Activity

Initiating. Proposing tasks or goals, defining the problem, suggesting a procedure or ideas for solving the problem.

Information seeking. Requesting facts, seeking relevant data about a problem, asking for suggestions or ideas.

Clarifying. Clearing up confusion, indicating alternatives and issues, giving examples.

Summarizing. Restating suggestions, synthesizing ideas, offering a decision or direction for the team to accept or reject.

Consensus testing. Setting up straw men to see if the team is near conclusion, checking to see how much agreement has been reached.

Maintenance Activity

Encouraging. Being friendly, recognizing others.

Expressing group feelings. Sensing moods, feelings, relationships with others, sharing feelings.

Harmonizing. Reconciling disagreements, reducing tensions, getting others to explore their differences.

Keeping Track

Many facilitators use checklists to track the behaviors—both good and bad—of team members. This allows the facilitator to provide accurate feedback at the end of the meeting. Keeping track of the team members' behaviors can make criticism specific, objective, and, therefore, easier to take. And it helps to know everyone on the team is receiving the same type of commentary.

But keep in mind that checklists could make team members uncomfortable. If you make such a list, do it with the team's approval and agreement on how the data will be used and discussed.

The checklists are generally a row-and-column grid. If group process is being monitored, the facilitator may put the team's rating in the second column. The facilitator then keeps a tally of how many times an individual engages in a particular behavior. For example, the team members may feel that, as a group, they interrupt each other too much. The facilitator may be asked to monitor that one aspect and report to the team members at the end of the meeting. Conversely, many facilitators use the tally sheet as a confidence-builder by tracking various desirable leadership behaviors and reporting them back. A sample grid follows:

Roles	Members										
Task Activity											
Initiator											
Information Seeker											
Clarifier											
Summarizer											
Consensus Tester											
Information Giver											
Maintenance Activity											
Encourager											
Expresser of Group Feelings											
Harmonizer											
Compromiser											
Gatekeeper											
Standard Setter											
Coach											
Collaborator											
Individual Activity											
Blocker											
Avoider											
Digressor											
Recognition Seeker											
Dominator											

Compromising. Admitting error, disciplining one-self to maintain group cohesion.

Gatekeeping. Trying to keep communication channels open, suggesting procedures to induce discussion of group problems.

Setting standards. Expressing standards to achieve, applying standards to evaluate the group and its output, evaluating frequently.

Coaching and consulting. Working with team members and management outside of meetings.

Individual Activity

Blocking. Interfering with group progress by arguing, resisting, disagreeing, or beating a dead horse.

Avoiding. Withdrawing from the discussion, day-dreaming, doing something else, whispering, leaving the room.

Digressing. Going off the subject, filibustering, discussing personal issues.

Other areas may also be observed that help the team function better. The facilitator may want to customize the list to suit the organization's culture or team environment. Among these other areas are:

- group rules
- clarity of ideas
- handling group problems
- favoritism
- group status
- sensitivity to needs of the group
- positive or negative body language
- seating arrangements
- tension
- program planning
- hidden agendas
- invisible committees
- making others aware of their own contributions

Feedback

These above categories also provide a framework for individual and group feedback. Gaining permission from the team members to keep track of their behaviors and explaining what impact these different behaviors have on the group will help the facilitator give useful feedback. In general, feedback should be:

■ *Descriptive*
Feedback is intended to provide others with a reading of what we are experiencing. For facilitators, this may mean pointing out someone's reaction to the action or statement of another, such as "What happened when you failed to post an agenda for the meeting?"

■ *Specific*
General feedback makes no value judgment of the person the facilitator is attempting to help: "I noticed you stared out the window when Bonnie was talking. It appears to me you may not be listening to Bonnie."

■ *Mindful of the Needs of Both Parties*
Feedback, especially when it is being given by the facilitator, should not be aimed at relieving one person's feelings or at relieving the facilitator's own feelings. Such feedback, Carr notes, tends to be destructive or hurtful, cuts off or reduces communication, and does little to change the behavior. (See *Info-line* No. 9006, "Coaching and Feedback," for more information about feedback.)

Facilitators also observe how teams make decisions. Edgar H. Schein notes that observing how decisions are made helps the facilitator "assess the appropriateness of the method to the matter being decided on." Decisions made by groups are "notoriously hard to undo," Schein continues, adding that "often we can undo the decision only if we reconstruct it and understand how we made it and whether this method was appropriate." He lists some group decision-making methods:

Plop. Group decision by omission. "I think we ought to introduce ourselves." Silence.

Self-authorized agenda. Decision by one. "I think we should introduce ourselves. I'm John Smith."

Handclasp. Decision by two. "I wonder if it would be helpful if we introduced ourselves." "I think so. I'm John Smith."

Does anyone object? Decision by minority—one or more. "We all agree that introductions are appropriate."

Voting. Decision by majority.

Polling. "Let's see where everyone stands. What do you think?"

Consensus taking. Test for opposition, or find out if the opposition feels strongly enough to block the implementation of a decision. "Can you live with this?"

References & Resources

Articles

Allcorn, Seth. "Understanding Groups at Work." *Personnel,* August 1989, pp. 28-36.

Bettenhausen, Kenneth L. "Five Years of Group Research: What We Have Learned and What Needs to Be Addressed." *Journal of Management,* June 1991, pp. 345-381.

Cooper, Colleen, and Mary Ploor. "Challenges That Make or Break a Group." *Training & Development Journal,* April 1986, pp. 31-33.

Crapo, Raymond F. "It's Time To Stop Training…and Start Facilitating." *Public Personnel Management,* Winter 1986, pp. 433-449.

Driskell, James E., et al. "Task Cues, Dominance Cues, and Influence in Task Groups." *Journal of Applied Psychology,* February 1993, pp. 51-60.

Head, Thomas C. "Impressions on What Makes a Good Facilitator from a Frustrated Teamplayer." *Organization Development Journal,* Winter 1992, pp. 61-63.

Kaczmarek, Patricia S. "Planning and Conducting Facilitated Workshops— Part 2: Conducting the Session." *Performance and Instruction,* January 1993, pp. 31-34.

Kaye, Beverly. "Advisory Groups on the Seven Cs." *Training & Development,* January 1992, pp. 54-59.

Kochery, Timothy S. "Conflict Versus Consensus: Processes and Their Effect on Team Decision Making." *Human Resource Development Quarterly,* Summer 1993, pp. 185-191.

Levine, John M., and Richard L. Moreland. "Progress in Small Group Research." *Annual Review of Psychology,* 1990, pp. 585-634.

Rogelberg, Steven G., et al. "The Stepladder Technique: An Alternative Group Structure Facilitating Effective Group Decision Making." *Journal of Applied Psychology,* October 1992, pp. 730-737.

Sugar, Steve. "The RAT Race: An Exercise in Group Dynamics." *Performance & Instruction,* August 1990, pp. 13-17.

Thiagarajan, Sivasailam. "Secrets of Successful Facilitators." *Journal for Quality & Participation,* 1992, pp. 70-72.

Thornton, Paul B. "Teamwork: Focus, Frame, Facilitate." *Management Review,* November 1992, pp. 46-47.

Varney, Glenn H. "Helping a Team Find All the Answers." *Training & Development Journal,* February 1991, pp. 15-18.

Weingart, Laurie R. "Impact of Group Goals, Task Component Complexity, Effort, and Planning on Group Performance." *Journal of Applied Psychology,* October 1992, pp. 682-683.

Weingart, Laurie R., et al. "The Impact of Consideration of Issues and Motivational Orientation on Group Negotiation Process and Outcome." *Journal of Applied Psychology,* June 1993, pp. 504-517.

Williams, Bill. "Ten Commandments for Group Leaders." *Supervisory Management,* September 1992, pp. 1-2.

Books

Dimock, Hedley G. *Groups: Leadership and Group Development.* San Diego: University Associates, 1987.

Fox, William M. *Effective Group Problem Solving.* San Francisco: Jossey-Bass, 1987.

Heron, John. *The Facilitator's Handbook.* New York: Nichols Publishing, 1989.

Kayser, Thomas A. *Mining Group Gold: How to Cash In on the Collaborative Brain Power of a Group.* El Segundo, CA: Serif Publishing, 1990.

Mink, Oscar G., et al. *Groups at Work.* Englewood Cliffs, NJ: Educational Technology Publications, 1987.

Nutt, Paulo C. *Making Tough Decisions.* San Francisco: Jossey-Bass, 1989.

Quinlivan-Hall, David, and Peter Renner. *In Search of Solutions: Sixty Ways to Guide Your Problem-Solving Group.* Vancouver: PFR Training Associates, 1990.

Ulshak, Francis L., et al. *Small Group Problem Solving.* Reading, MA: Addison-Wesley, 1981.

Info-lines

Kirrane, Diane E. "Listening to Learn; Learning to Listen." No. 8806 (revised 1997).

Meyer, Kathy M. "Coming to Agreement: How to Resolve Conflict." No. 8909 (out of print).

"Coaching and Feedback." No. 9006 (revised 1997).

Intervention Starters

Interventions during facilitation often take the form of questions the facilitator asks of the group. The text discusses four forms of questions: objective, reflective, interpretive, and decision making. Following are suggested openers for each type of intervention.

Objective

What happened?

Do we need to get back on track?

Have we strayed from the topic?

Do we need to take a break?

Summarize the group's activity.

Reflective

How do you feel?

Would you like to say something?

Maybe we misunderstood our roles.

I'm sorry it appears that way.

How would you like me to provide feedback?

Hey, you wanted an enforcer!

Interpretive

What did you learn?

Is this what the team thinks?

What are the specifics?

What's our common ground?

Do you understand the other's point of view or work process?

Decision Making

What do you want to do?

The material appearing on this page is not covered by copyright and may be reproduced at will.

Create Effective Workshops

Issue 8604

Create Effective Workshops

AUTHORS

Geoffrey M. Bellman
President, GMB Associates, Ltd.
Seattle, WA

Leslie A. Kelly
President, Kelly & Associates
Indianapolis, IN

Editorial Staff for 8604

Managing Editor
Madelyn R. Callahan

ASTD Internal Consultant
Eileen West

Revised 1997

Editor
Cat Sharpe

Contributing Editor
Ann Bruen

Designer
Steven M. Blackwood

Create Effective Workshops

Workshop training can save an organization time and money, and offers long-term performance benefits because of the special emphasis on practicing skills and transferring them to the job. More efficiently than many other methods, workshops can close the gap between desired and actual job performance, and are most valuable if practical and relevant to both organizational and individual training needs. They concentrate training within a minimal time frame of 40 hours at most.

What's the key to creating an effective workshop? Designers and facilitators should focus on job-specific objectives benefiting both employee and employer, and should always include participants as resource persons in both the planning and the delivery of training.

Workshops generally provide training in three areas—knowledge, skills, and attitudes—and can be designed and delivered in-house by company staff, or custom designed by outside consultants and conducted in their facilities. But experts agree that the most effective workshops are those that involve participants and their managers and supervisors in the planning, from preliminary or preworkshop stages through the workshop itself and the follow-up phase.

Early input from these groups ensures that the training will directly address trainees' specific job concerns and needs. Two ways of acquiring input are: discussions of the training plan among workshop designers, facilitators, managers, and participants; and questionnaires or surveys on their expectations and objectives.

This issue of *Info-line* covers successful methods and techniques for planning and conducting workshops, gathering data for drafting workshop plans, designing the workshop format, and preparing leaders and facilitators to motivate participants and help them to accomplish objectives.

Planning

The most important aspect of workshop design is the planning phase. Front-end work involves comprehensive needs assessment studies involving surveys, interviews, and both structured and unstructured observation. As the workshop progresses, planning remains a vital process of the experience. At every stage of the workshop, from preworkshop planning through follow-up, designers and facilitators must be prepared to make changes and make new plans to better meet learners' training needs. Here are some guidelines for wise planning:

Basic Steps

1. Define the need. Identify training needs from perceived job behaviors. Bring managers and participants together for preworkshop meetings to discuss needs and agree on action plans.

    By studying the audience profile, determine whether participants will need briefing or preworkshop activities to be prepared sufficiently for the activities, exercises, and information. During preworkshop planning, obtain input from participants by verifying their needs, expectations, and experience.

2. Set the program objective. Define practical objectives based on training needs. Write objectives clearly in terms of expected behavior changes during the workshop. Develop a budget and determine the maximum amounts of time and money needed to best support workshop objectives. Also, develop a strategy for presenting and selling your budget to management. Present your workshop to line management for review and make adjustments based on managers' recommendations.

3. Determine workshop subject matter content. Select activities and exercises to support workshop content. Draw up a schedule of the various sections of the workshop in sequence.

Workshop Checklist

Workshops that are well planned and designed can offer valuable instructional experiences to participants. Good planning and research efforts can ensure long life for the workshop and cost savings over the long term. To make sure you've thought through vital issues for creating an effective workshop experience, consult the following checklist:

☐ What are the group's training needs? How will you determine these needs—through observations, surveys, interviews, and so forth?

☐ What is the size of the training population? What do they expect of the training? Is the group diverse, or do they hold relatively similar positions in the organization? Do they have basically the same qualifications and capabilities for handling the workshop content and methods?

☐ How will you involve participants in drafting and designing the workshop instruction? Will you establish a system for preworkshop planning sessions, or will you simply query participants for their input at each stage of the planning?

☐ How many training objectives will you select for your workshop? Will you have sufficient time to cover each objective? How will these objectives specifically address each of the identified training needs?

☐ What kinds of instructional training will you employ to help participants achieve workshop objectives? Do you have access to the equipment and resources, or will you need to rent or buy them? Do you have the skills, staff, and budget allowances to support these media?

☐ Can you justify your expenses in terms of expected gains? Have you drafted a document regarding these justifications? How will you present this information to management? Can you count on management support?

☐ Is the workshop the most cost-effective and efficient method for your training purposes? Are there other ways to present your design that would be less costly but as effective?

Concentrate on designing activities that are as close as possible to actual workplace conditions and organizational issues. In organization-centered workshops, clarify roles and responsibilities. In workshops that focus on individuals, concentrate on what action must be performed, how to undertake it, and when it is necessary or appropriate to do so. Arrange activities, exercises, and information in sequential order from either simplest to most complex, or the order in which they occur on the job.

4. Consider program delivery. Put together workshop materials and presentations, obtain media equipment, visual aids, and so forth, and select the training room and facilities for the best seating arrangements and space to support workshop objectives. (For an in-depth treatment of media, see *Info-line* No. 8410, "How to Prepare and Use Effective Visual Aids.")

5. Provide for ample participation. If appropriate, organize participants into job-related groups during the workshop. Throughout the workshop, encourage participants to suggest ways of applying workshop objectives in their particular job environments. Encourage them to state barriers to expected job performance and to think of ways to overcome them.

6. Evaluate workshop effectiveness. When the workshop is over, hold meetings between participants and managers to discuss the action planned and management approval. Evaluate the workshop in terms of results and learner improvement, paying close attention to whether participants achieved the workshop objectives. When participants are back on the job, follow up the training with sessions or meetings to work on newly acquired behaviors.

Guidelines for Planning

Determine needs by picking up clues in the workplace. Observe the workforce in action and listen to their concerns. New technologies or plans to automate can create a training need by changing the nature of an employee's job. Executives and managers may discover performance problems during appraisal periods and productivity research.

Early in the workshop planning process, consult with learners in order to respond to their needs and maximize the relevance of the training. Ask them for specific input on what the content should be and how the workshop should be structured.

Pay attention to organizational needs. To make sure the training addresses them, consider the following issues: Is the workshop practical? Can the learning be put to use immediately? Is it relevant to the company's daily activities, to the organization's environment and culture? Does the instructional design process involve learners as resource persons?

Give your workshop draft this test for practicality: Look at the training from the learner's perspective. Does the draft address the particular performance problem or skill deficiency? Does it give you answers or tools to achieve the solution? Take a relevance test: Look at the workshop from an adult learner's perspective. This particular group of learners focuses on immediate and practical solutions to on-the-job problems. They want on-target training, especially when it takes time away from their jobs.

If you're designing training to make changes in organizational practices and elements, think of how the workshop should address current communication styles and procedures, processes for establishing objectives, methods for involving departments, relations among departments and between superiors and employees, employee attitudes, and procedures for resolving conflicts.

Make sure the workshop covers key issues by gathering data: Use a poll to get managers' views, conduct formal and informal interviews, and hand out surveys and needs assessment instruments. (For more details, see *Info-lines* No. 8502, "Be a Better Needs Analyst"; No. 9401, "Needs Assessment by Focus Group"; No. 9408, "Strategic Needs Analysis"; and No. 9611, "Conducting a Mini Needs Assessment.")

Use an open-ended interview style to uncover hidden issues that may not be revealed by the workshop designer's structured question/answer format. Encourage interviewees to discuss what they like best and least about their jobs and about the workplace. Listen closely to their comments and suggestions for clues that reveal training needs. Use instruments for sensitive issues that may be hard to discuss face-to-face. For example, managers may feel more comfortable filling out a questionnaire on values than discussing this topic.

Questionnaires

Besides indicating preferences for training content, questionnaires reveal how organizational behavior should change to achieve workshop objectives. For example, if a company aims to use technology to upgrade its performance, questionnaires can determine which departments require more sophisticated technology and what individuals think of the new automation. Here are tips for writing pre-workshop planning questionnaires:

Be brief and specific. Questionnaires should be short enough to complete in a matter of minutes. In addition to fill-in and short-answer questions, include sufficient space for comments. Write clearly and aim for practicality. Concentrate on questions that address daily behavior on the job, general attitudes, and opinions.

Easy tabulation. Design the questionnaire so that it can be tabulated easily with a calculator. Use a scale of one to five, with five being the highest value. When appropriate, use open-ended formats rather than numerical scales. For example, if you're designing a workshop on developing leadership skills, ask the participants to draw up a list of the most important qualities of an effective leader.

Confidentiality. Keep questionnaire responses confidential. No one should be embarrassed because they've answered the survey honestly. If participants feel comfortable with one another, hold a discussion of preworkshop questionnaire results to address concerns and clarify issues.

Evaluation. Once the workshop is under way, discuss the results to find out if the training is meeting participants' expectations as stated in their responses to the questionnaires.

Questionnaire Standards

Use these quality standards to ensure valuable results:

- Content of the questionnaire relates directly to the training topic.

- Each item addresses only one action or behavior.

- All items are written in simple sentence structure and are stated in a positive manner.

- Points on the scale measure only one dimension of the behavior or action.

- Realistic measurement terms are used to describe behavior (for example, use *infrequently* rather than *never*.)

- Items and spaces for answers are approximately the same length so as not to signal responses.

Involve participants in workshop design. Seek their input and be sure your design is flexible enough to accommodate their ideas. This establishes ownership and a reason to buy into the training. Participants can give designers valuable information about their training needs, their jobs, and the workplace.

Involve Participants

When you've established the basic purpose for your workshop, use a variety of methods to involve participants in the planning and design phases.

- Give participants questionnaires about their expectations of the workshop and a list of possible training objectives. Explain that these forms will ensure their input in preworkshop planning.

- Provide managers and participants information from the questionnaires and the list of preliminary objectives. Managers need this information to approve the training, and participants need to know what to expect and how they can contribute to the plan.

- Revise the preliminary objectives of the workshop according to responses to the questionnaires. Use results of tabulated surveys to establish final objectives and to plan the type and sequence of the learning activities. When there isn't sufficient time to follow this course, the plan for learning activities can be presented to the managers and participants along with the questionnaires and lists of objectives. In this case, the respondents should be told to limit their changes to a minimum.

- Consult with managers. They are usually closer to employees than trainers and designers, and, for this reason, are able to help you match your design views with employees' expectations.

- Schedule a time for managers and participants to get together to discuss the workshop plan.

Workshop Objectives

Once workshop designers determine participant needs, analyze organizational needs, understand participants' expectations, and gather all the necessary data to begin constructing a final design, they are ready to establish workshop objectives, the measurement by which participants assess their progress during the workshop and the basis for evaluating the workshop at its completion. Follow these guidelines for writing effective objectives:

1. Use objectives to impart the organization's purpose for conducting the workshop.

2. Write statements that clearly describe the desired behavior participants should be able to demonstrate at the end of the workshop.

3. Identify those behaviors as evidence that participants have achieved workshop objectives.

4. Describe criteria for measuring acceptable performance, specifying degrees of acceptability.

5. State clearly what you expect participants to be able to do and describe the conditions under which they are expected to perform. For example, "Given the number of publications you are expected to produce under tight deadlines, and the amount of projects you're assigned on short notice, be able to draft a schedule for producing and distributing by January 1 the company's report to investors."

6. Use action-oriented words like *compare, contrast, solve, identify,* and *write* rather than vague ones such as *understand, know,* and *grasp.*

7. Write objectives that are easy to demonstrate. (For a more in-depth treatment of objectives, see these *Info-line*s: No. 8505, "Write Better Behavioral Objectives"; No. 9110, "Measuring Affective and Behavioral Change"; and No. 9512, "Transfer of Training.")

Ideally, workshop instruction moves from simple concepts to complex ones, from helping participants become familiar with ideal behaviors to making them competent. To progress from introductory to advanced stages, structure workshops according to four major learning levels: knowledge, comprehension, practice, and performance. Each level requires a specific method of teaching.

■ *Knowledge*

This segment of the workshop provides participants with information about specific objectives and standards for learning. Tools for communicating this knowledge include films, tapes, panel discussions, readings, and lectures.

■ *Comprehension*

To completely understand the instruction, workshop participants need to be able to make associations and connections between their current behavior and new behaviors being taught, to relate the workshop content to current and future job-related behaviors. Tools for this aspect of the workshop include demonstrations, simulation, and dialogue.

■ *Practice*

On this level learners try out the new behaviors. Practice opportunities help them begin to accept and apply what they've learned. Teaching tools for this level are straightforward activities and exercises. During this preliminary application stage, it is very important for workshop leaders to give participants strong and positive reinforcement.

■ *Performance*

More demanding workshop exercises and activities give participants opportunities to acquire and practice skills. These teaching tools commonly include simulations, problem-solving case studies, role plays, planning for on-the-job applications, and follow-up or postworkshop activities.

Transfer Tips

Tie the learning levels to job transfer by using action planning during the workshop. Give participants assignments and exercises to encourage them to plan actions they will take to change their on-the-job behaviors by using the new skills and knowledge they have.

To help transfer skills, create an atmosphere of reality in the workshop environment. Use simulations and role plays and make sure all training content is job specific. The workshop must relate directly to organizational concerns and targeted results.

Ensure that participants will apply the new behaviors by consistently providing positive reinforcement. Managers, supervisors, workshop leaders, and other administrators participating in the training should make a special effort to applaud good behavior and offer positive feedback when needed.

Take a practical approach, making sure the workshop actively involves participants and maintains a sharp focus on applying new behaviors. Encourage positive attitudes and high levels of skill and competency. Acquiring new behaviors depends more on these elements than on knowledge and understanding.

Basic Steps for Changing Behavior

The following are steps individuals undergo to change their behavior:

1. Recognize the significance and value of changing the behavior.

2. Determine which behaviors must be changed and how to go about changing them.

3. Learn new behavior patterns.

4. Test these ways by practicing them to find out which get the best results and are the most appropriate in different situations.

5. Get feedback on the new behaviors. Find out how others respond, and consider their suggestions for improvement.

6. Use positive reinforcement to build on good behaviors and develop performance confidence.

Exercises and Activities

Learning exercises and activities are the most valuable aspect of a workshop. This is where on-the-job behavior changes begin to happen. New knowledge alone is rarely sufficient to effect a change. The following are some approaches to organizing and conducting exercises and activities:

■ Deductive

This approach involves first presenting information and then applying it. Experts say the deductive approach works best for technical and administrative topics. For example, the workshop designer presents a case study depicting scheduling problems in a production department. Part of the presentation involves explaining administrative solutions. The next phase of this process requires participants to apply those solutions to the case.

■ Behavior Modeling

This is a variation on the deductive approach because it explains how learners should perform a task or skill. Modeling involves a step-by-step demonstration of desired behavior (usually on a videocassette or computer screen) and a subsequent discussion of key actions and principles. This approach translates theory into practice (role plays and simulations), which provides opportunities for critiques and reinforcement. The most effective uses for behavior modeling are supervisory skills training and instruction in conceptual or theoretical subject matter that may be difficult to comprehend without practical applications.

■ Inductive

This approach involves first observing participants' behaviors and then analyzing the effects of these actions. It is most useful in such situations as crisis management and interpersonal skills training. The designer presents a related case, such as an increase in errors made by the production department, and participants try to solve the problem. The workshop leader and the group observe their behavior skills and later offer feedback on their performance. Some feedback criticisms may include the following: based decisions on insufficient information; too hesitant to make decisions; made too many snap decisions; took a limited view of the situation; used wrong criteria in making decisions.

A videocassette recorder would be a good teaching tool for the inductive approach, to back up the commentary and show participants where their performance was strongest and where it was weakest.

■ Discovery

This is a variation of the inductive approach. Designers present a work-related problem, and teams or individuals consult with the workshop leader, talk with other participants, and use workshop resources to reach a decision or solution.

■ Combined Inductive and Deductive

By combining the approaches, workshop leaders use the diagnostic and instructional benefits of both. Participants receive structured information and also have the opportunity to practice and experiment with new behaviors. This combined approach will take more time, but it is highly effective.

Design Tips

Managers as trainers. Maximize the workshop's effectiveness by planning to use managers as trainers. Managers have the greatest influence on the workforce and are better able to generate interest in training. When you use professional trainers, brief managers on content, encourage them to attend sessions, and ask them to reinforce results.

Job-specific workshops. To ensure that workshops are job specific and practical, design activities and exercises based on organizational concerns and issues. Organizations realize the value of workshops that are custom designed to support plans, decisions, and actions needed for job improvement.

Keep in mind that the best designs give participants the opportunity to perform tasks required by their jobs, and to apply new skills and knowledge to improve their performance. Use group size as a guide for designing activities. Remember, small groups of no more than 10 work best for discussions and interpersonal skills training.

Learner skills. Use flexible, open-ended designs to accommodate a variety of learners. Seasoned employees will work independently, making sophisticated contributions to the workshop, and will require minimal assistance from the workshop leader. Less-experienced employees will rely on the guidance and contributions of workshop leaders and will benefit from the experience and knowledge of the rest of the group.

How to Select Outside Workshops

Workshops may last from a few hours to several weeks. Their sponsors range from independent consultants to professional societies, colleges, and universities. To find out whether a particular program suits your training needs, consider the following issues:

- Does the workshop literature talk about specific learning objectives or vague "outcomes"?

- How are the objectives stated? Are they expressed clearly in behavioral terms?

- Are behaviors described in observable and measurable terms? Do they seem reasonable and realistic given the time constraints?

- What kinds of employees should register for this workshop? Does the literature specify level of experience, type of job, or particular background?

- Does the workshop brochure offer an outline of the topic and subject matter to be used in the workshop?

- Does it include a schedule with time allotted for participants to discuss issues and address questions?

- Does the schedule permit enough time for participants to think of ways to apply workshop content back on the job and to discuss these ideas?

- Does the schedule also permit time for feedback—for participants to let leaders know whether or not their training needs are being met during the program?

- What kinds of learning methods will be used? How does the literature explain these approaches?

- Are methods participative and action oriented? Are participants expected to get involved or just sit and listen?

- Does the workshop description mention opportunities for learners to consult with program leaders either in small groups or one-on-one?

- Do you have information about the workshop leaders? Have they published respected works on topics to be covered by the workshop? What are their credentials?

Check the sponsoring organization to find out if its past programs have met with success and its former clients are satisfied with the results of the program. The following are items you should consider:

- Is the workshop sponsored by an established organization that has been in operation for two or more years? (Don't dismiss reputable new organizations, but it's easier to gather information about older ones.)

- Does the organization have at least one year of experience conducting programs on topics of interest?

- Have the workshop leaders worked for this sponsor for one or more years? Do they offer programs like this throughout the area and the country?

If the program has been offered before, get rosters from the organizations and call former clients for recommendations and opinions. Find out how workshop participants are now using the training; this can be more important than finding out whether or not they liked the experience. To find out about the usefulness and quality of the workshop, ask previous workshop attendees these kinds of questions:

- As a result of the workshop, have participants instituted new policies and procedures on their jobs?

- What policies and procedures have they changed or canceled as a result of the workshop?

- What skills, knowledge, tools did participants bring back to the job for immediate application?

- What problems have they solved?

- Has your company realized any cost benefits from investing in this training?

- Would you use this program again?

- Did participants fit the advertised description of who should attend, or did the leaders simply accept anyone who paid the fee?

- Is preparation necessary for this workshop? How should participants prepare?

- Does this workshop provide for individualized attention and instruction from leaders?

If you design assignments and activities on interpersonal skills for managers and supervisors, give them sufficient time to prepare for effective discussions, observations, and feedback. Workshops on this kind of process-oriented training may be difficult for managers and supervisors who are accustomed to focusing on solutions. They may also be hesitant to critique or discuss each other's behavior unless they feel prepared to do so.

Feedback. To ensure that participants understand behaviors and the impact of certain actions, build structured observation into exercise and activity designs. Handouts such as checklists and questionnaires can help group members focus on interactions, skills performance, and interpersonal skills. Before beginning a process observation and feedback discussion, make sure the group has reached a comfort level that allows this kind of activity. Make sure that all feedback instruments, such as surveys, checklists, and questionnaires, address job-specific behaviors, actions, or attitudes.

Structure activities to include two observers in a group. If you're using specific exercises for developing interpersonal skills, require a facilitator for each group. This individual can assist participants in learning how to relate to others in the group. Require videocassette recorders as part of the activity sessions. These machines capture group process and support data gathered by observers.

Workshop Tools and Media

Today, workshop leaders and designers have a wealth of resources to choose from. Games, simulations, group activities and exercises, visual aids, computers, software, video equipment, books, and a variety of instruments can be used to enhance workshop learning. The following are some hints for developing and using resources:

- Buy professional materials from vendors when cost, relevance, approach, and job specifications fit both your instructional and budget plans.

- Create your own resources by starting with available materials and making improvements and changes to suit your own needs. But remember to make a distinction between using materials as sources and violating the copyrights of others.

- Use specific materials in workshops, such as case studies. Use short (maximum four paragraphs), to-the-point case studies for workshops. These are easiest and most effective with large groups working under strict time constraints.

- Think of the group itself as a resource. Try to set up workshops to encourage interaction and an exchange of ideas. Participants bring a great deal of information and experience to discussions and activities.

- Make sure that a consistent training philosophy guides your design. Workshop designers should explain to leaders and participants the theories that support each presentation and activity.

- Draw up a bibliography or supplementary resource list for participants interested in further investigation into the theory and philosophy of behaviors and practices covered in the workshop.

Uses of Media

For instructional media to be useful, they must contribute directly to communicating and accomplishing workshop objectives. The most effective kinds enhance participant involvement and activity.

Traditional media. Be careful not to limit yourself to traditional kinds of media. Visual aids like chalkboards and charts often are used to enhance a lecture, making participants passive recipients of knowledge. Though some elements of the workshop will require presentations of information, be sure to follow up this passive process with other media-supported activities such as videotaping a lively discussion of the lecture topic.

Use instructional media (films, tapes, computers) to communicate large amounts of subject matter. The use of media equipment eases the workload and time investment of a speaker who is expected to be very knowledgeable, pleasant, and patient. Encourage interaction between learners through the use of films and tapes that relate directly to jobs, involve the learner in active instruction, and demand problem-solving and decision-making skills in follow-up assignments.

Increase behavior changes by using both participant and media feedback. For example, teams of two learners can evaluate each other's performance with the assistance of a personal computer, which facilitates dialogue and interaction.

New technology. Use personal computers to bring an active dimension to the training before, during, and after the workshop. Some software programs can diagnose and analyze the effectiveness of organizational and individual behaviors. Software used for preworkshop instruction can teach background for learning a new skill or process, and prepare learners to focus on application and practice during the workshop. Programs that focus on improving job performance and current skills can last through the workshop to a follow-up phase.

Before purchasing sophisticated media, consider ease of operation, cost, and space requirements. (For more information on media uses and selection guidelines, see *Info-lines* No. 9610, "The Basics of Internet Technology"; and No. 9701, "Delivering Quick-Response IBT/CBT Training.")

The Facilitator or Leader

Workshop leaders are responsible for facilitating the accomplishment of training objectives. In group training situations, they focus more on process than on active leadership. The facilitator's role exists somewhere between group member and change agent who helps the group move toward achieving common goals. Here are some functions associated with the job of workshop leader or facilitator:

Planner

In preworkshop planning and early stages of conducting the workshop, the primary role of the leader or facilitator is to direct learners toward producing results and attaining objectives. Leaders begin planning by assessing participants' training needs and expectations, and continue through the design phase and the workshop in progress. They're prepared at each step to make adjustments and reorganize the training for the benefit of learners.

Other planning functions include identifying and defining instructional methods and techniques, and selecting media. Leaders also are responsible for

---

Case Study: Manufacturer Seeks Help

A corporation was looking for ways to simplify work processes and cut costs. A large number of employees in all departments would take part in the initiative. Their ideas would need management support in order to be adopted, and the endorsement of customers to be effective.

The solution:

A three-day workshop was designed. The first day was spent generating ideas. That evening, a panel of customers joined the company participants to react to ideas and suggest some of their own. The second day was devoted to translating the resultant ideas into workable form. On the third day, the ideas were presented to higher management for discussion and approval.

The workshop was held first for department managers. Because managers would have to review and approve ideas from their subordinates, they needed to understand the process. The workshop was then presented throughout the company. All departments participated, beginning with those deemed to have the most savings potential.

Adapted from Reitz and Manning, The One-Stop Guide to Workshops. *New York: Irwin, 1994.*

---

preparing environments that are physically comfortable and psychologically conducive to learning.

The leader or facilitator is concerned with the following planning issues throughout the workshop:

- Is the group taking directions toward accomplishing objectives?

- Are individual and group needs being addressed?

- Is the psychological environment of the workshop secure so that changes can take place without difficulty?

- Do participants have the opportunity to try new behaviors according to workshop objectives?

- Do participants have the time to think through their subject content and experience it?

- Is the group developing an identity as a cohesive and supportive network?

Guide

The leader guides the group by exhibiting appropriate behaviors during the workshop. This is an informal way of setting behavioral norms or standards that encourage effective growth and change. The following are some guidelines for appropriate behavior during the workshop:

Demonstrate your respect for participants. Show that you value them by listening and not interrupting them. If you disagree with an idea or comment, make it clear that you're rejecting the words, not the person.

Facilitate learning. Create a physically and psychologically comfortable workshop environment. Indicate by your actions that the climate is safe for experimenting and trying out new behaviors and ideas. Never criticize participants for expressing their feelings and opinions.

Listen to and respond to feelings. Expressions of anger, frustration, happiness, and enthusiasm indicate how the group is progressing and represent the dynamics of group interaction. Honest expressions of feelings are part of the growth and change necessary for workshop participants to attain objectives. Never take these expressions personally. If you view them as a natural and normal aspect of group experience, you'll be able to channel them in a productive manner.

Demonstrate correct learning process. Begin sessions with activities and learning experiences that involve everyone. Invite participants to set up cases or scenarios in which they will take an active part by trying to reach solutions and accomplish goals. Workshops should provide an opportunity for participants to examine their actions and experiences.

Address current workshop happenings. Let participants know the learning process at hand is most important. Talk about past experiences, other workshops, or groups only when these tie directly to the accomplishment of current workshop assignments.

Share responsibilities for learning. Demonstrate your belief that the workshop is an experience of planning together. Never surprise the group with new tasks and topics. Don't pull rank over others. Let the group take some responsibility for achieving objectives and determining the best direction for pursuing their achievements.

Assist with exercises and activities. Assist the group in constructing and adapting exercises and activities to help participants accomplish their personal learning goals. Use methods such as role plays and small groups (dyads and triads).

Guide group analyses. Make comments, state generalizations, raise questions, provoke thoughts about the workshop experience, and lead participants in a thoughtful discussion of issues. Analysis should include interpreting the group experience and the learning, asking participants what they think is missing in the workshop, introducing a concept for discussion, and asking participants to explain the implications of their ideas.

Provide support to group members. Emotional support is crucial in learning situations that require group analysis of new and existing behaviors. The leader's intervention and supportive comments will establish a standard of behavior that the rest of the group can use as a model.

Encourage involvement and responsibility. Help the group to think through issues and assist one another. As participants develop together and gain experience, the leader can, for example, encourage them to select role plays and scenarios. The leader can also turn questions back to the group and ask for group opinions and interpretations of what is going on in the workshop.

Value your role. As a member of the group, the leader shouldn't try to maintain a psychological or emotional distance from other participants or demand special status as the leader. These two extremes may cause the group to withdraw from the leader. Try to maintain a delicate balance as facilitator, guide, or resource person and group member.

References & Resources

Articles

Benabou, Charles. "Assessing the Impact of Training Programs on the Bottom Line." *National Productivity Review*, Summer 1996, pp. 91-99.

Boyce, Ann. "Effective Training Begins With Needs Assessment." *Occupational Health & Safety*, August 1996, pp. 72-73.

Broadwell, Martin M. "Ten Commandments for Successful Training." *Training*, August 1996, p. 16.

Broadwell, Martin M., and Carol Broadwell Dietrich. "How to Get Trainees Into the Action." *Training*, February 1996, pp. 52-56.

Brookshaw, Chip, and Dan Seoane. "Training Effectiveness." *InfoWorld*, October 14, 1996, pp. 76-80.

Costanzo, Joe. "Diving Into Digital." *Training & Development*, August 1996, pp. 55-56.

Gordon, Jack, et al. "Asking Questions That Make Them Think." *Training*, September 1996, pp. 12-14.

———. "Go Beyond Surveys to Assess Needs." *Training*, May 1996, pp. 15-16.

———. "How to Help Them Get the Most From Training." *Training*, September 1996, p. 17.

Hall, Brandon. "Easing Into Multimedia." *Training & Development*, April 1996, pp. 61-62.

Hequet, Marc. "Fighting Fear." *Training*, July 1996, pp. 36-40.

———. "Instructive Moments." *Training*, January 1996, pp. 68-74.

———. "There, There…." *Training*, July 1996, p. 38.

Huang, Zhuoran. "Making Training Friendly to Other Cultures." *Training & Development*, September 1996, pp. 13-14.

Katz, Cynthia J., and Peter L. Katz. "A Training Solution for Lean and Mean Times." *Personnel Journal*, Product News Supplement, July 1996, pp. S8, S10.

Krause, Hal. "5 Training Myths." *Franchising World*, July/August 1996, pp. 22-23.

Lightfoot, Ethan, and Jo Bennett. "Train Me… If You Can!" *Occupational Health & Safety*, February 1996, pp. 47-49.

Lincoff, Richard L. "It's Show Time!" *Training & Development*, November 1995, pp. 15-16.

Malouf, Doug. "The Seven Deadly Sins of Speakers." *Training & Development*, November 1995, pp. 13-15.

Pescuric, Alice, and William C. Byham. "The New Look of Behavior Modeling." *Training & Development*, July 1996, pp. 24-30.

Phillips, Jack J. "Was It the Training?" *Training & Development*, March 1996, pp. 28-32.

Rinke, Wolf J. "The A-B-Cs of Keeping Your Audience Tuned In." *Training & Development*, May 1996, pp. 22-23.

Stone, Florence. "Developing an Effective Team-Training Program." *Getting Results… for the Hands-on Manager*, October 1996, p. 5.

Williams, Leigh Ann. "Measurement Made Simple." *Training & Development*, July 1996, pp. 43-45.

Books

Jolles, Robert L. *How to Run Seminars and Workshops.* New York: John Wiley & Sons, 1993.

Knowles, Malcolm S. *Designs for Adult Learning.* Alexandria, VA: ASTD, 1995.

Munson, Lawrence S. *How to Conduct Training Seminars.* 2d edition. New York: McGraw-Hill, 1992.

Rietz, Helen L., and Marilyn Manning. *The One-Stop Guide to Workshops.* Burr Ridge, IL: Irwin Professional Publishing, 1994.

Simerly, Robert G. *Planning and Marketing Conferences and Workshops.* San Francisco: Jossey-Bass, 1990.

Info-lines

Bensimon, Helen. "How to Accommodate Different Learning Styles." No. 9604.

Finn, Tom. "Valuing and Managing Diversity." No. 9305 (revised 1999).

O'Neill, Mary. "How to Focus a Training Evaluation." No. 9605.

———. "Linking Training to Performance Goals." No. 9606 (revised 1998).

Job Aid

Workshop Planner

1. List the training needs identified during front-end work and needs assessment procedures.

   a. _____

   b. _____

   c. _____

2. List the training objectives based on the needs stated above.

   a. _____

   b. _____

   c. _____

3. Describe your workshop audience.

   a. How many participants will be attending the workshop?

   _____

   b. What are the position levels, titles, and experiences of the group members? Explain your audience profile.

   _____

   _____

   _____

   _____

   c. What managers and administrators will you ask to attend the workshop? List titles.

   _____

   _____

   _____

   _____

4. Describe the physical workshop environment.

   a. What are the dimensions of the workshop room?

   _____

   b. What kinds of media and equipment will be necessary for the training? List the name of the piece and the number of pieces you will need.

   _____

   _____

   _____

   _____

5. Describe the limitations you'll be working with.

   a. What is the budget allowance you're requesting, and what is the actual approval amount?

   Amount requested is_____

   Amount approved is_____

   b. How much time will you need to complete the training and how much actual time will you have?

   Amount of time needed_____

   Amount of actual time_____

6. List ways that you can overcome any limitations. (For example, restrict number of attendees, cut back on workshop resources, have materials developed in-house to save costs.)

   a._____

   b._____

   c._____

Successful Orientation Programs

Issue 8708

**REVISION
CONSULTANT**

Stewart Hickman

Successful Orientation Programs

Editorial Staff for 8708

Editor
Gerry Spruell

Revised 1999

Editor
Cat Sharpe

Contributing Editor
Ann Bruen

Production Design
Anne Morgan

Orientation Process

The "joys" of job hunting are nothing compared with the "fun" of starting work at a firm. For many people, self-confidence and enthusiasm about a new job give way on the first day to anxiety and confusion. (What am I doing here? What do they expect of me? Whom can I go to for help?) How long this mental mayhem lasts—an hour or a few months—can depend a great deal on employee orientation.

Orientation is a process...not an event. It is part of the overall integration of new employees into the organization by which the organization helps the new hire adapt to the work environment and the job. Orientation is, in fact, a training opportunity to promote organizational effectiveness from the start of a person's employment. Successful orientation speeds up the adaptation process, helping new employees feel comfortable at the organization and making them more productive on the job. The process approach to orientation also results in reduced employee turnover.

There are a number of ways to conduct the orientation process, but all programs achieve the following outcomes:

1. The employee feels welcomed.

2. The employee understands the organization in a broad sense (its past, present, and its vision for the future) as well as specifics in key areas (its structure, culture, policies, and procedures).

3. The employee is clear about what is expected of him or her in terms of work and behavior.

The first day is all-important; new hires can acquire a greater understanding of the organization later through a formal, group orientation presentation. Newcomers should have their employment decision reinforced by being made to feel that the organization is happy to have them. They should receive the information they need to be immediately productive and meet the people who will provide continuing support during the orientation process: supervisors, a peer adviser or "buddy," and the human resources manager. A nice touch is to give them information about the surrounding community: community events, shopping, restaurants, places to go for a walk, and so forth. Another important welcoming gesture is to make sure that someone—the supervisor or buddy—takes the newcomer to lunch the first day.

While the organization provides a framework and the necessary tools, newcomers share in the responsibility for their own orientation process—through reading, self-study, training, observation, and taking advantage of coaching or mentoring opportunities. They can work out their own objectives for future development, and learn more about the organization by asking for informational interviews with co-workers. Since, ideally, all the other employees in an organization will contribute in one way or another to the orientation process—as supervisors, trainers, mentors, information suppliers, or just day-to-day contacts—employees at all levels should be involved in developing and implementing the process.

An unsuccessful orientation can mean more than slow adaptation for employees—it can mean *no* adaptation. No subsiding of first-day anxieties. No clearing up of confusion. Loss of interest in pursuing a career at the organization. Resignations by still-new employees. Poor work from those with so much potential.

Once you have organization-wide understanding of orientation's importance, you can begin a successful process. This issue of *Info-line* tells you how. You will learn the conditions necessary for good orientations, how to develop objectives, details of orientation development and implementation, and orientation evaluation. You also will find tips for training supervisors for their roles and conducting orientation tours.

Absolute "Musts"

The following conditions are integral to effective orientation programs:

1. All employees, existing and new, must understand the importance of orientation. Employees from entry level to senior level must be made aware of the tie between orientation practices and productivity, and they must take orientation seriously.

2. The organization must be willing to invest the amount of time, effort, and resources necessary to develop and maintain an effective orientation program.

3. The orientation program must be flexible enough to address the diverse needs of employees. The program developer must acknowledge differences in employee positions, work hours, experience levels, education levels, ages, and backgrounds.

4. To ensure ongoing effectiveness, one person or group within the organization must be ultimately responsible for the program. The orientation process must be owned by the entire organization, however. Integration of new employees into the workplace is a shared responsibility.

5. The person or group ultimately responsible for orientation must devote the necessary time and effort to training all others involved in implementing the program.

6. The orientation program must remain current. This means that those responsible must periodically assess organizational needs and how well the orientation program is meeting those needs. They also must conduct surveys of program participants for opinions about effectiveness and continually explore opportunities for program improvement.

Orientation Objectives

As with any training, well-thought-out objectives are essential for the orientation program. Follow these checkpoints when developing your program objectives:

☐ Assess the needs of the organization. How can the orientation program address them? (For additional information, see *Info-line* No. 8502, "Be a Better Needs Analyst.")

☐ Survey employees at all levels. What do employees from entry level to top management think the objectives of orientation should be? (For more details, see the face-to-face interviews and written questionnaires sections of *Info-line* No. 8612, "Surveys from Start to Finish.")

☐ Consider complaints voiced by current employees. What negative comments have been heard, and how can the orientation program promote more positive feelings from the start of employment?

☐ Consider comments made by employees in exit interviews. What problems with the organization have exiting employees expressed to the personnel manager, and how can the orientation program address these problems?

The complete list of orientation program objectives varies from firm to firm, but certain basics are found almost everywhere. Tailor the following basic list to your organization's needs:

● Reduce the common anxiety of new employees by making them feel a part of the organization.

● Promote in new employees positive attitudes toward their jobs and the organization.

● Establish from the start of employment open communication between the organization and its employees.

- Communicate to new employees exactly what the organization expects of them in terms of work performance and behavior.

- Acquaint new employees with the organizational strategy, goals, philosophy, values, products and services, structure, culture, systems, and people.

Retention

One casualty in a work environment that seemingly encourages downsizing and limited advancement openings may be company loyalty. As a result, organizations must pay extra attention to getting the right employees—and then keeping them. Employee loyalty needs to be cemented early on and nurtured on a continuing basis.

There are ways to address the problem of retention, such as networking and mentoring systems, flexible work arrangements, recognition, praise, and advancement opportunities. But the most important ingredient for successful retention, fostered by an ongoing orientation program, is **giving employees a sense of being valued and important.** For a case study illustrating how retention rates can rise dramatically as a result of a good orientation, see *Keeping Good Employees* at right.

Organizational Culture and Values

In concert with the retention problem is the need to foster a sense of "belonging" among new hires. Productivity suffers when employees are:

- overwhelmed or confused

- don't understand the link between their jobs and the organization as a whole

- feel frustrated by a seeming lack of opportunity

Keeping Good Employees

With good initiation, an organization can build employee loyalty from the beginning. In the 1980s, Corning, Inc., implemented an orientation program that resulted in a marked rise in employee retention rates. The New York-based company considers a smooth introduction so important that on the first day, their employees report directly to an orientation class instead of their place of work.

These classes, which are available each Monday to as few as two new hires, introduce the new employees to the Corning history, heritage, values, and the various positions within the company. During the second half of the day, the new hires sign up for benefits and receive their security badges. They also receive a new-employee workbook, covering each of the seven learning modules that they will go through, along with questions and summaries of each section.

Corning waits six weeks before finishing the remaining five modules of orientation, permitting new employees to become more familiar with the company. They then attend a two-day orientation session that covers topics such as the following:

- Corning's performance development and review process

- a module called Valuing the Individual that signals how much the organization values diversity

- how to read the annual report

- acceptable spending habits

- use of company resources, such as the Employee Assistance Program

- projects sponsored by the company's research and development and engineering groups

Corning's philosophy is that employees decide within the first six to eight weeks whether they are going to stay with a company. Since the first impression is a lasting one, the company tries to get the orientation done within that time frame in order to give its new employees a sense of being valued and important.

Adapted from "Attracting the Right Employees—and Keeping Them," by Gillian Flynn, Personnel Journal, *December 1994.*

Learning an Organization's Culture

When the human resources staff at Micron Technologies evaluated the company's orientation process, they discovered that new employees were not receiving the information they needed to become effective team members. In response, the training department developed a 15-hour training class designed to introduce employees to the organization. They enlisted the aid of employees from different areas of the company and sought feedback of managers and supervisors to design a course that reflected the company's philosophy and direction.

The course includes sessions that address the following topics:

Joining the company team: history and mission, stages of team development, and individual team behavior styles.

Participating in groups: expectations for participation in meetings, group dynamics, and specific techniques for becoming more effective contributors.

Gaining responsibility: taking charge of new assignments, asking questions and clarifying responsibilities.

Planning employee development: career development over the long term, analysis of job responsibilities, tasks, and standards, and the performance evaluation process.

Resolving workplace issues: conflict resolution and the company's problem-solving procedure.

Dealing with change: effects of unwelcome change and how to respond effectively to such changes.

Each segment incorporates in-class activities and on-the-job assignments and is co-facilitated by a supervisor or manager from various departments in the organization. The course concludes with an assessment of how each team moved through the stages of group development, their profit-and-loss statements, and how the differences in their behavior were reflected in the team's dynamics. Through this course, the company hopes to effect greater employee motivation, initiative, and job satisfaction by providing an understanding of the organization's values and how each employee's efforts support those values.

Adapted from "From New Recruit to Team Member," by Karen Bridges, et al., Training & Development, *August 1993.*

Frequently, new hires are immersed in the organizational culture without an adequate understanding of it. A successful orientation process will communicate this culture in an interesting and useful way in order to help employees understand the company's values and how their department's goals support those values. For an example of an innovative program developed to achieve these goals, see *Learning an Organization's Culture* at left.

Orientation and Productivity

A focus on what it takes for a new employee to be effective immediately can be an important element in the orientation process. One approach is to develop training classes involving highly interactive and experiential learning techniques that engage participants in applying their skills immediately. Program designers can determine which pieces of information new employees can use right away and which can be offered in other formats at other times.

Information about company history and culture is woven into the activities of these workshops, which can include:

- team and meeting skills
- problem solving and decision making
- quality control tools
- diversity appreciation
- change management

When carefully designed and implemented, the use of these training techniques in the orientation process can meet all the "traditional" objectives while fostering a more rapid assimilation and consequent increase in productivity for new employees.

Development and Implementation

Once you have determined the orientation objectives, it is time to develop the program. To do so, you will need assistance—information and opinions—from a variety of people. You will call on different people for more than program development help, however; you will also rely on others to help implement the program. Supervisors and co-workers of the new employees, and perhaps even the firm's president, play roles in conducting orientations.

Following are recommendations for an umbrella program, encompassing core content as well as departmental or individual content. These recommendations include general guidelines and what topics to cover—how to cover them, who should cover them, where, and when. Remember to build in flexibility; revise your umbrella program as needed to address diverse employee groups or to address the changing needs of your organization.

Guidelines for Groups and Individuals

Here are helpful guidelines on developing an orientation process. If you have a number of new employees, regularly scheduled group orientation sessions are the most efficient way to disseminate information about the organization, but keep in mind that job-specific orientation information should be presented one-on-one on the first day of employment.

Groups

Send new employees written orientation materials the first day on the job. This gives them a chance to skim information and prepare questions for the orientation sessions. In addition, the employee can refer to the materials for any information he or she wants immediately that may not be presented for a while. Along with the orientation materials also send a schedule of any job training sessions, such as computer training, that will occur during the orientation period.

Plan orientation sessions for no longer than 90 minutes. If you have a lot of information to cover on one orientation topic, break it into 90-minute presentation segments and plan sessions on successive days. Sticking to this time limit prevents information overload. New employees can easily become overwhelmed by fact after fact on the firm's background, beliefs, benefits, or other orientation topics.

You may not need to develop two-part or three-part orientation sessions. But if you do, here is a benefit: Participants have a good opportunity (an entire day, at least) between sessions to consider questions they may have. Some people have difficulty pinpointing their area of confusion on the spot during a postpresentation question-and-answer period. The total amount of time necessary for orientation sessions depends on the size and complexity of the organization, the complexity of the jobs new employees assume, and the number of orientation objectives to be fulfilled.

Individuals

Focus on orienting each new employee, not just a group. Keep individual needs in mind. Make the supervisor key to the program (see *Supervisor Training Tips* on the next page). Supervisors are responsible for their personnel, and that responsibility begins on each employee's first day. Give supervisors an active part to play in orientation, and train them well. The long-term success of a new employee can depend a great deal on how involved the supervisor is in orientation and how well he or she carries out orientation responsibilities.

Ask supervisors to assign each new employee a "buddy" for the initial orientation period—a peer-level co-worker. The buddy provides day-to-day support: to help the new employee feel at home, to answer questions, and to orient the employee to informal rules and social norms at the organization. The co-worker chosen must have excellent work behaviors, a positive attitude toward the organization, and enough experience to correctly answer the new employee's questions. The supervisor or buddy should take the new employee on a tour of the facilities during the first week of employment (see *Facility Tours* for guidelines).

Strange as it sounds, even a top manager should have a buddy, although the assigning of one may be much more informal. This buddy could be the new employee's mentor if a mentoring system is in place.

Supervisor Training Tips

Make sure supervisors are well prepared for their orientation roles. Following are guidelines for a supervisor training session:

- Explain the orientation objectives and the rationale behind the program.

- Emphasize the importance of orientation and how it affects performance and retention of employees and organizational productivity.

- Explain the entire program, highlighting supervisors' roles.

- Let supervisors rehearse their roles. Ask them to pair off and take turns playing supervisor and new employee. Coach supervisors in their performance. (For assistance in conducting this part of the training, see *Info-line* No. 8412, "Simulation and Role Play.")

- Set up small-group discussions. Ask supervisors to talk about employee problems that might be prevented by the orientation program. Ask them to think back to their own orientations, or lack thereof, and consider the benefits of your orientation program.

Relocated Employees

Assist new employees from out of town, who have a harder time feeling "at home," by preparing packages of information about local services and events. Include such things as public transportation brochures and listings of restaurants, shopping centers, parks, libraries, churches, synagogues, and hospitals. Send these packages ahead of employment time if possible.

If your organization believes this much help is beyond the call of duty, at least make a few information suggestions to the new employees during orientation sessions. You may even consider suggesting to management that your organization host one or two social events each year for employees and their families. Experts believe such events are excellent ways to help new employees assimilate at the organization and keep them employed longer.

Temporary Employees

As a cost-cutting measure, many of today's streamlined organizations make frequent use of temporary employees. When you have "casual hires" coming and going, you need an orientation program that ensures proper training and creates instant rapport with full-time employees.

Begin your orientation with a welcome and general information about the organization. Explain company policies, such as dress guidelines and attendance, and basic work information, such as hours of operation, breaks, lunches, and general ethical work expectations. Try to give the temporary employee a quick tour of the work area, and pair them up with a supervisor or co-worker who can address any concerns they may have.

Focus your orientation for temporary employees on the following essentials:

- What do they need to know?

- Do they have the necessary skills to do the job?

- What would it take for them to be more effective immediately? Can you provide job aids that will assist them?

- Are there any differences in language or culture that need to be addressed?

- Is there someone nearby who can answer their questions and make them feel welcome?

If your organization is hiring a number of temporary employees at the same time, consider beginning a general orientation session with an icebreaker to give them an opportunity to get to know one another. (For examples, see *Info-line* No. 8911, "Icebreakers.") Fostering an atmosphere of teamwork is just as important for temporary employees as it is for permanent workers. If they feel that they belong and enjoy the work environment, they will stay longer and be more productive.

What to Cover

Following are topics that must be covered in any orientation program. Based on the needs of your organization and employees, determine a timeline for distributing the orientation content. You cannot cover all the information in one day, but you should not wait too long to cover the important topics. Decide what your new hires need to know the first day, the first week, the first three months—then decide what should be reinforced as a part of your ongoing orientation efforts.

■ *Organization Overview*
Cover the history, philosophies, goals, and managerial style of the organization.

■ *Nature of the Business*
This part of the orientation covers the type of business; profile of customers or clients; facilities; functions of various divisions; products and services offered; overview of how products work and how services are provided; competitive products and services; financial background of the firm.

■ *Structure*
Distribute an organization chart showing all divisions and reporting relationships. Give the new employee a chart or handout showing the structure of his or her department. Provide the names and positions of personnel who are key to the new employee's job, including names of all top management team members.

Facility Tours

Often the new employee's supervisor or buddy conducts facility tours, but the orientation program manager should handle the tour planning. Following are tips for planning effective facility tours:

■ *Employee Needs*
Keep the needs of individual new employees in mind. Specify the route and include stops at all work areas relating to each employee's job. Leave out work areas unnecessary to the orientation of the particular employee or group of employees going on the tour. Include in your plan a list of staff members the new employees should meet on the tour.

Point out fire extinguishers, fire escapes, and exit stairways and discuss evacuation procedures. Check the restrictions imposed for visitors at work areas you want to include in the tour, ensuring in advance that visitors are allowed access.

■ *Time Requirements*
Include approximations of time to be spent in each work area and with staff members to be met. Some employees, due to the nature of their jobs, need more exposure to certain parts of the organization than other employees. Specify which staff members introduced on the tour are to give brief overviews or demonstrations of their work. Notify these staff members in advance of the tour date and time, offering any assistance they might require. Consider the noise level at the areas where these staff members work—if it is too high, find another location for their presentations.

Consider how much time all the stops will take. Tour participants can tire easily and lose attention, so make sure the tour will not run too long. If the tour is necessarily long, however, build in rest and refreshment breaks.

■ *Number of Participants*
Do not schedule too many new employees for one tour. Set the limit at three or four so you can plan the tour to meet their particular needs—too many participants with too many different needs means too long a tour. In addition, if too many people are taken on one tour, the tour guide and staff members speaking along the way will have to shout.

■ *Performance Expectations*

Include what the organization expects of employees in terms of work performance: expected levels of productivity, expected work habits and ethics, and so forth. Also present what employees can expect from the organization in terms of equitable treatment, professional development opportunities, and financial rewards.

■ *Behavior Expectations*

Distribute and discuss a list of organizational norms—rules of expected behavior for the organization and employees. Typical norms incorporate culture, philosophies, and values of the organization. A sample norm for the organization might be: "The equality, dignity, worth, and potential of individuals will be recognized." Sample norms for employees might be: "We will conduct ourselves professionally: responsibly, ethically, and legally." "We will resolve conflicts at the lowest possible levels and with willingness to negotiate." "We will support group decisions."

■ *Policies*

Distribute a brochure or manual prepared by human resources that covers organizational policies, procedures, compensation practices, and benefits. Provide details on the following areas of interest:

- how and when performance appraisals are conducted

- how often salary is increased, how increases are determined, and how they are computed

- benefits offered: health and life insurance, retirement plans, profit sharing, vacation and personal days, holidays, employee services

- policies and procedures: work hours, overtime, comp days, inclement weather days, sick leave, funeral leave, military leave, jury duty, maternity/paternity leave, leaves of absence, probation, discipline, and security

■ *Safety Rules and Health Requirements*

If the industry you are in requires extensive coverage of safety rules and health requirements, provide a manual and a special safety and health audiovisual presentation. If only a few rules and requirements need explanation, they can be included in the policies and procedures brochure.

■ *Office Procedures and Supplies*

Explain procedures for such things as sending interoffice correspondence, ordering supplies, requesting checks, and filling out expense reports. Show the new employee how the telephone system works, how to use the copy machine, where supplies are kept, and so forth.

■ *Individual Job Specifics*

On the first day of employment, the supervisor should discuss the content of the individual employee's job in a private office. The discussion should cover the job description, work objectives, and performance expectations as well as a review of the performance appraisal process. This is the time to clarify any confusion over functions and responsibilities and to tell the employee how his or her job fits in with and affects others in the organization. The supervisor should emphasize the importance of this particular job, describing how it contributes to organizational success.

Orientation Follow-Up

As a part of the ongoing orientation process, supervisors should conduct private follow-up meetings with new employees. During these sessions, the supervisor should do the following things, and then share the result with the orientation program director:

1. Answer any questions the employee still has about items covered in the orientation.

2. Encourage the employee to share any problems encountered with the organization thus far and to express any concerns. Address those concerns.

3. Gauge the employee's comfort level at this point with the organization and his or her job.

4. Determine the need for additional training, remembering that orientation is a process, not an event.

Preemployment Orientation

A number of organizations use the period between an employee's hire date and start date to begin the orientation process early. They send some or all of the written orientation materials to the new employee, all at once or distributed over time. This usually depends on how much orientation material there is and how long a period there is between hire and start dates. The materials sent include those ordinarily distributed on the employee's first day:

- a handout or brochure on the organization's history, philosophies, goals, and managerial style

- product and service brochures; information on customers, clients, and competitors; the organization's annual report

- organizational and departmental charts

- the policy and procedure brochure or manual

- the list of organizational norms

- a tentative schedule of orientation sessions once the employee begins work

Depending on the length of time before the employee starts work—it may be months if the new hire is still finishing school or is relocating—the materials sent can also include the following:

Correspondence from employee's supervisor: weekly or monthly notes to stay in touch and to keep the employee on top of what is happening in the department.

Internal publications and memos: information about current organizational activities (the employee is put on a weekly or monthly mailing list, or is contacted by email).

Preliminary job training materials: schedules of sessions the employee will attend, job information sheets, self-study manuals and workbooks.

Advantages

An early start on orientation is advantageous for both employer and employee. Here is why:

Employer

- Strengthened employee commitment to the organization. A long period between hire and start dates gives new hires a lot of time to change their minds. By regularly sending them organizational materials, the employer keeps their interest and helps ensure they will not seek out better offers.

- Anticipation of working with a self-confident employee.

- Expectation for early productivity of a new hire who feels comfortable at the organization.

- Simpler training; high levels of productivity begin sooner.

Employee

- Reassurance that the organization is holding his or her job—especially important if the hire-to-start period is a long one.

- Assurance that the supervisor is happy to have him or her on board. Preemployment correspondence exudes interest.

- Reduced anxiety about fitting in at the firm prior to the first day of work. Through preemployment materials, the new hire gets a feel for the organizational culture and gets familiar with staff members in advance.

- A jump start on learning job functions, which makes the formal training easier to complete successfully.

Online Orientation Programming

Many organizations are now delivering their basic orientation information via CD-ROM or the intranet. The idea is not to replace but to supplement traditional face-to-face methods of delivery. The advantages of online delivery are many:

Eliminates information overload. New hires can access the orientation data when and where they want to—and as often as they like.

Reduces or eliminates the cost of transporting new hires into a central location for orientation.

Provides a useful method of delivery for overseas employees, or during preemployment orientations.

Produces a consistent orientation message for all new employees. Permits easy updating of organizational policies and operations.

Reduces the number of follow-up questions for supervisors. New hires can go back to the online resource for a refresher.

There are disadvantages to a total reliance on this type of orientation, not the least of which is the ready availability of computer access for all new hires. Furthermore, it constitutes an impersonal introduction to the new work environment, which makes it difficult for a new employee to feel welcome. A number of organizations are finding that their new hires like technical delivery, however, as long as the program is easy to use and the quality of the content is good.

Evaluating Orientation Programs

To evaluate the effectiveness of employee orientation programs, get feedback from the new employees and the supervisors who participated. Measuring participant reaction is, according to Donald Kirkpatrick's four-level approach to evaluation, a Level 1 evaluation. This type of evaluation is important because it determines customer satisfaction.

The participant must see some value in the program and usefulness of the knowledge acquired. Managers want the investment in training and development to produce a measurable impact on business performance standards. Reaction evaluation will help determine if you have achieved the outcomes you wanted. (For details, see *Info-lines* No. 9813, "Level 1 Evaluation: Reaction and Planned Action," and No. 8612, "Surveys from Start to Finish.")

Employee Reactions

Send oriented employees a questionnaire, asking the following questions:

1. Did the orientation program in general prepare you well for your job?

2. Which program topics were most important to your job:

   - organizational history, culture, philosophies, goals, and managerial style

   - nature of the business; facilities; products and services; profile of customers or clients and competitors; financial background

   - organizational and departmental structure and introduction to staff members

   - general performance expectations

   - behavior expectations

   - organizational policies, procedures, compensation practices, and benefits

   - safety rules and health requirements

- office procedures, equipment, and supplies

- specific job requirements and expectations

3. Do you think enough orientation time was devoted to the most important topics? Do you think too much time was spent on any topics?

4. How effective was the training in each of the program topics? Was the training on target with your needs? Was it thorough? Was it interesting? Were the people conducting the training well prepared? Did they communicate well?

5. Did the sequence, timing, and duration of orientation sessions fit your schedule and information needs?

6. Do you have any suggestions for improving the orientation program?

Supervisor Reactions

Interview supervisors for their thoughts on orientation effectiveness. Ask these questions:

1. How well are oriented employees performing on the job? Do you think orientation is helping, hindering, or having no effect on performance?

2. Do just-oriented employees seem comfortable with the organization? Do they fit in well with your department? Do they display positive attitudes? Do you relate any of these outcomes to their orientation?

3. Are you comfortable with your role in the orientation program? Should your participation be different in any way?

4. Do you have any suggestions for the orientation program in terms of the following:

    - topics covered

    - activities and materials used to cover topics

    - person responsible for covering each topic

- time devoted to each topic

- scheduling of sessions

Successful Outcomes

Do not simply collect employee and supervisor feedback—use it! Revise your program as needed to address employee and supervisor concerns and to stay current with organizational changes. The result will be continuous successful orientation outcomes. You will know if your orientation program has been successful if you can say that the new employee:

- feels at ease and welcome at the organization

- has a good grasp on organizational history, values, and goals

- understands the industry the organization is in and the functions of different divisions and departments

- understands what the organization expects in terms of work and behavior

- knows the importance of his or her job and how it fits in with the work of others

- knows everything necessary to start performing his or her job

- knows where and who to go to for help with work matters

- knows the policies and procedures of the organization

- is happy to be a part of the organization

- has a positive first impression

These outcomes can become part of a post-orientation follow-up evaluation to answer the question: "How did we do?" Be open to any changes that are suggested, and continually strive for a more effective process.

Final Words on Good Starts

New employees are interested in the total organization. They *want* information on organizational history; they *want* introductions to different departments and personnel. They *want* a feel for the corporate culture and structure; they *want* to know where they fit in. They want to know what the organization expects of them, and they want to know what to expect of the organization. And they want all of this early on so they can feel comfortable on the job as soon as possible.

Good impressions at the start are essential. When new employees are welcomed, made to feel wanted and valued, given complete information, trained, coached, and supported, their feelings about the organization are enhanced. If, however, they are ignored, their feelings about the organization suffer and it is likely they will never fully recover from that experience.

As the old saying has it, "You never get a second chance to make a first impression." Poor early impressions of the organization stick with employees and send them looking for work elsewhere. Orientation is not, however, a one-time event but an ongoing process—employees who experience a continued learning and growth environment within the organization are likely to remain happy and productive in their jobs.

References & Resources

Articles

Austin, Nancy. "Getting Oriented." *Incentive,* October 1995, p. 24.

Bridges, Karen, Gail Hawkins, and Keli Elledge. "From New Recruit to Team Member." *Training & Development,* August 1993, pp. 55-58.

Brinkley, Cynthia, and Ken Florian. "Geneer Specializes in 'Growing' People in a High-Tech Environment." *Corporate University Review,* November/December 1998, pp. 36-39.

Carter, Janet H., and Nancy Hayek. "Using Peers As Resources: Orienting the New Manager." *Performance & Instruction,* February 1993, pp. 18-22.

Cooke, Rhonda. "Welcome Aboard!" *Credit Union Management,* July 1998, pp. 46-47.

Estrin, Chere B. "Orientation." *Legal Assistant Today,* January/February 1997, pp. 70-72.

Filipczak, Bob. "Trained by Starbucks (and Born to Be Wired)." *Training,* June 1995, pp. 73-81.

Flynn, Gillian. "Attracting the Right Employees—and Keeping Them." *Personnel Journal,* December 1994, pp. 44-49.

France, Debra R., and Robin L. Jarvis. "Quick Starts for New Employees." *Training & Development,* October 1996, pp. 47-50.

Ganzel, Rebecca. "Putting Out the Welcome Mat." *Training,* March 1998, pp. 54-62.

George, Marie A., and Kelly D. Miller. "Assimilating New Employees." *Training & Development,* July 1996, pp. 49-50.

"Intranets and CD-ROMs Replace the Face to Face in New-Hire Training." *Training Directors' Forum Newsletter,* May 1997, pp. 1-3.

Loraine, Kaye. "Orientation Is As Simple As 1-2-3." *Nursing Management,* January 1997, pp. 35-36.

LeBleu, Ronald E., and Roger T. Sobkowiak. "Help New Managers Get Started Better." *Human Resources Professional,* March/April 1996, pp. 18-21.

Seaver, Jean B. "An Orientation Process for New Nurse Managers." *Nursing Management,* October 1997, pp. 53-55.

Starcke, Alice M. "Building a Better Orientation Program." *HRMagazine,* November 1996, pp. 107-114.

Sunoo, Brenda P. "How Fun Flies at Southwest Airlines." *Personnel Journal,* June 1995, pp. 62-73.

Tyler, Kathryn. "Take New Employee Orientation Off the Back Burner." *HRMagazine,* May 1998, pp. 49-57.

West, Karen L. "Effective Training for a Revolving Door." *Training & Development,* September 1996, pp. 50-52.

Winkler, Kitty, and Inez Janger. "You're Hired! Now How Do We Keep You?" *Across the Board,* July/August 1998, pp. 16-23.

Young, Cheri A., and Craig C. Lundberg. "Creating a Good First Day on the Job." *Cornell Hotel & Restaurant Association Quarterly,* December 1996, pp. 26-33.

Books

Desatnick, R.L. *Managing to Keep the Customer.* Revised edition. San Francisco: Jossey-Bass, 1993.

Jerris, Linda A. *Effective Employee Orientation.* New York: AMACOM, 1993.

Shea, G.F. "Induction and Orientation." In *Human Resources Management and Development Handbook,* edited by W.R. Tracey. 2d edition. New York: AMACOM, 1994.

Smalley, Larry R. *On-the-Job Orientation and Training.* Irvine, CA: Richard Chang, 1994.

Info-lines

Buckner, Marilyn. "Simulation and Role Play." No. 8412 (revised 1999).

Callahan, Madelyn R., ed. "Be a Better Needs Analyst." No. 8502 (revised 1998).

Long, Lori. "Surveys from Start to Finish." No. 8612 (revised 1998).

Phillips, Jack J., et al. "Level 1 Evaluation: Reaction and Planned Action." No. 9813.

Preziosi, Bob. "Icebreakers." No. 8911 (revised 1999).

Orientation Checklist

This checklist is a guide for everyone involved in the orientation process. The new employee carries it throughout the orientation process and the person who covers each topic fills in the appropriate boxes, then initials and dates the document. Upon completion of the orientation process, copies of the checklists are then reviewed and retained by human resources personnel.

New Employee: _____

Start Date: _____

Position: _____

Department: _____

Supervisor: _____

Buddy: _____

Program Administrator: _____

Topics	Informal Discussion	Formal Presentation	Training	Materials Distributed (check if applicable)	Initials	Date
Part 1: Organizational Background						
☐ Distribute handout or brochure.						
☐ Review and discuss informally:						
organizational history						
organizational philosophies						
organizational goals						
managerial style						
☐ Review and discuss in session:						
organizational history						
organizational philosophies						
organizational goals						
managerial style						
Part 2: Nature of Business or Facilities						
☐ Distribute handout or brochure.						
☐ Review and discuss informally:						
nature of the business						
profile of customers/clients						
facilities						
functions of various divisions						
products and services (offered)/how they work						

Job Aid

Topics	Informal Discussion	Formal Presentation	Training	Materials Distributed (check if applicable)	Initials	Date
Part 2: Nature of Business or Facilities (continued)						
competitive products and services						
financial background of the organization						
☐ Conduct tour of facilities, introduce new employee to personnel.						
☐ Review and discuss in session:						
nature of the business						
profile of customers/clients						
facilities						
functions of various divisions						
products and services (offered)/how they work						
competitive products and services						
financial background of the organization						
Part 3: Organizational Structure						
☐ Distribute organizational and departmental charts.						
☐ Review organizational and departmental structures and reporting relationships.						
☐ Introduce new employee to department staff.						
Part 4: General Performance Expectations						
☐ Review and discuss in session:						
expected levels of productivity						
expected work habits and ethics						
equitable treatment						
professional development opportunities						
career advancement opportunities						
financial rewards						
Part 5: Behavior Expectations						
☐ Distribute, review, and discuss organizational norms.						
Part 6: Policies						
☐ Distribute brochure or manual.						
☐ Review:						
performance appraisal procedures						
compensation practices						

(Job Aid continued on page 50)

The material appearing on this page is not covered by copyright and may be reproduced at will.

Job Aid

Topics	Informal Discussion	Formal Presentation	Training	Materials Distributed (check if applicable)	Initials	Date
Part 6: Policies (continued)						
insurance benefits (health and life)						
retirement plan						
vacation/holidays						
work hours/overtime						
inclement weather days						
sick, funeral, military leave						
jury duty						
security						
Part 7: Safety and Health Requirements						
☐ Distribute manual.						
☐ Deliver demonstration (if required).						
Part 8: Office Procedures, Equipment, and Supplies						
☐ Explain procedures for:						
interoffice correspondence						
ordering supplies						
requesting checks						
expense reports						
☐ Demonstrate/show:						
operation of telephone system						
operation of copy machine						
where supplies are kept						
Part 9: Specific Job Requirements						
☐ Review:						
job functions						
job responsibilities						
work objectives						
job performance expectations						
how job fits into the organization						
Part 10: Orientation Follow-Up						
☐ Answer questions, discuss orientation experience, assess additional training needs.						

Mentoring

Issue 0004

AUTHORS

Beverly Kaye, Ph.D.
Beverly Kaye & Associates, Inc.
3545 Alana Drive
Sherman Oaks, CA 91403
Tel: 818.995.6454
Fax: 818.995.0984
Email: Beverly.Kaye@csibka.com

Devon Scheef
Scheef Organizational
    Development & Training
4840 Coyote Wells Circle
Westlake Village, CA 91362
Tel/Fax: 805.494.0124
Email: DevonScheef@cs.com

Editor
Cat Sharpe Russo

Managing Editor
Sabrina E. Hicks

Contributing Editor
Ann Bruen

Production Design
Leah Cohen

Mentoring

The ROI of Mentoring

It is ironic that in this time of technological achievement, the lifeblood of corporations is the accumulated insight of the people who choose to give their gifts of talent and commitment to any given organization. So, the question is this: How do we ensure that the intellectual legacy of our people continues?

A large portion of the answer lies with mentoring initiatives. Mentoring is a powerful, dynamic process—for both employees and organizations. To share wisdom is to share life experience. No matter which methodology is used, mentoring has the potential to elevate corporate dialogue from the mundane to the truly transformational.

The case for mentoring is compelling. According to an emerging workforce study done by Louis Harris & Associates, 35 percent of employees who do not receive regular mentoring are likely to look for another job within 12 months. In contrast, just 16 percent of those with good mentors expect to leave their jobs. Through mentoring programs, protégés develop vision and expertise, and mentors become reinvigorated, knowing that they are leaving a legacy to their organization, profession, and community.

Once an organization has accepted the value of a mentoring program, what approach is the best? While still popular, one-to-one mentoring is no longer viewed as the only or best approach. Many organizations find that group mentoring and virtual mentoring are attractive alternatives or supplements to traditional mentoring. Based on information contained in a previous *Info-line* on mentoring, this issue expands that focus and provides additional mentoring ideas. Here you will find an overview of the three approaches to mentoring, as well as techniques, guidelines, and tips to make your mentoring programs successful.

The Business Case for Mentoring

Among other trends reflected in the changing workforce is a growing employee commitment to careers, rather than jobs. Beginning with their first job out of college, today's employees are looking ahead to a solid career, and any individual job may be little more than a convenient stepping stone to a more ambitious end. Because of that, employers stand a better chance of retaining top-performing

employees if they take an active interest in their careers—and even help shape those careers through mentoring initiatives.

Career Development: Tradition With a Twist

A key benefit to mentoring programs is that they offer something other career development programs do not: individual attention. In a complex organization, it is particularly beneficial for an employee to learn how the system operates from someone who is better educated or more experienced. It is also worth noting that when a mentor relationship works, it is the easiest way for an organization to support career development; once in place, it usually no longer requires much involvement from the organization.

Traditionally, organizations are interested in grooming employees to take over jobs of increasing responsibility. On another level, they might be concerned with retaining the bright young graduates who are still "testing the waters" but could easily take their skills and enthusiasm elsewhere if they are not quickly involved with the excitement, goals, and—most important—people of the organization. The more specific the overall goal, the easier the mentoring program is to design and the better chance the organization has of receiving a return on its investment.

Employers stand to gain as much as employees through such efforts. Among other things, mentoring programs can help resolve such organizational problems as the premature departure of young professionals, the stagnation and boredom of solid performers, or the lack of qualified people to fill senior management positions vacated by retirees.

Succession Planning Initiatives

Organizations often look toward a formalized mentoring program as a means of instituting a management continuity system at a variety of levels. Some use the program to groom middle management for senior-level jobs. Mentoring programs are an effective means of increasing the political savvy, exposure, and visibility middle managers need if they are going to succeed in top-level management positions.

Why We Mentor

Mentoring is a tool to accomplish the following goals:

- Attract and retain high performers.
- Upgrade employee skills and knowledge.
- Promote diversity of thought and style.
- Develop leadership talent.
- Preserve institutional memory.
- Create inclusion.
- Develop a line of succession.
- Foster a collaborative environment.
- Ease the transition to new assignments.
- Strengthen corporate competitive advantage.

Because many organizations are challenged by ever-evolving work environments, the implementation of such a succession, or replacement, planning program requires using change management strategies that put the right people in the right places at the right times. To find those employees who have the skills to meet organizational challenges, the planning process entails the following elements:

- identification and analysis of key positions

- assessment of candidates against job and personal requirements

- creation of individual development plans

- selection of candidates

To meet the goals of their succession planning programs, organizations are asking managers to coach and mentor in more intensive ways than they have in the past. Mentoring helps develop future executives through structured activities that allow employees to acquire leadership skills as a part of their natural rate of development.

Types of Mentoring Programs

Mentoring can take at least three forms, and many variations of each are possible depending on the organization's needs. **One-to-one mentoring** uses mentoring partners, traditionally called protégés and mentors. Historically, this relationship was seen as rather patriarchal, with a powerful mentor responsible for guiding the career of a junior up-and-coming employee. The updated view of one-to-one mentoring is that of two partners, each with areas of expertise and contribution, who work together to achieve the development or learning goals of the protégé partner. The new view of one-to-one mentoring acknowledges that mentors often gain as much from the relationship as the protégés.

Group mentoring is a format in which small groups of people commit to jointly support and pursue one another's learning goals. The group has a learning facilitator, who takes on the role of group mentor. In addition, each group member is considered a mentor to the others, serving as feedback giver, supporter, and ally. This mentoring method leverages the power of group motivation and knowledge exchange. It is an appropriate model for many of today's fast-paced and flexible organizations that rely on knowledge networks and include everyone in the decision-making process.

Virtual mentoring is a form of one-to-one or group mentoring that is conducted by telephone, email, and video conferencing. Once considered a "last resort" mentoring method, it is growing in popularity because of geographic considerations. While it overcomes the challenges of distance, it requires special rigor and disciplined implementation to compensate for lack of face-to-face contact.

One-to-One Mentoring

Despite all their advantages, one-to-one mentoring programs are not easy to establish. To set up a mentoring program you need to be familiar with program components, mentor selection, and what mentors and protégés do.

Program Components

There are five essential components of mentoring programs.

1. Determine the purpose of the mentoring initiative and set specific goals. Frequently cited outcomes include high potential development, leadership development, support for diversity initiatives, knowledge transfer, and retention of key individuals.

2. Identify and match mentors and protégés. Select participants based on fair, attainable, and known criteria, and make sure that matching mentors and protégés is voluntary. Experts have found that the best matches occur based on the development needs of the protégés. Some companies find cross-functional matching valuable as well.

3. Train mentors and prepare protégés. Good mentor/protégé matches alone do not guarantee success. Improve chances for successful mentoring by training mentors how and when to apply skills such as empathetic listening, conflict resolution, flexible leadership, assertiveness, providing feedback and positive reinforcement, motivating, and using effective instructional techniques. Prepare protégés by helping them define their goals for the mentoring relationship.

4. Monitor the mentoring process to make sure that protégés are achieving their goals. The monitoring phase offers opportunities to identify poor matches and allow participants to request specific persons to replace their current mentor or protégé.

5. Evaluate the program. Base your program evaluation on the overall objectives for the mentoring initiatives.

Selecting a Mentor

Mentors find their roles to be rewarding and developmental, but they must be seasoned employees who fulfill specific criteria. Here are items to consider when selecting mentors:

Mentoring Myths

There are several common myths about mentors:

- All mentors are good communicators.

- Mentors control the next career step.

- Mentors have the latest information available on the organization.

- It is the mentor's job to keep the protégé's boss informed.

- A mentor should have information on special career path possibilities.

- People should have the same mentor for their entire careers.

Job Performance

- Are prospective mentors recognized as effective leaders, and have they performed well in leadership roles?

- Are they considered role models of character and values consistent with their leadership competencies?

- Do prospective mentors support the organization's vision and goals?

- Do they develop subordinates well?

Business Acumen

- Do prospective mentors have a long-view perspective? Are they comfortable with strategic business outlook planning and thinking?

- Do they deal well with the inherent ambiguity and complexity of any organization? Are they role models of flexibility and change management?

What Protégés Do

Protégés bring their own personalities and perspectives to the mentoring relationship. Their fresh outlook and enthusiasm can make a real contribution to the organization, as they and their mentors develop their relationship. These are the characteristics found in good protégés:

Proactive Learner

Nowhere is the notion of "active learning" more important than in mentoring relationships. While the mentor is a respected and valuable resource, it is the role of the protégé to grasp learning opportunities, take learning risks, and engage the mentor as an active development partner.

Change Agent

The best mentoring relationships are action oriented and emphasize doing, trying, and practicing versus telling, listening, and passive learning. The role of change agent means that the protégé realizes that growth and development are goals of the process. Indeed, the protégé's role is to change based on this learning relationship.

Contributor

A hallmark of a successful relationship is that the mentor learns as much from the protégé as the protégé does from the mentor. A key role of the protégé is to share ideas and expertise with the mentor, and view the relationship as one of reciprocal learning.

Interpersonal Skills

- Do prospective mentors have a history of positive relationships with a broad scope of individuals?

- Are they seen as trusted resources in their own organization?

- Do they have a history of freely sharing expertise and insight with others?

Learning Capacity

- Are prospective mentors aware of their strengths and weaknesses? Are they willing to talk about these with others?

- Are they personally committed to continuous growth and receptive to new approaches and ideas?

What Mentors Do

Every mentor brings unique experience and expertise to the relationship. Here are the roles most mentors perform:

Guide. A guide takes you through a journey, shows you a path, and helps you see important things along the way. This role can be accomplished in two forms. The *wise owl* offers perspective about what is going on in the organization; while the *teacher* helps people teach themselves by asking the right questions, throwing out ideas, and keeping conversation moving. These mentors lead with questions, share their views freely, and reflect on their own journeys.

Ally. An ally can help by offering honesty and friendship while helping others understand how they are seen in the organization. The role can be one of a *sounding board*, where the mentor creates an environment for venting feelings and frustrations. Or the ally can take the form of a *straight talker*, where the mentor provides honest and candid feedback from his or her vantage point. Allies tell it like it is, feel comfortable when others are venting, and freely offer their own feelings and views.

Catalyst. A catalyst may use ideas and knowledge from his or her own experiences to stimulate others to explore the culture and environment that surrounds them. This mentor can be an *entrepreneur*, helping the protégé to see the organization in a new light, or a *creative motivator*, stimulating the person to discuss feelings, ideas, visions, and creative concepts. Catalysts know the inner workings of the organization, think of themselves as creative or idea persons, and get excited when they see others get excited about new possibilities.

Savvy Insider. The savvy insider knows the ropes. Insiders understand how things really get accomplished in the organization. They can be *people connectors*, putting protégés in touch with people in the organization who can take their learning to another level, or they can be *information providers*, supplying specific data that comes from their connections and activities.

Advocate. The advocate actively seeks to propel the protégé's growth and helps him or her develop action plans. Advocates may be *champions*, using their positions to help protégés gain visibility and exposure, or serve as a *powerful voice*, taking action on one or more of the protégés. These mentors go to bat for their people, let others take responsibility and share credit, and enjoy strong credibility and the respect of their peers.

Tips for One-to-One Mentors

Here are some ideas for achieving success in the mentoring relationship:

■ *Get in Gear*
Every mentoring relationship needs two elements. First, what are the protégé's goals for the relationship, and what are your own—what do you want to learn or achieve as well? Second, what role does the protégé want you to play? Are you comfortable with that role? Explore these questions at your first, and most important, mentoring meeting—it is the foundation for the relationship.

■ *Recognize the Power of Feedback*
Mentors provide the gift of feedback. By sharing unbiased perceptions in a kind and honest way, mentors have tremendous impact. Be sure to provide coaching points, and recognize growth and change. Feedback given in the spirit of helpfulness and progress is appreciated and acted on, as long as it is specific and direct, solicits the protégé's input, and points the way to change in the future.

■ *Be Yourself*
Be straightforward about your own strengths and weaknesses. By doing so, you model how a successful person deals with reality. Offer your own lessons learned, struggles, and successes. Being a mentor does not mean being perfect. Many protégés report that their mentors helped them by disclosing how they had handled difficult aspects of their own personalities.

Conversation Starters for Mentors

At first, it may be difficult for mentors who are new to the role to get started in the relationship-building process. Here are a few suggested ways to get the conversation going:

● Which assignments in the past have provided you with the most challenge? The least challenge? Why?

● Tell me about an accomplishment of which you are particularly proud.

● What are your most important values? Which values are met and not met at work?

● What makes you unique? What about your values, interests, competencies and skills, personal traits, and style?

● What part of your education or work experience has been the most valuable to you over the years?

● What actions have you taken to manage your career? What assistance may I provide?

● What lessons have you learned from your successes and failures?

● What is your biggest challenge in trying to balance your work life and personal life?

■ *Be a Question Coach*
Mentors do not have all the answers, but they can help their partners self-discover. Use questions to help others reflect on their experience and draw out key learning points. The fast-paced action orientation of the business day does not allow much time for reflection, so promote insight by asking questions such as these: "What did you learn from this situation?" "How might you approach this situation in the future?" "What patterns are you noticing about yourself?"

■ *Shine a New Light*
Mentors have the luxury of being distant from their protégé's work problems and trials. Use this distance to provide the "big picture" as a context for daily ups and downs. Take the long view, and teach your protégé to do the same.

■ *Let Actions Speak Louder Than Words*

Ask your protégé to accompany you on projects that will expand his or her point of view. Look at your own job for situations that could provide learning experiences. Most people learn by doing, so bring the protégé along. Afterward, spend time debriefing the events and relating them to the protégé's development. Share your thought process regarding how you handled or acted in the situation. In the process, the protégé may have some valuable feedback to contribute.

Group Mentoring

Today's organizations are flat, sparse, team based, and self-directed. They must constantly learn new ways to serve customers and beat competitors. Employees are required to look everywhere, even outward, not just upward. In these environments, structuring one-to-one relationships may be the wrong way to go. Such relationships only strengthen patriarchy, and the notion that someone "else"—at a higher level—must have the answers. Furthermore, copying the one-to-one relationships that work so well in the informal system gives us a different animal when we try to "formalize" them. So, why replicate? Why not invent something totally different?

A group approach, whereby a mentor works with a group of protégés, sets very different dynamics in motion. Protégés are responsible for the group agenda—setting it, requesting what they need for their development, and working together. Peers recognize how much they can learn from one another, and group mentors, when freed from the responsibility of coming up with an agenda, can respond more candidly to real concerns and issues. All participants feel better about the process and learn more as a result.

Mentors look forward to the group meetings. With shared agendas, they learn too. Some bring their own current organization issues to these meetings, to elicit the fresh viewpoints of their protégés who have a different status and tenure in the organiza-

tion. Many group mentors do not look upon this as the added burden they felt in earlier one-to-one efforts.

The group mentoring concept has a number of pluses. It places a successful organization veteran with a group of four to six less-experienced protégés. As a group they do the following things:

● exchange ideas
● analyze development issues
● receive feedback and guidance
● build team-development skills
● build interpersonal interaction skills
● become a "learning group"

The Learning Group

The mentoring group should be assembled with care. Participant qualifications include not only demonstrated ability to perform, but also interpersonal skills and a willingness to learn from others.

Group composition. The ideal protégé group consists of four to six high-performing employees who are seen as making important contributions to the organization currently and in the future. Typically, their names are on the succession-planning lists. They have expertise the organization does not want to lose—whether the expertise is technical, managerial, or administrative.

In selecting high-performing people for a protégé group, it is important to consider the interaction and the synthesis of the group as a whole. Diversity in position levels, functions, gender, race, and career goals serves several purposes. A diverse protégé group creates a unique opportunity for the members to learn the perspectives of people in different positions and areas of the organization. It also helps create a peer network of contacts. In addition, when people in a group do not think alike, valuable interaction is more likely. But achieving diversity in a small group is usually deliberate. The members must be selected with diversity in mind.

Mentoring Do's and Don'ts

The difference between mentoring success and failure lies in the ability to retain intellectual capital and integrate learning continuously. Here are some do's and don'ts for successfully rolling out a mentoring program:

Do	Don't
Look at employee retention rates, the percentage of senior managers who will reach retirement in the next five to 10 years, and current bench strength; then develop objectives.	Develop a mentoring program because it is popular or because you have read that it works for other organizations.
Set long-term goals that will help make your organization a better place to work, increase productivity, make people more savvy about managing their careers, connect people, increase diversity, and build trust and communication.	Develop a mentoring program without setting goals.
Benchmark the practices of other successful mentoring programs. Consider the limited use of outside consultants to advise and provide feedback to the program developers.	Develop a mentoring program that relies solely on internal resources.
Publicize the program in a variety of forms and forums. Conduct briefings, enlist champions, and create mentoring resource centers.	Expect employees to flock to the program without an aggressive internal marketing plan.
Carefully screen protégés and mentors to assess their level of interest and commitment. Pair participants who can and want to help reach learning goals.	Develop a program that mandates relationships or is limited to certain employees, such as high-potentials.
Provide training and coaching to participants about creating specific and appropriate learning goals, building trust, communicating, and defining roles and responsibilities.	Expect people to know how to mentor and be mentored— even senior-level executives who have had significant mentors in their lives need guidance.
Encourage mentoring partners to meet face-to-face and connect via telephone or email at least once a month. Recommend that they plan at least one event outside of the office during their relationship.	Let more than three or four weeks go by without contact between mentoring partners, or the relationship may falter.
Make continuous improvements to your program based on what you learn along the way. Use surveys and exit interviews to assess effectiveness.	Rest on your laurels.

Adapted from "Play '20 Questions' to Develop a Successful Mentoring Program,"
by J.G. Lindenberger and L.J. Zachary, Training & Development, *February 1999,* © ASTD.

Organizing Mentoring Groups

When forming mentoring groups, take into consideration the following guidelines:

- Diversity makes a difference. Select groups with diverse racial and gender representation to foster different ways of thinking about careers and success.

- Group mentors do not necessarily need to be the very highest-level executives in the organization. Choose people who are about two levels above the protégés.

- Group mentors should be outside the protégés' functional chain of command.

- Don't forget the protégés' immediate managers. Their roles are crucial too. Plan some meetings that include the protégés' managers, in order to help clarify those roles.

- Give group mentors some ideas for getting dialogue started—questions to ask, concepts to discuss, and experiences to share. But mentors are not in charge of the process. They should encourage the group to set the agenda.

Learning needs. Protégés need many broad opportunities for growth to attain their potential. Development assignments outside the group setting are a vital program component. Such assignments provide an excellent laboratory for a research and development manager who has not had much experience in a business unit. Or, a budget officer who needs field experience in what it takes to manage a profit center. Many protégés have never managed teams, run meetings, negotiated contracts, or planned client presentations. Consequently, they need opportunities to round out their repertoires. Group members must be willing to experiment. Testing new waters should be a stimulating challenge, providing grist for group meetings.

The learning continues when group members come together again to discuss the meaning of their on-the-job experiences. But the key is to make the learning deliberate. Ask group participants to take on specific development assignments that will offer growth opportunities in the workplace. Such assignments fall into the following three categories:

1. Platform. These assignments enable group members to learn new skills in a temporary work assignment or short-term project constructed specifically for them. After the assignment is completed, the "platform" is dismantled.

2. On-the-job. These assignments enable group members to try out new skills and responsibilities while working at their jobs.

3. Dedicated. These assignments enable group members to gain exposure and experience in different areas of the organization. The members are accountable for the work they do while on the assignment, and they must live with the consequences.

Managers and mentors need to continually debrief the learning embedded in these assignments.

Group action. Typically, a protégé group meets with its mentor each month for several hours. The agenda should accommodate any topics or concerns, and anyone should be permitted to initiate a dialogue. The leader and group members share the responsibility for learning every step of the way. In *The Fifth Discipline*, Peter Senge suggests that through an open framework of shared responsibility, groups are able to pursue dialogue rather than discussion. Discussion involves:

- attempting to influence others
- seeking solutions
- determining actions
- making decisions
- gaining consensus
- maintaining hierarchy

Dialog, which is critical to the group model, entails the following elements:

- thinking more freely at deeper levels
- talking about beliefs
- exploring ideas and gaining insight
- adding knowledge
- stretching oneself
- diverging toward varied interests

The Group Mentor

The ideal group mentor is someone concerned with his or her own learning, the learning of others, and the future of the organization. The group mentor should be a senior person on the technical or management track, preferably at the manager or director level. The mentor's experience must be broad (acquired at different organizational levels), and his or her insight should stem from having done the job.

Specifically, a group mentor's track record should include the following things:

- success in his or her field
- contact with a wide variety of people
- vast accumulated experience
- substantial power
- history of fostering employees' development
- control of substantial resources
- broad organizational experience
- success in managing teams
- reputation for competence

It is crucial for group mentors to be sensitive to diversity. They must approach diversity issues with candor and understanding, especially when differences related to gender, race, or ethnicity arise in the learning group. Group mentors also must have, and be able to pass on, appreciation for the paradox of organizational life, which is not necessarily rational, formula driven, or goal oriented. It is full of variables with competing and conflicting demands. This awareness and admission can help people deal with ambiguity just when they thought they had things figured out.

Tips for the Group Mentor

To make a group mentoring process successful, do the following things:

■ Ask the Right Questions
This is often more important than giving the right answers. Opening the conversation so that the group can take charge of the process is essential to success. Do not push them to look for answers to problems and issues, but rather to look for all the various options and consider what they really think about the issues. Preparation is a critical factor in making a group meeting successful. Simply jotting down four or five questions that will get the group thinking can be your best prework.

■ Listen More Than You Talk
Do not feel that just because you are the leader of the group, it is your responsibility to do most of the talking. Once the group has jelled, members should be able to generate dialogue themselves, and you should not need to spend much of your time talking. It may be easy to get into the trap of being seen as the guru or the leader of this small group and always being there to provide insight and advice. Yet for true learning to take place, it is necessary for you to hold back and allow the group to find their own answers and solutions. You are more of a facilitator of this process.

■ Let the Group Create the Agenda
If group members feel that they are responsible for what is being discussed at each session, they will have a much greater sense of ownership in the process. This, in turn, will stimulate attendance because the sessions are of their own making. You can guide and assist members in the process of creating the agenda, but do not let this be your sole responsibility.

■ Do Not Have All the Answers
Many questions and issues will come up in this group for which you do not have the answers, and there is no reason you should assume that you must have answers for every situation. It will be far more interesting for everyone if the group brainstorms answers or ways to obtain answers together, rather than looking to the learning leader. You do not want to create a student-teacher environment where there is a built-in sense of inequality. The group

Mentoring in Action

Many organizations have been successful in establishing mentoring programs. Here are just two examples:

Chemical Company

Begun originally by one business unit as an effort to gain vertical parity for its women and minorities and develop leadership capabilities, group mentoring gradually spread throughout a global chemical company. Approximately 30 protégés moved through the year-long program each time it was offered. Protégé groups included six to eight high-potentials from diverse locations. Each group was assigned to a mentor who met with the group once a month for a minimum of two hours.

Mentors were selected by senior management. Protégés were those tapped for succession planning and continuity planning. Groups developed their own agendas and asked their mentor for the kinds of interaction and discussions they felt were important. Managers of the protégés met with mentors at the beginning of the process and kept in touch on an individual basis after that. All groups were brought together four times during the year to join in a learning community and hear from other senior leaders. Groups reported that the interaction with their peers was as important in their learning as the interaction with their mentor.

City Government

When the engineering group of a large California city saw that it needed to develop not only its future leadership but also its middle managers, it launched its own group mentoring effort. Protégés self-selected into the program by completing an application describing their interest in the process and talking about their career goals. Members of the protégé group selected mentors they thought demonstrated a concern for development. All protégés attended a career development class and then used the subsequent meetings with their mentors to discuss various aspects of this learning. Mentors attended a brief training session, followed by get-togethers to learn more about each other's experience in the mentor groups. Groups met for a year, decided their own agendas, and also decided whether or not to continue once the year had ended.

should feel collegial, recognizing that answers grow out of its collective intelligence, and work together rather than exclusively.

■ *Give Advice Through Storytelling*
Often the best way to give examples is to use the lessons of your own experiences. This will increase your credibility and breathe real life into your suggestions so that the group can identify with you on an intimate level. You can make the dialogue richer by considering articles that the group has read in advance of the meeting. But if the conversation becomes theoretical or didactic rather than personal, it will not have the same learning potential. Encourage the group to tell stories and give individual examples related to their readings and assignments so that they personalize the learning.

■ *Have Something Up Your Sleeve*
Do not assume that just because you are not responsible for the agenda you should not have some ideas for group dialogue ready to interject. For the most part, conversation will come easily as the members of the group get to know one another and the issues with which they are most concerned. If the easy flow of dialogue gets jammed up, however, you will want to be prepared to get things moving again.

The Manager

Because protégé group activities go beyond group meetings, it is crucial that the managers of the protégés be committed to making the group experience a success. Some managers may view learning groups as tugging at the allegiance of their own direct reports, taking them away from job tasks and work groups. To that end, managers should receive orientation or training on the benefits of the mentoring process. An orientation leads managers through several activities that teach them how to help employees think through a development assignment.

Managers explore their roles in facilitating development conversations and providing feedback and coaching. They also link high-performing employees to organizational information and networks, helping them to shape goals and process learning on an ongoing basis. Development-minded managers enrich the process by encouraging members

Mentoring Strategies

When deciding to harness the benefits of informal mentoring activity, organizations should take the time to plan management strategies that guarantee results. These are the issues they should consider:

Business Case for Mentoring

What are your reasons for developing the program? What business impact do you want to achieve? What success indicators will tell you that the mentoring initiative is succeeding? (Consider both quantitative and qualitative measures.)

Organizational Concerns

What is your organizational history with mentoring programs? How have previous mentoring efforts been perceived? How will this history affect how you implement and communicate the current initiative? Do you have organization-wide cooperation and support from top management? Will you request organization-wide input or advice from a limited number of experts and decision makers? Does the organization have positions for the new talent it develops in mentoring programs?

Communication

What will you name this mentoring initiative? How will you present the program? What will you say about its purpose, objectives, goals, mechanics, and benefits? What are the benefits to the organization and the program partici-

pants? How will you publicize the program? What resources do you have (memos, discussions, meetings)? How will you regularly communicate the purpose, progress, and results?

Roles and Responsibilities

Who will be the process owner? Who will be the day-to-day manager? What other resources and roles are needed?

Implementation

How will you select participants for the program? What will the selection criteria entail? How will you present these criteria to interested candidates? Will participation be voluntary or mandatory? Why? How will the program foster and support mentor-protégé relationships? Will it provide opportunities for mentors and protégés to meet and exchange views and opinions so they can assess their own suitability? Or will the program assign mentors to protégés?

Evaluation

How will you evaluate the results and outcomes of the program? When will you make adjustments to ensure accomplishment of program goals? Is the mentoring program the best way to impart skills and knowledge and to develop human resource potential? What are its advantages over other training methods?

to explore new ways of contributing to the job while still monitoring their continued responsibility. Such managers understand their role in terms of day-to-day authority and skill building.

As partners in the process, managers perform the following functions:

- Provide personal feedback to learners on values and mindsets that arise in group meetings.

- Cultivate people's capabilities for their current and future jobs.

- Help craft and debrief challenging learning assignments in partnership with learning leaders and learning group members.

- Endorse experimentation, applaud new approaches, and permit mistakes.

- Ask questions to encourage discussion on what participants are learning and how.

Mentoring Guidelines

Use the following guidelines for organizations setting up programs, mentors working with protégés, and protégés seeking mentoring relationships.

Organizations

☐ Get top management support of the program. Managers should endorse and be willing to fund the program as well as give mentors, protégés, and learning groups time away from the job to meet and form relationships.

☐ Make the mentoring program part of succession planning, or a larger career or management development effort to help employees.

☐ Start with a short program—six months at most—to accomplish specified learning goals without imposing a long-term, burdensome commitment.

☐ Minimize the dropout rate by making the program voluntary and by establishing clear expectations.

☐ Publicly announce the criteria for selecting program participants. Selection criteria should be fair and attainable so as not to invite the resentment of those who feel they have been unfairly excluded.

☐ Select mentors with high levels of expertise, rank, and power. Select protégés who have basic skills and capabilities, but most important, the desire to learn from mentors.

☐ Give mentors and protégés an orientation that addresses the concerns, expectations, and benefits to participants and the organization.

☐ Allow for diverse mentoring styles, providing structure but permitting flexibility. Prevent problems by specifying responsibilities of mentors, protégés, and their immediate supervisors or managers.

☐ Document the progress of the mentoring program using evaluation instruments, meetings, reports, and logs, and use this documentation to recommend maintaining, expanding, or eliminating the program.

Mentors

☐ Expect to invest considerable time and effort. Like any other strong relationship, the one between mentor and protégé or learning group requires a solid foundation of mutual trust and understanding.

☐ Be prepared to initiate the relationship; protégés often are apprehensive about approaching senior advisers.

☐ When the time is right, let protégés or learning groups go. If they are gradually given more independence to act and make decisions on their own, protégés will be prepared mentally for separation.

☐ Have realistic expectations of the relationship. Do not expect lifelong gratitude; some protégés may consider this a business arrangement to which they owe improved job performance only.

Protégés

☐ Look for a mentor among the ranks of middle and senior managers. Observe work and communication styles to select the kind of mentor who would be right for you.

☐ Do not wait to be chosen. Express your interest by asking middle and senior managers for advice.

☐ Know what you want from the relationship, based on your current situation. Think about your competencies, the skills you would like to develop, and your long-range career plans.

☐ Know what is expected of you in the relationship. Besides providing mentors with respect and psychological support, as your relationship develops into one of mutual assistance, you will be returning the mentor's help by acting as his or her agent.

☐ Have realistic expectations. Relationships may not last a lifetime and most cannot fulfill *every* need, because individual mentoring styles vary as do degrees of mentoring.

Virtual Mentoring

Cross-site or distance mentoring often involves alternative communication such as telephone, email, and video conferencing. Whichever methods you choose, you will want to use some strategies to compensate for less face-to-face time. Communication research shows that it takes about 25 to 30 percent more time to build a personal relationship when you build it at a distance. That is because you miss the gestures, body language, and subtle communication of direct contact. The *good* news is that people involved in distance mentoring report high satisfaction because they often develop better listening skills and plan their time more carefully than face-to-face mentoring partners.

Tips for Virtual Mentoring

To make virtual mentoring programs successful, consider the following suggestions:

- Pay special attention to outcomes and objectives. Be clear and precise about the relationship's purpose.

- Exchange photos. If you are not familiar with each other's sites, send some photos of your facilities, work areas, co-workers and anything else that would help your partner get to know you.

- Exchange "artifact" boxes. Package up and send items that will help your partner understand your site's products and your job. Use your imagination.

- Establish a "mentor hotline time." This is periodically designated time dedicated to mentor-learning partner conversation.

- Keep commitments. If you view conversations as "just a telephone call," it is easy to cancel or postpone them. Follow through on plans and activities. Dependability contributes to strong partnerships.

- Exchange information that paints a "whole picture" of each person's work environment on a routine basis. For example, share regular status reports.

- Do not begin by replacing teleconferencing with email. Email is very useful, but early on you will want to hear each other's voices, and the spontaneity associated with live conversation is important.

- Combine communication methods. For example, use email to supply detailed information in conjunction with a planned teleconference or project review. Send a follow-up email after a telephone conversation.

- Listen with a third ear. Be sensitive to tone of voice as a substitute for seeing body language.

- Ask "why" and "how" questions to obtain deeper understanding in conversations.

- Connect at conferences or organization-sponsored events.

- Create a mentoring group at your site for people who have distance mentors. Form a collaborative group to support mutual development.

- Plan field trips to your partner's site when you have opportunities to be near or at his or her location.

Putting It All Together

While the time-honored practice of mentoring has always been with us, today it is a dynamic tool for employee development. Whether you select one-to-one mentoring, learning groups, or virtual mentoring, know that relationship learning forges an environment that reduces learning curves and development cycles.

Yes, there is time investment. And mentoring in any form requires careful preparation and fit with business objectives. The payback comes not just in rewards for the organization, however, but also in personal dividends for the participants. Use the ideas and tools in this *Info-line* to unleash the potential for you and your organization.

References & Resources

Articles

Benabou, Charles, and Raphael Benabou. "Establishing a Formal Mentoring Program for Organizational Success." *National Productivity Review,* Spring 1999, pp. 7-14.

Coley, Denise Bolden. "Mentoring Two by Two." *Training & Development,* July 1996, pp. 46-48.

Gunn, Erik. "Mentoring: The Democratic Version." *Training,* August 1995, pp. 64-67.

Jossi, Frank. "Mentoring in Changing Times." *Training,* August 1997, pp. 50-54.

Kaye, Bev, and B. Jacobson. "Mentoring: A Group Guide." *Training & Development,* April 1995, pp. 22-27.

———. "Mentoring: A New Model for Building Learning Organizations." *OD Practitioner,* vol. 28, no. 3 (1996), pp. 35-44.

———. "Reframing Mentoring." *Training & Development,* August 1996, pp. 44-47.

Kaye, Bev, and Devon Scheef. "Shared Brain Power." *National Business Employment Weekly,* Nov. 23-29, 1997, pp. 11-12.

Lindenberger, Judith G., and Lois J. Zachary. "Play '20 Questions' to Develop a Successful Mentoring Program." *Training & Development,* February 1999, pp. 12-14.

Messmer, Max. "Mentoring: Building Your Company's Intellectual Capital." *HR Focus,* September 1998, pp. S11-12.

Robinson, S. "Mentoring Has Merit in Formal and Informal Formats." *Training Directors' Forum Newsletter,* May 1990, p. 6.

Scandura, Terri A. "Mentorship and Career Mobility." *Journal of Organizational Behavior,* March 1992, pp. 169-174.

Simmons, Kathy. "Growing a Successful Mentor Program." *Executive Update,* December 1999, pp. 42-45.

Tyler, Kathryn. "Mentoring Programs Link Employees and Experienced Execs." *HRMagazine,* April 1998, pp. 98-103.

Van Collie, Shimon-Craig. "Moving Up through Mentoring." *Workforce,* March 1998, pp. 36-42.

Van Slyke, Erik J., and Bud Van Slyke. "Mentoring: A Results-Oriented Approach." *HR Focus,* February 1998, p. 14.

Books

Bell, Chip R. *Managers As Mentors.* San Francisco: Berrett-Koehler, 1996.

Caruso, Richard E. *Mentoring and the Business Environment.* Brookfield, VT: Dartmouth Publishing, 1992.

Fritts, Patricia J. *The New Managerial Mentor.* Palo Alto, CA: Davies-Black, 1998.

Huang, Chungliang Al, and Jerry Lynch. *Mentoring: The Tao of Giving and Receiving Wisdom.* New York: Harper San Francisco, 1995.

Jeruchim, Joan, and Shapiro Jeruchim. *Women, Mentors and Success.* New York: Fawcett Columbine, 1992.

Kaye, Bev. *Up Is Not the Only Way.* Palo Alto, CA: Davies-Black, 1997.

Kaye, Bev, and B. Bernstein. *MentWorking™—Building Relationships for the 21st Century.* Scranton, PA: Career Systems International, 1998.

Kaye, Bev, and B. Jacobson. *Learning Group Guide.* Scranton, PA: Career Systems International, 1998.

Kaye, Bev, and Sharon Jordan-Evans. *Love 'Em or Lose 'Em.* San Francisco: Berrett-Koehler, 1999.

Kram, Kathy E. *Mentoring Relationships at Work.* Lanham, MD: University Press of America, 1988.

Murray, Margo, and Marna Owen. *Beyond the Myths and Magic of Mentoring.* San Francisco: Jossey-Bass, 1991.

Peddy, Shirley. *The Art of Mentoring.* Houston: Bullion Books, 1998.

Senge, Peter. *The Fifth Discipline.* New York: Doubleday, 1990.

Wickman, Floyd, and Terri Sjodin. *Mentoring: A Success Guide for Mentors and Protégés.* New York: McGraw Hill, 1997.

Zeldin, Michael, and Sara S. Lee, eds. *Touching the Future.* Los Angeles: Hebrew Union College, 1995.

Zey, Michael G. *The Mentor Connection.* Homewood, IL: Dow Jones-Irwin, 1984.

Info-lines

Callahan, Madelyn R., ed. "Alternatives to Lecture." No. 8602.

———. "Design Productive Mentoring Programs." No. 8609 (out of print).

Gibson, Richard. "Selecting a Coach." No. 9812.

Slavenski, Lynn, and Marilyn Buckner. "Succession Planning." No. 9312 (revised 1998).

Younger, Sandra Millers. "Learning Organizations: The Trainer's Role." No. 9306 (revised 1999).

Program Outline/Planner

When you are charged with setting up a mentoring program for your organization, use this outline as a guide. In it you will find the questions you need to address in order to have a successful program.

1. State the objectives of the mentoring program:

_____

_____

2. List the benefits of the mentoring program for each of the following:

a. Organization:

_____

_____

b. Mentor:

_____

_____

c. Protégé:

_____

_____

3. Which mentoring method(s) can help you achieve your goals?

☐   One-to-one mentoring

☐   Group mentoring

☐   Virtual mentoring

4. Who are the key stakeholders in the mentoring initiative, and what will their involvement look like?

Stakeholder   *Involvement*

_____   _____

_____   _____

_____   _____

5. Consider the following questions concerning the structure of your mentoring program:

a. What criteria will you use to select mentors?

_____

_____

b. What criteria will you use to select protégés?

_____

_____

c. What role do you see for the managers of the protégés?

_____

_____

d. How will you orient mentors, protégés, and managers to the mentoring process and prepare them to be successful?

_____

_____

(Job Aid continued on page 68)

e. How will you "match" mentors and protégés?

_____

_____

f. What plans do you have to follow up on the process and gather periodic input from all participants?

_____

_____

g. How will you recognize and reward all those involved?

_____

_____

6.   How will you present the benefits and selection criteria (bulletin board, employee newsletter, and so forth)?

_____

7.   How will the program foster mentor/protégé relationships? List ways of providing support for the participants (program guidelines, weekly meetings, councils, and so forth).

_____

_____

8.   List the positions that the organization has for the protégés. Are there enough? Will the organization create new ones?

_____

_____

9.   Consider the following when deciding on evaluation factors:

a. How will you evaluate the program? State your method(s)—questionnaires, surveys, interviews, and observations.

_____

_____

b. How did the program affect protégés?

_____

_____

- Attitudinal effect: _____
- Behavioral effect: _____
- Accomplishments: _____

c. How did the program affect mentors?
- Attitudinal effect: _____
- Behavioral effect: _____
- Accomplishments: _____

d. How did the program affect the organization?
- Overall performance rating: _____
- Productivity: _____
- Condition of corporate climate: _____

Succession Planning

Issue 9312

Succession Planning

AUTHORS

Marilyn Buckner, Ph.D.
Lynn Slavenski
National Training Systems, Inc.
P.O. Box 8436
Atlanta, GA 31106
Tel: 404.875.1953
Fax: 404.875.0947

Editorial Staff for 9312

Editor
Barbara Darraugh

Revised 1998

Editor
Cat Sharpe Russo

Contributing Editor
Ann Bruen

Succession Planning

In today's dynamic world of mergers, acquisitions, downsizing, shrinking markets, and flattening organizations, many companies are asking two key questions about succession planning:

● Do we have qualified people ready to fill key positions now and grow the business in the next three to five years? (Short-term emphasis.)

● Will we have a sufficient number of qualified candidates ready in five to 10 years to fill key positions? (Long-term emphasis.)

Because many organizations are challenged by ever-evolving work environments, the implementation of a succession planning program requires the use of change management strategies. It is well known that **changing organizations succeed by having the right people in the right places at the right times.** Research done by the Center for Creative Leadership in Greensboro, North Carolina, on how executives develop stresses the importance of planning structured activities that will allow individuals to acquire leadership skills as a part of their natural rate of development.

In addition, research conducted in 1997 by the Advisory Board, located in Washington, D.C., emphasizes the shortage of leadership at all levels and its impact on the future of organizations. The key to designing a successful succession planning program is not accomplished by copying somebody else's. The key is asking the questions that pertain to the specific issues of your changing organization now and continuing to ask these questions as your organization progresses through inevitable transformations. A good succession planning program is always part of continuous improvement.

What Is Succession Planning?

Succession, or replacement, planning entails the identification of those employees who have the right skills to meet the challenges the organization faces. During this process:

● key positions are identified and analyzed

● candidates are assessed against job and personal requirements

● individual development plans are created

● people are selected

Succession planning normally focuses on replacements for specific, top positions. In some cases where a number of people can fill certain positions (for example, general managers, business leaders, domestic or international representatives), organizations use a pool or group approach. In this situation, a group of individuals is groomed to fill any number of similar positions. This approach has become more prevalent as specific positions change within organizations, but at the top executive levels, traditional succession planning for specific positions still takes place.

Succession planning is used to help organizations solve real business problems, such as the following:

● Who will move into this key financial position when Ron retires?

● In view of our vulnerable domestic situation, who can be spared to open the new European market?

● Pat could move into any of these three positions, but if we place her in one, who will fill the other two?

● Why aren't more female and minority employees in the executive suite?

● Joan is not quite ready for this assignment, but if we hire externally, will we lose her?

● How can we keep John from leaving us? He is a key player.

If your company raises questions like these and finds no ready answers or solutions, it is probably time to develop and implement a succession planning process. Obviously, every organization needs to develop its own culture-sensitive system. While no one system fits all, this *Info-line* can provide the framework for system design.

System Components

There are five basic succession planning components: replacement planning, human resource audit, high-potential employee identification, employment input, and development programs. Some systems incorporate all five, while others may rely on only one or two.

Replacement Planning

The primary component of a succession planning system is the identification of replacement personnel. At its simplest, this is a statement of who will fill a given job because it comes open. At its best, replacement identification includes an evaluation of the quality and "readiness" of the named successors.

Although the group approach to succession planning is currently being implemented in many large companies, at the very top, basic replacement planning still occurs. In fact, according to Jeffrey Sonnenfeld in *The Hero's Farewell*, boards of directors of large companies increasingly want to know not only who the replacements for key positions are but also their qualifications. In small to medium-sized companies, traditional succession planning for managerial positions may take place throughout the organization. Because of the increased need for technical expertise across all organizations, a form of replacement planning for filling key technical positions is also occurring.

A useful tool for succession planning is the *Succession Summary* work sheet opposite, which can be used by a manager of a unit to choose successors.

Planning Tips

When conducting your replacement planning, follow these suggestions:

- Create a bottom-up approach—either specific positions or a pool for similar positions—whereby managers at lower levels make initial recommendations as to who can be replacements for their direct reports.

- Have each higher level of management review the recommendations and make revisions. (If a cross-movement strategy is being used, managers should include recommendations from other parts of the organization.)

- Identify competencies for all key positions in highly technical, detailed, and stable organizations through a formal job analysis process. Managers, or a panel of managers, can evaluate individuals against these standards (see *Info-line* No. 9503, "Understanding Core Competencies").

- Use group meetings in more flexible organizations to discuss replacement skill level, readiness, and potential to get a fairly accurate judgment of a person's capability. Use group consensus for general skills for the future.

Human Resource Audit

The human resource audit, the second component of a succession planning system, builds on the identification of successors and addresses assessment of employee mobility to various positions. This process identifies whether employees at various levels should stay in their current positions, or move to other positions, and distinguishes key developmental strategies. It also helps designate the pools of people qualified for specific positions.

Each manager conducts a human resource audit by reviewing each direct report, including his or her:

- time in current position
- performance
- readiness for advancement
- potential to move to a new position
- development required

This plan ensures that all employees are reviewed whether they are successors or not, alleviating management's concern that succession planning is an elitist program that ignores the development of all employees.

If your system is linked to a staffing process, you must then collect information on "recommended next positions." A job-function code (sales, manufacturing, legal, human resources, or quality control, and so forth), combined with salary information, can help you locate candidates for open positions in other parts of the organization. This way, a person who is not a "natural" successor in his or her own unit could be considered in another part of the organization.

Succession Summary

The position is listed first on the form because it is the focus of the planning process. Some optional pieces of data can be collected on the incumbents and replacements, such as Social Security or other employee identification numbers that are used in computer systems for retrieval of information. (International organizations often have employees who do not have Social Security numbers, so they would have to develop a numbering system.)

A job-function code identifies the type of job that an incumbent occupies or can fill in the future. This code is helpful if the system is expected to do candidate searches for similar positions. The probability of vacancy (PV) rating alerts the organization if a manager will be leaving in less than one year. The successor(s) are listed on the right of the form with their potential (PO), readiness (RE), and performance (PR) ratings.

Division: _____

Department: _____

Unit: _____

RATING MANAGER (Manager of Unit)	JOB FUNCTION CODE _____ SUCCESSION NAMES	PV	PO	RE	PR
POSITION:	(List candidates in order of preference.)				
NAME:	**1.** NAME:	____	____	____	____
ID#	ID#				
	2. NAME:	____	____	____	____
	ID#				
	3. NAME:	____	____	____	____
	ID#				

DIRECT REPORT POSITIONS	JOB FUNCTION CODE SUCCESSION NAMES	PV	PO	RE	PR
POSITION:	(List candidates in order of preference.)				
NAME:	**1.** NAME:	____	____	____	____
ID#	ID#				
	2. NAME:	____	____	____	____
	ID#				
	3. NAME:	____	____	____	____
	ID#				

NOTE: If you do not have an ID# for a person on the list, please contact your personnel or human resources representative for assistance.

PROBABILITY OF VACANCY
1. Within 12 months
2. Within 1-2 years
3. Beyond 2 years

POTENTIAL
1. Advance 2-3 levels
2. Advance at least 1 level
3. Move to a lateral position

READINESS
R. Ready now
F. Ready 1-3 years
Q. Promotability within 5 years is questionable
? Too early to evaluate

PERFORMANCE
1. Exceptional
2. Exceeds expectations
3. Meets expectations
4. Does not meet expectations
X. New in Position

JOB FUNCTION CODES

01	Finance/Accounting	**09**	Data Processing	**16**	Publications
02	Contracts Administration	**10**	Library	**17**	Technical
03	Sales	**11**	Purchasing	**18**	Technical Support
04	Account Management	**12**	Material Handling & Distribution	**20**	Airplane Operations
05	Public Relations & External Affairs	**13**	Facilities & Plant Maintenance	**21**	Manufacturing Managers
07	Human Resources	**14**	Communications & Administrative Services	**23**	General Managers & Executives
08	Security	**15**	Executive Support & Planning & Business Development	**40**	Legal

Succession planning should be supported by performance appraisal programs or other means of providing viable, dependable employee skill information. With high-quality assessment information, managers can provide employees with effective development for future assignments.

Audit Tips

Apply the following principles to human resource audits:

■ *Use Multiple Reviewers*
This is effective, particularly with a good supply of promotable employees. In such a process, at least two levels of management review the employees and agree on their candidacy for specified positions. More formal evaluation processes, such as the following, may be warranted under these conditions:

● Manager judgments or experience levels are weak.

● There is a shortage of identified talent.

● The organizational culture supports structured programs.

■ *Use Assessment Centers*
Because employees are evaluated on job-sample exercises that closely resemble the actual job, assessment centers provide extremely accurate measures of performance and capability. Organizations using assessment centers have seen a high degree of predictability of employee success at more senior levels. These can be used for selection or development purposes, but the trend is more to use the assessment center for development.

■ *Ensure Managers Have Good Judgment Skills*
The quality of the judgment skills of the managers in your organization is critical. If hiring and promoting employees are infrequent events, managers may need training in performance appraisal and assessment to identify the most promotable employees.

Identifying High-Potential Employees

Experts recommend including a high-potential identification process for the next generation of leaders. These high-potential programs can either be stand-alone or incorporated into the entire succession planning process. The more comprehensive programs utilized by many successful groups generally integrate high-potential identification. In addition, high-potentials can even be grouped into pools of successors.

The simplest definition of a high-potential employee is someone who has the ability to move into (and perhaps above) a particular level, such as a vice president or other key position in an organization. This definition becomes increasingly selective by identifying necessary competencies (based on previous or future success) and failure factors associated with certain positions.

To narrowly define *high-potential*, look at critical competency areas for leaders. High-potentials need to have management, as well as growth, potential. Predicting leadership capacity potential has led some experts to observe a set of common factors possessed by these individuals:

Results driven—has completed many challenging assignments.

People skill—influences, motivates, works with a wide range of people.

Mental ability—street smart, asks insightful questions.

Lifelong learning—seeks challenging opportunities for new knowledge, learns from successes and failures.

Integrated thinking—links ideas, sees essence of problem.

Flexible—adjusts priorities, takes risks, embraces change.

Energy—gets energy from work and energizes others.

In addition to the above-listed personal skill competencies, there are also organization competency requirements. According to corporate strategy experts C.K. Prahalad and Gary Hamel, managers need to

High-Potential Definitions

Only 5 percent of those in a salary range mentioned below should be high-potential. (This is the norm in many organizations.) The following are definitions of high-potential employees:

Potential to be a senior-level officer in any sector

- Can advance two job levels within five years.

- Demonstrates quantifiable accomplishments.

- If in field, willing to relocate.

- If at headquarters, willing to get field experience (relocate) if needed to become senior officer in their career ladder.

- Has potential for at least 10 to 15 more years with the company.

These candidates should have the following characteristics:

- People skills.

- Management skills (decision making, planning and organization, leadership, oral communication).

- Background, knowledge (understand business, technical knowledge, experience).

- Traits such as results orientation, ability to deal with change, flexibility.

- Willingness to move from sector to sector.

Potential to be at least regional or staff executive

- Can advance two job levels within five years.

- If in field, willingness to relocate.

- If at headquarters, willingness to relocate if needed in their career ladder.

- Demonstrates quantifiable accomplishments.

These candidates should have the following characteristics:

- People skills.

- Management skills (decision making, planning and organization, leadership, oral communication).

- Background, knowledge (understand business, technical knowledge, experience).

- Traits such as results orientation, ability to deal with change, flexibility.

- Willingness to move from sector to sector.

Potential to be general manager, department head

- Same criteria as above.

In some cases, sectors will also provide definitions of sector high-potentials.

identify employees who possess skills related to the core products of the organization. These people are corporate resources, to be shared throughout the company.

As a result, an organization may need more than one classification of "high-potential." A second classification might be high-potentials who can be general managers. A third classification might include a pool of employees lower down in the organization who can move upward at least two levels. A fourth category might even be necessary if your organization needs employees who can move into specialty areas, such as international positions, key technical management, or nonmanagement positions. Even with precise definitions, most organizations can never expect to have total accuracy in identification. As a result, people will drop off the high-potential lists in successive years. Generally, most organizations target 5 percent of their population as "high-potential." For a listing of high-potential definitions, see the sidebar on the preceding page.

Another driving force is the globalization of companies, which demands that employees possess a broad spectrum of specific personality and character traits. Recent research conducted by the Canadian Imperial Bank of Commerce has identified the factors that best produce global executives. It cites the following 10 key competencies as a requirement for increasing global business:

1. Cross-cultural awareness.

2. Ability to value differences in people.

3. Flexibility.

4. Language skills.

5. Emotional adaptability and stability.

6. Interpersonal skills in listening and coaching.

7. Sensitivity.

8. Ability to deal effectively with conflict and ambiguity.

9. Social intelligence.

10. Ability to understand nonverbal communication styles.

Identification Tips

When conducting high-potential employee identification programs, follow these guidelines:

- Define high-potential employees.

- Determine whether you have a large supply of high-potentials or a minimal supply (use this information to define the scope of the program).

- Assess candidates against competencies and criteria.

- Hold group meetings for final selection at which managers discuss their high-potential employees.

- Determine if you need to "grow" or "buy" high-potentials and at what organizational levels.

- Create developmental plans (see opposite) and corresponding follow-up plans.

- Track the loss of high-potentials and establish a retention plan.

- Determine whether to tell high-potential employees that they are considered high-potentials.

Employee Input

The fourth component of succession planning is employee input via a career development process. Successful planning must respond to workforce demands, and this includes employee input. Such responsiveness is a vital link between human resource planning and business strategy. Employees list career interests, qualifications, and willingness to relocate on an employee input form. This form should trigger a career development discussion between the manager and the employee. If a computerized system is used, candidate information for the employee can be combined into career profiles. You can use this career profile in review meetings and for selection information when openings occur. It contains information generated by both the employee and the organization.

Gathering Tips

When seeking employee input for career development programs, consider the following:

- Obtain employee data through manager-employee career discussions that focus on employee interests, goals, and development. Managers can capture the data informally by taking notes during these discussions.

- Have employees complete career interest forms—which address relocation, dual career issues, language fluencies, and career objectives—for formal information gathering.

- Enter job preference data into a database. This data can be searched to fill positions that have no successors or to assist management in finding future replacements in other parts of the organization.

- Use computer networks/intranets to make career information accessible to all employees. (Some organizations have set up career Websites that contain job information, company information, assessment capability, and a planning process.)

Development Programs

The fifth component of succession planning is the design and implementation of career development programs for employees. As a result of the accelerated rate of change, development is becoming increasingly critical. Organizations need more people faster to fill key positions—and they must have them ready now. The skills needed for positions are changing so rapidly that people cannot keep up without having planned development. Many organizations use leadership development programs to fast-track their high-potentials. Some of the more innovative and effective programs use action learning (participants diagnose, discuss, and resolve actual business challenges) and business simulations. In addition, managers are being asked to coach and mentor people in more intensive ways than they have in the past.

Unless development is a strong part of a succession planning program, the actual replacement will not be able to move into a designated position, and high-potentials will not be prepared. Development

Developmental Plan

Name: _____

Date: _____

Current Position: _____

Department: _____

Manager: _____

Possible Future Positions	Skill or Functional Development Area
1.	1.
2.	2.
3.	3.

Development Activities	Time Frame
Innovation/Creativity (Attend senior-level meetings)	
Strategic Planning (On-the-job training)	
International Key Experiences (Job rotation)	
Corporate Knowledge (Job enrichment)	
Financial Knowledge (Training & development programs)	
Interpersonal/Leadership Skills (Task force assignments)	

takes succession planning from a plan to a process. (See *12 Development Strategies* for more methods of developing employees.)

Use a format that emphasizes key assignments to encourage people to think beyond just the use of their education. For further information, refer to *Info-line* No. 8804, "Training and Learning Styles." Another important ingredient of development is a vehicle for measuring accomplishments (see *Learning Plan*).

Development Program Tips

When devising a development program, follow these guidelines:

● Determine if you should use a skill-based plan or a job strategy-based plan focusing on the proper mix of job experiences—or a combination of the two.

● Use instruments to assess the skills of high-potentials and to identify their developmental needs. (A popular trend is to use instruments that collect data from subordinates, peers, and supervisors, called 360-degree feedback. See *Info-line* No. 9508, "How to Build and Use a 360-Degree Feedback System.")

● Match content of development plans to reflect how people actually learn. People learn primarily from challenging assignments, relationships with people outside their regular environment, and hardships. Some examples of challenging assignments include turnaround, fix-it, starting things from scratch, and significant shifts in scope and scale of activities.

Factors for Success

Simply knowing the necessary components of succession planning is not a guarantee of success. What does it take to really make a succession planning program work? Below is a list of best practices from organizations with successful programs.

■ *Get Top Management Support*
This is obtained by clearly identifying needs within the organization and tying programs to business strategy and results. A sense of urgency and importance in getting things done is probably the single most important factor in running a successful program. (For example, the business strategy may call for anticipating the staffing of future positions because of organizational growth, decline, or changes. A clear identification of business strategies is needed to obtain proper resources and commitment to ensure your program will be successful.)

Management also needs to realize that it takes time to put these programs into operation. An organization must commit the time and resources necessary to get the plan moving. Many organizations find that it takes three to five years to fully implement a planning process, and even longer to make the development process a part of the fabric of the organization. Managers will be committed if they can see the problems the process is beginning to solve.

■ *Conduct Management Review Meetings*
Review meetings create energy for completion of the process and give top management the opportunity to provide support. They address only the most critical issues: top-level successors, a few high-potentials, cross-organizational movement, international candidates, progress of candidates, or diversity programs. These discussions are necessary because actual job movements and developmental actions are more likely to happen when managers are talking about candidates frankly. Review meetings should include representatives from all parts of the organization involved in the succession planning process and be facilitated by a human resources representative, who takes notes on action items and provides follow-up to make sure there is progress.

■ *Put Development First*
Succession planning can be successful only if high-potential employees are given the opportunity to develop their skills, knowledge, and attitudes through an ongoing learning process. Key decision makers in an organization need to make development a priority and hold managers accountable for emphasizing people planning in their departments. One way to ensure accountability for development is through reporting measurements of progress or tying development to a bonus or appraisal system. This will ensure that managers take the development of their employees seriously.

■ *Move People Effectively*
Organizations must have systems in place that ensure smooth moves of employees either within a department, across the organization, or across the

12 Development Strategies

Many people think that development is something that just happens in the classroom. But only 1 percent of people's time is actually spent in the classroom, suggesting that the bulk of development takes place during the other 99 percent of the time. In other words, people develop on the job; the expenses associated with "learning while doing" are part of the investment in development. Following is a list of development strategies and activities that will help you learn:

1. Variety of Job Assignments
People learn lessons from different job assignments—line to staff switches, starting from scratch, fix-it opportunities, larger- or smaller-scope jobs, project or task force assignments—and even from setbacks.

2. Training Sessions
These can take several forms: inside courses relating to professional, management, and technical programs; courses contracted from sources outside the organization; or business-specific training provided from within the organization.

3. Self-Study
This employs a variety of media from which to learn—CD-ROM, audio, print, and video.

4. On-the-Job Coaching
This approach is particularly useful for developing improved job performance and involves day-to-day discussions between the manager and individual. It may be used to upgrade skills or technical knowledge and may involve progress discussions, question-and-answer sessions, or working through an actual problem with the individual to provide direction and guidance.

5. Understudy
Here, the employee works closely with a manager as an "understudy" to develop potential for assuming a manager's position or understanding his or her supervisor's job better. This technique is particularly useful for developing both knowledge and skill areas.

6. Shadowing
Following another person around and watching what they do—"shadowing" them—can be helpful in learning about a particular area or function. The process could entail an hour, a day, a week, or a month of observing, going to meetings with the person, and so forth.

7. Job Enrichment
This involves expanding present responsibilities to include a wider variety of assignments and duties. It is effective for improving both skill and knowledge areas, but should be limited to those who already are effective in their present positions, since it requires expanding work performance rather than simply adding more of the same work.

8. Job Rotation and Lateral Moves
This involves moving to other, same-level jobs within the organization. Different functions increase employees' knowledge of the organization and require a different skill set. This is becoming a common development move and is particularly useful for exposing employees to new areas.

9. Task Force Assignments
Here, employees are assigned to committees or task forces composed of specialists from a single functional area or a combination of functional areas. This is beneficial to acquiring skills for complex problem resolution or issues that involve broad organizational scope. This strategy develops current job performance and promotion potential.

10. Higher-Level Meeting Attendance
Here, employees attend and participate in selected meetings. Involvement may include preparation of materials, participation in discussions, or just observation. Knowledge or management skills can be acquired, depending on the role of the individual at such meetings as well as exposure to the thinking and procedures of higher management.

11. "Acting" or Replacement Assignments
Employees are given temporary assignments that are vacant because of illness, vacation, or other reasons. This strategy is particularly useful for developing skills and knowledge critical to promotion potential.

12. Serving as a Conference Leader or Instructor
This is beneficial to developing both skills and knowledge. Preparation and research for teaching can provide valuable knowledge, while serving as a leader or instructor may provide development in a range of skill areas. Employees who attend training classes should be encouraged to return and share this knowledge with fellow employees.

globe. If employees go to new areas and cannot transition well, replacement plans cannot be effective. All managers must be involved and supportive of moving people between organizational areas. To implement this, having a policy of mandatory release of candidates may be necessary. Such a policy might state that a manager may refuse to release a candidate the first time for business reasons, but that on the second request, the employee must be released.

Avoid common problems associated with moving employees by having these solutions in place:

- a good placement and development process

- funding to allow people to move between areas

- a talent pool to move

- policies for employees to move from their locations in a timely and appropriate manner

Another problem is moving people too often. In his study of general managers in *The Dynamics of Taking Charge*, John J. Gabarro found that it takes anywhere from two to two and one-half years for managers to acquire an in-depth understanding of their new situation and become truly effective. Moving them in less time does not allow them to develop sufficiently.

■ *Link Programs and Staffing Needs*
To meet the organization's overall business goals, you need to align succession planning with other organizational programs and staffing decisions (see the sidebar *Identifying Critical Human Resource Issues*).

Changes in an organization's structure or workforce require an overall human resource strategy that links employee development programs. For example, a high-potential program is connected with career development, whereby employees provide input into deciding what types of positions they would like to fill. The high-potential program also is linked to a management development training program, which moves people through a series of training programs, from the professional ranks through supervisor and middle-management levels, until they can reach senior management.

Providing managers with viable candidates may be the most important product of a succession planning and high-potential system as well as the most effective way of gaining long-term management support. An effective human resources manager is able to influence staffing decisions, including those that involve external staffing in which the decision may be made that talent needs to be bought when internal talent is not available.

■ *Develop Leadership Skills*
Leadership is the main reason for successful employee development programs. The chief executive officer and senior executives have to show active leadership by holding people accountable for achieving goals and communicating that succession planning and high-potential development are essential to the management process. Senior management should identify leaders who not only possess those qualities required to develop people but also are committed to making identification programs work.

Organizations that are good at developing future talent identify people early in their careers, give them challenging assignments, and move them around to different departments. Managers tasked with developing their employees' leadership potential can identify solutions to common problems by reviewing the *Key Issues* sidebar.

■ *Use Computer Capability If Appropriate*
Computers are helpful, but not critical to the success of the replacement planning and high-potential identification process. You can use computers to simplify data collection and documentation and to integrate personnel information from different sources to create documents for presentations. You also may use them for analysis and review. Various succession planning software packages are available, but if you decide to buy a computer program, make sure it is flexible in changing the data elements as well as the reporting features. Most programs need to change as the succession planning and high-potential identification system evolves.

Learning Plan

Name: _____ Area: _____

Date: _____ Name of Coach: _____

Assignments
- a project with senior levels
- job scope increase or change
- start-up project
- key presentation
- represent manager
- benchmarking other companies
- fix-it project
- project team leader
- project in another area

Coaching
- specific ongoing behavioral coaching
- practice presentations
- watch role models
- refer them to other colleagues as advisers
- schedule follow-up meetings

Education
- courses
- self-study
- books
- periodicals
- videos
- audios
- CD-ROMS
- professional associations

Future Career Goals (not exact positions) _____

Learning Objective _____

	Actions	Target Date	Date Completed	Involvement of Others	Type **A, C, E**
1.					
2.					
3.					
4.					

Learning Objective _____

	Actions	Target Date	Date Completed	Involvement of Others	Type **A, C, E**
1.					
2.					
3.					
4.					

Learning Objective _____

	Actions	Target Date	Date Completed	Involvement of Others	Type **A, C, E**
1.					
2.					
3.					
4.					

Learning partners who will observe you and give candid feedback _____

Evaluation of Plan: _____ % of activities completed as of _____ (date)

Completed Review Meetings (dates) _____

Identifying Critical Human Resource Issues

Answer the following questions to identify and probe the critical human resource (HR) issues existent in each key business objective:

Organizational Structure

☐ What changes in the organization's structure are suggested?

Workforce Planning

☐ What changes are needed in the number and types (diversity) of people who will be needed in the future?

☐ Is a planning process in place to help answer this question?

Management Skills

☐ What is the significance of changing business strategies to current management skills?

☐ What new management capabilities and resources will be required?

☐ What are the implications for attracting high-talent individuals to the organization?

☐ What current management strengths or capabilities will require a change in priority and emphasis?

☐ What HR emphasis will be needed to change the focus? (Consider performance appraisal, compensation, training, labor relations, and other management strategies to accomplish needed changes.)

Consequences for Not Implementing Programs

☐ What is the impact of loss in competitive edge of continuing without change?

☐ What external factors (government, unions, and so forth) will influence your ability to attract, retain, and grow productive employees?

Recent research has uncovered the following trends in organizations that are reexamining their current succession planning processes. These companies are:

- developing a leadership framework for executive development

- using the pool approach for flexible employee selection

- redefining the involvement of the senior management team

- preparing the leadership cadre to create successful selection programs that are linked to mission and values

The implementation of these programs will help ensure that organizations are ready and able to deal with the constantly changing workplace of the future.

Key Issues

As you develop your succession planning program, a number of issues will arise. Here are some solutions to common problems.

Issue	Solution
Managers may feel unsure as to whether the best candidates are filling positions.	A systematic process of review will reassure them.
Employees may perceive that you get ahead by whom you know.	Knowing there is a complete review process for staffing will help alleviate their concerns.
Losing high-potential professionals may be a problem.	A targeted development and retention program can address this situation.
You may have a lack of candidates at certain levels.	A plan to fast-track people or buy talent may be needed.
Some high-potentials may become "bottle-necked" and frustrated and may need to be moved laterally to keep them challenged.	You will need to communicate that it is OK to move laterally and create opportunities.
Some organizations get so large that managers do not really know whom they need to promote.	A refined list of names for job openings will be the key to meeting this need.
High-potentials may sometimes be identified, but there may not be a targeted management development program.	You will need to link your design to obtaining internal or external training resources.
High-potentials may or may not be willing to move to other locations.	You will need a career development component to integrate this vital piece of information into the staffing process.
You should determine whether you should buy or grow high-potential individuals.	Very often in some organizations the grass looks greener on the outside. You may need to look at assessment centers to help prove to your managers that internal people are as good as those outside the organization.
You have a major problem with bias toward internal candidates from other divisions.	A management development program in which you give people exposure to employees from other divisions may help to break down the biases.

References & Resources

Articles

Brookes, Donald V. "In Management Succession, Who Moves Up?" *World of Banking*, Summer 1996, pp. 30-32.

Caudron, Shari. "Plan Today for an Unexpected Tomorrow." *Personnel Journal*, September 1996, pp. 40-45.

Fulmer, Robert M., and Kenneth R. Graham. "A New Era of Management Education." *Journal of Management Development*, vol. 12, no. 3 (1993), p. 35.

Hayes, Cassandra. "Passing on the Baton." *Black Enterprise*, September 1996, p. 52.

Johnson, Randall. "Downsizing Presents New Challenges for Succession Plans." *Training Directors' Forum Newsletter*, February 1995, p. 5.

Joinson, Carla. "Developing a Strong Bench." *HRMagazine*, January 1998, pp. 92-96.

Kelley, Bill. "King Makers." *Human Resource Executive*, February 1997, pp. 18-21.

Liebman, M., et al. "Succession Management." *Human Resource Planning*, vol. 19, no. 3 (1996), pp. 16-29.

McConnell, Charles R. "Succeeding with Succession Planning." *Health Care Supervisor*, December 1996, pp. 69-78.

Nowack, Kenneth M. "The Secrets of Succession." *Training & Development*, November 1994, pp. 49-54.

Prahalad, C.K., and G. Hamel. "The Core Competence of the Corporation." *Harvard Business Review*, May/June 1990, pp. 79-91.

Richards, Randall R. "Lending a Hand to the Leaders of Tomorrow." *Association Management*, January 1997, pp. 35-37.

Vicere, Albert A., and Kenneth R. Graham. "Crafting Competitiveness." *Human Resource Planning*, vol. 13, no. 4 (1990), pp. 281-295.

Werther, William B. Jr., et al. "Global Deployment of Executive Talent." *Human Resource Planning*, vol. 18, no. 1 (1995), pp. 20-29.

Books

Bell, Chip R. *Managers as Mentors*. San Francisco: Berrett-Koehler, 1996.

Buckner, M., and L. Slavenski. "Succession Planning." In *Human Resources Management and Development Handbook*, edited by William R. Tracey. New York: AMA-COM, 1993.

Burack, Elmer H. *Creative Human Resource Planning & Applications*. Lake Forest, IL: Brace-Park, 1994.

Dalton, Maxine A., and George P. Hollenbeck. *How to Design an Effective System for Developing Managers and Executives*. Greensboro, NC: Center for Creative Leadership, 1996.

Davis, Brian L., et al. *Successful Managers Handbook*. Minneapolis, MN: Personnel Decisions International, 1996.

Eastman, Lorrina J. *Succession Planning*. Greensboro, NC: Center for Creative Leadership, 1995.

Gabarro, John J. *The Dynamics of Taking Charge*. Boston: Harvard Business School Press, 1988.

Hill, Linda A. *Becoming a Manager*. Boston: Harvard Business School Press, 1996.

Kotter, John P. *Leading Change*. Boston: Harvard Business School Press, 1996.

Potts, Tom, and Arnold Sykes. Executive Talent. New York: Irwin, 1992.

Rothwell, William J. *Effective Succession Planning*. New York: AMACOM, 1994.

Sonnenfeld, Jeffrey. *The Hero's Farewell*. New York: Oxford University Press, 1988.

Ulrich, Dave, and Dale Lake. *Organizational Capability*. New York: John Wiley & Sons, 1990.

Vicere, Albert A., and Robert M. Fullmer. *Crafting Competitiveness*. Oxford, UK: Capstone Publishing, 1996.

Walker, James W. *Human Resource Strategy*. New York: McGraw-Hill, 1992.

White, Randall P., et al. *The Future of Leadership*. Southport, UK: Pitman Publishing, 1996.

Wolfe, Rebecca L. *Systematic Succession Planning*. Menlo Park, CA: Crisp Publications, 1996.

Info-lines

Russell, Susan. "Training and Learning Styles." No. 8804 (revised 1998).

Shaver, Warren, Jr. "How to Build and Use a 360-degree Feedback System." No. 9508 (revised 1998).

Younger, Sandra Millers. "Understanding Core Competencies." No. 9503 (revised 1998).

Career Interest Form

Employee Name/Title_____

Social Security Number _____

Manager Name/Title_____ Company/Sector _____

Department/Branch_____ Location _____

1. Company Experience (most recent jobs first)

From _____ to _____   From _____ to _____

Title _____   Title _____

Department/Branch _____   Department/Branch _____

2. Product Experience

_____

_____

_____

_____

3. Additional Experience (relevant experience only)

From _____ to _____   From _____ to _____

Title _____   Title _____

Organization _____   Organization _____

4. Education—Formal Education/Degree

Year _____ Degree _____

Institution _____ Major or Specialization _____

Certification/Licenses/Memberships _____

_____

_____

_____

5. Other In-Depth Training. List long-term assignments, courses, or programs through which you have increased your work skills and abilities (for example: Management Institute, Insurance Associations Claims course, extended university programs).

_____

_____

_____

_____

_____

(Job Aid continued on page 86)

6. Career Interest. As you look ahead, what do you see as your "ideal" career future? Please describe long-range goals, as well as intermediate and short-range options and assignments that may be interesting, challenging, or that you see as prerequisites for helping you accomplish your goals within the company.

_____
_____
_____
_____

7. Language. Indicate which languages you write and speak fluently.

_____
_____
_____
_____

8. Mobility. Are you willing to geographically relocate?_____ Are you willing to move to another sector?_____
Please describe any special circumstances that affect your geographic mobility at this time.

_____
_____
_____
_____

8a. Career Achievements/Skills. As you look back over your career, what key achievements have you accomplished? Please briefly describe two or three of these here and the results accomplished. Use numbers where applicable. Be specific. Also describe key skills you feel you have developed.

_____
_____
_____
_____

9. Development Strategy. What do you see as your development strategy/plan?

_____
_____
_____
_____

Employee's Signature _____ Date _____

Reviewing Manager's Signature _____ Date _____
(denotes that preceding information is accurate to your best knowledge)

This Career Experience Employee's Statement does not constitute or create an express or implied employment contract, but rather is intended for information purposes only. No representative of the company has the authority to enter into any agreement for employment other than on an at-will basis, unless specifically agreed to in writing and signed by an officer of the company.

Change Management

Issue 9904

Change Management

A U T H O R

Stella Louise Cowan, M.Ed.
Tel.: 313.393.0050
Fax: 313.393.0051
Email: Indybridge@msn.com

Stella Cowan has worked in training design and delivery and organizational development for over 14 years. Her work experience is vast—ranging from acting as a learning systems consultant to a leadership education specialist. She now operates a business in instructional design. Stella is also an adjunct professor in management at Spring Arbor College and Baker College.

Editor
Cat Sharpe

Associate Editor
Sabrina E. Hicks

Production Design
Anne Morgan

ASTD Internal Consultant
Phil Anderson

Change: The Inevitable Reality

Organizations are under siege by a relentless business environment—relentless due to its ability to change at an exponential rate. As a result, negative realities such as the following persist:

- shrinking market share
- increasing customer demands
- continuing inefficient, obsolete processes
- altering workforce due to demographic changes

Creating solutions to harness these changes and providing practitioners to guide the helm of change are hot topics for people like us in the training or human resources (HR) profession. Organizations need change practitioners who can not only conceive of the broad, *aerial* strategy but can also break down this strategy into specific action-oriented activities that move the change forward (that is, operationalize the strategy). We call this the *ground* view.

You must have an aerial, big picture view of your organization's approach to change. This big picture falls flat, however, if you do not operationalize it. Listed below are the key players in managing the change for your organization:

- organizational development specialist
- trainer
- HR expert

Although there is no magic elixir to ease organizational change, certain tactics can help you manage your organization's change efforts. Use this issue of *Info-line* as a primer on change management tactics and the skills needed to facilitate change and implementation roadblocks. This issue includes a number of tools, hands-on examples, and models for change practitioners to use as resources and ideas. With the continued increase in mergers, downsizing, and reengineering, these tools are beneficial because possessing a high level of such change practitioner skills is extremely valuable and marketable.

The Broad or Aerial View

The emphasis of this *Info-line* is the tactical side of change management; however, we must start by taking a look at a typical broad view. The *Six-Phase Change Strategy Model* sidebar on the following page represents the phases of change along a continuum. It shows that progress can be forward or backward, depending on what is going on in the organization.

You must remember that change is incremental relative to both the redesign or reengineering of processes and the transformation of employee attitudes and behaviors. Attitudes and behaviors such as sliding trust, increasing disengagement, and growing fear are challenging to manage and require most of the actions described in the six steps of the model. The change manager (whether he or she is an organizational development specialist, trainer, or HR practitioner) supports forward movement through programs and active advocacy of change. The bottom line is that successful change demands a multipronged approach.

The Dynamics of Change

Having a broad, aerial view for the change process is just the first step. You need perspective on the challenge of moving each employee through the different phases of change acceptance, which we will refer to as the Adaptation/Acceptance Spectrum (consult the sidebar by that title). Keep in mind this phrase: "Change is a process, not an event." Change takes time and typically occurs in overlapping increments—plus, it does not occur as a result of a single effort.

Change is an emotional experience for those involved, and people adjust to change at different rates. It can bring pain, confusion, uncertainty, guilt (for change survivors), and even excitement for those who see personal advantages in it. Understanding the characteristics of each phase of the Adaptation/Acceptance Spectrum helps you manage the change in your organization.

Six-Phase Change Strategy Model

This model depicts each phase as an independent item. It is important to remember, however, that the actions involved are not necessarily independent of each other. Some can occur concurrently. For example, monitoring impact (phase 4) and responding to feedback (phase 5) should occur at almost all points. In addition, actions like training and communications are common threads, punctuating most of the phases.

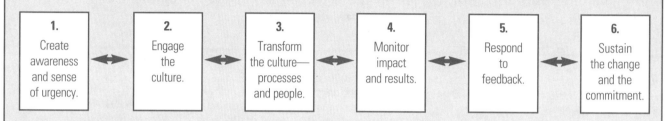

The Six Phases

Phase 1: Create awareness and a sense of urgency. Communicate information on the need for change on a consistent and timely basis. Communicate a clear vision for the organization's future. Share the business case for the specific change strategies selected. Share the financial picture and financial recovery plan to the extent possible.

Phase 2: Engage the culture. Implement programs like town meetings, merger or integration hot lines with prerecorded updates, support circles, and cross-division and cross-level change leadership councils. Create avenues for employee input and involvement.

Phase 3: Transform the culture—processes and people. Implement specific actions such as training, coaching, job counseling, redesign of performance system, and restructure of job roles.

Phase 4: Monitor impact and results. Obtain and analyze data on employees' adaptation to the change, effect of the change on meeting customer requirements, and degree of progress on system or process modifications.

Phase 5: Respond to feedback. Make ongoing, appropriate adjustments to the change strategies and tactics.

Phase 6: Sustain the change and the commitment. Ensure that you align HR systems like recruitment, rewards, training, and involvement to carry the new culture forward. Ensure management systems (like decision making and communication) reflect the new culture. Ensure the physical structure of the organization is consistent with the needs of the new culture.

Phase 1: Thrusting into the Unknown

For the most part, people like the comfort and perceived certainty of their current state. Managing their move from rejection to acceptance (and ideally to embrace) takes time and depends on the stimuli prompting the change. As shown in the sidebar on the following page, change begins for employees with the act of "thrusting" them into the unknown or uncertain. The unknown or uncertain can be any number of events:

- a new procedure
- a change in job responsibilities
- a change in reporting relationships
- a change in business practices
- the loss of a job

People tend to freeze or become paralyzed in this phase of the spectrum.

The literature and theories on involvement indicate that people are more likely to resist change in which they have no input, which is disturbing because people are usually put in a new situation unexpectedly and without their input or involvement. Input or involvement engenders a sense of ownership of the situation. Such ownership does not mean that

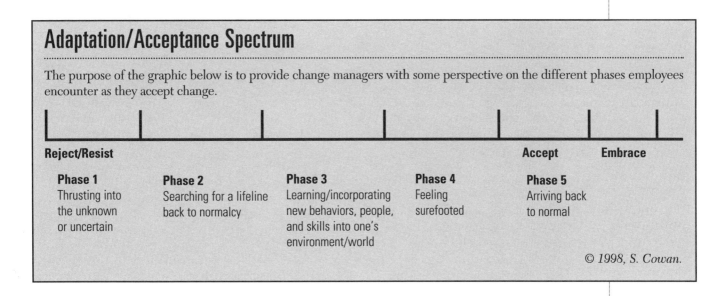

Adaptation/Acceptance Spectrum

The purpose of the graphic below is to provide change managers with some perspective on the different phases employees encounter as they accept change.

Reject/Resist ... Accept ... Embrace

Phase 1
Thrusting into the unknown or uncertain

Phase 2
Searching for a lifeline back to normalcy

Phase 3
Learning/incorporating new behaviors, people, and skills into one's environment/world

Phase 4
Feeling surefooted

Phase 5
Arriving back to normal

© 1998, S. Cowan.

employees who are required to change expect to be the decision makers. But it does mean this: They want you to consider their ideas, and they want you to inform them about events leading to decisions affecting them.

Even if the situation of change cannot be avoided, letting them know ahead of time can lessen the resistance. When it comes to communication and involvement, more is better. To manage the fear of the unknown and lessen resistance, tactics such as the following will help as you communicate change:

- regularly scheduled voice or email messages on the state of the change

- cross-functional reengineering teams with rotating membership

- periodic focus groups to solicit ideas

- change readiness or climate surveys

Phase 2: Searching for Normalcy

Despite communication and involvement, the "searching for a lifeline back to normalcy" phase can be difficult and long lasting. Employees may understand the change and feel involved to some degree, but grabbing that lifeline is no easy task.

Even at this stage, people are still somewhat frozen or paralyzed by change. Your role in change management is pivotal in constructing the lifeline.

The lifeline consists of support actions needed to facilitate release from the frozen state. This does not imply that there is a quick fix. But support actions like the ones described below can help the thaw.

Coping skills. Effective coping techniques are important for managing change. Coping techniques include the following:

- implementing stress and grief management (typically, people experience loss and go through the stages of grief when responding to a drastic change like job elimination)

- handling ambiguity

- confronting fears

Facilitator-led workshops, counseling, videotapes, and audiotapes are formats for teaching coping skills. Employee assistance providers can also support this effort. Keep in mind that coping skills are valuable through the entire change cycle. Change is a process, and as it unfolds it brings new disruptions to handle.

Decision making. If jobs are relocating or changing substantially and employees have the opportunity to decide whether they want to relocate or retrain, the quality of their decision making is important. That is why items like a worksheet or pamphlet containing the pertinent decision factors and tips for reaching the best personal decision are valuable. They help employees feel as if they have some control over their circumstances.

Emotional support. You cannot underestimate the value of emotional support. People need understanding and empathy (not to be confused with sympathy). They need to know that although you cannot necessarily fix their pain, you can relate to it. Moreover, people need to connect with others experiencing similar circumstances.

Support groups, either in person or virtual, can address this need. The groups can be informal or facilitated. The group format provides an arena for expressing and receiving empathy and for divesting emotionally. Employees that benefit particularly from the group format are the survivors of downsizing. Very often, these people suffer from *survivor's guilt* and need their own special emotional support.

Career or job planning. Today, more than ever, people need to be adept at career or job planning. One of the most difficult changes for people can be workforce transition (that is, movement of people to different jobs, elimination of jobs, or transfer of jobs). People are sometimes wedded to their job with no concept of how to transfer their skill sets to a different job. Understanding the concept of transferring skill sets opens up new opportunities for the individual and the organization. In fact, from the organization's viewpoint, redeployment of resources can be a strategic option.

Getting to "Normal"

The road from phase 3 ("learning/incorporating new behaviors") to phase 5 ("arriving back to normal") requires a host of actions. However, it bears repeating that there is no magic formula. The information described under the next sections, "Change Management Skills" and "Operationalizing the Change Strategy," speak to those actions.

Change Management Skills

Successful change management weaves together two key threads:

1. People considerations (for example, emotions associated with job or work elimination or survival).

2. Process considerations (such as restructuring of tasks and responsibilities).

Change is a two-sided coin that involves both people transformation and business strategy innovation. Sometimes, however, the emphasis on reengineering the processes and systems eclipses the people side. This is a mistake. The human or high-touch side of change management is a necessary ingredient. An effective change manager, therefore, is a combination of strategist, process consultant, diagnostician, and *humanist*. Characteristics of a successful change manager include the following:

- appreciates that organizational change unearths interpersonal or emotional issues (that is, the "people" side of change)

- understands the implications of change to production and management systems

- knows how to take in, sort through, and frame information in a way that creates a foundation for a change strategy

- can build an appropriate strategy that integrates the "people" and the "process" side of change management

- can operationalize the broad strategy into specific tactics

More specifically, the 12 groups of behaviors described in the *Implementation Skills* sidebar at right are key to success at change management. The behaviors are particularly relevant to the critical objective of balancing people transformation with business innovation or process redesign.

Implementation Skills

Having a sound, detailed plan; top leadership support; the resources; and the manpower for your organization's change is ammunition for success. But to win the battle, you need certain skills to implement the change effectively. While there is no definitive list of skills for change managers, the list below is applicable to fueling an atmosphere of change and implementing appropriate change tactics. Also, depending on your organization's particular change situation (for example, wide scale versus limited or targeted change, merger versus spin-off of a division or business segment), the frequency and extent you use the skills may vary.

Skill Sets	Behaviors
1. Thinking Analytically	● Evaluating data or information systematically to identify surface, as well as underlying, causes of problems (for example, performance gaps or process misalignment). ● Assessing the impact of solutions and making appropriate modifications.
2. Seeing the "Big Picture"	● Looking beyond details to see the overarching goals and results. ● Understanding the impact of business decisions on the entire change strategy. ● Making appropriate modifications to the general strategy based on business decisions and customer input.
3. Thinking Out-of-the-Box	● Designing new or innovative ways to address organization initiatives and customer needs.
4. Using Technology	● Using existing or new technology to design products, create solutions, deliver programs, and market services.
5. Using Human Relations	● Working collaboratively with others to build understanding and trust and to achieve common goals. ● Establishing and maintaining rapport with individuals and groups.
6. Learning Continuously	● Being self-directed and persistent in pursuing new information, technology, and ideas.
7. Creating Partnerships/ Networks	● Building ownership and support for change among affected individuals or groups.
8. Thinking Holistically	● Recognizing that an organization is a living, breathing entity. ● Identifying the parts of an organizational process or operation. ● Understanding how the parts fit together and the impact of misalignment of one part on another. ● Understanding the impact of modifying one part on another.
9. Using Project Leadership Methods	● Acting as a lead contact or focal point for components (for example, program, intervention, or event) of the change strategy. ● Directing the activities of others contributing to the component. ● Overseeing project deadlines, deliverables, and customer expectations. ● Adapting to constraints and unexpected roadblocks.
10. Leveraging Power/ Influence	● Establishing and using a power base through unique knowledge or expertise or through alignment with power brokers in the organization.
11. Creating Solutions	● Customizing or designing solutions that best fit the problem. ● Implementing the solutions. ● Tracking the impact of the solutions and making adjustments as appropriate.
12. Responding to Clients	● Interpreting client needs and expectations through various actions (for example, feedback system, survey, and consistent in-person contact). ● Developing effective solutions (for example, coaching, training, or intervention) to close the gap if needs or expectations are not met.

As is evident by the 12 groups of behaviors, in your role as a change practitioner you will wear many hats. These hats or skill sets serve different but related purposes and complement each other.

■ *Analyzing and Designing Hat*

The hat for analyzing issues and designing appropriate solutions represents foundation skills:

- thinking analytically
- thinking "out-of-the-box"
- learning continuously
- creating solutions

These skills allow you, through tactics like surveys, focus groups, observation, and data collection, to see and design the best solution fit for change-related problems. They help to develop and make use of instruments like the *Performance/Issue Analysis* sidebar and the *Change Management Planning* job aid (parts I and II) to achieve this. These types of tools help you ask the right questions and organize the information in a way that creates a visual framework of the problem.

■ *Strategy Hat*

Seeing the big picture, thinking holistically, and responding to clients are important when deciding what broad strategies to use in the change plan. It is simply a matter of identifying factors in the business, economic, political, and social environment (like those shown in the sidebar bottom left). You must also realize that customer demands drive the need for change and dictate the required response to it.

■ *Change Agent Hat*

Everyone in the organization is in essence a change agent. Change management is not one department or one person; therefore, building a network of advocates and champions is critical. You should not underestimate the value of good press or word-of-mouth advertising. It creates needed momentum. To create that momentum, skills such as using human relations techniques, creating partnerships, and leveraging influence are desirable for your change management role.

■ *Technology and Leadership Hat*

Using technology and project leadership methods are two skills that can prove to be your best friends in fostering change. Technology can support creative change programs or solutions, such as performance coaching through videoconferencing or virtual brainstorming using bulletin boards on an intranet.

Virtual brainstorming is a creative way to foster idea sharing across geographic and department boundaries because there is not always the opportunity to meet in person. It can also foster involvement and network building. The actual brainstorming process would involve posting questions or needs on the intranet bulletin board. Employees would place responses to questions or needs (adding to each other's ideas) on the board either independently (that is, asynchronous postings) or employees would be online at the same time for a designated period (that is, a synchronous chat). The responses could be in narrative form, lists, or even mind maps. Creativity would be the key, and visual images (words or pictures) stimulate creativity. The responses would remain on the intranet as information resources.

Finally, in your change management role you will orchestrate a number of wide-ranging activities such as the following:

- breaking large tasks down into specific activities
- ensuring adequate time for those activities
- conducting a cost analysis

Big Picture/Holistic View

External Environment
- competitors
- government regulations
- societal changes (for example demographic shifts)
- globalization
- expanding technology
- decreasing product appeal
- growing niche markets
- politics

Internal Environment
- formal and informal communication
- financial picture
- decision making
- rewards
- predominant leadership style
- selection and promotion
- training and development
- performance measurement and feedback

Performance/Issue Analysis

Use the performance/issue analysis tool to map out a problem from a holistic viewpoint. It will help you to determine what systems or processes in the organization have an impact on the problem and to what degree. This process is key to ensuring that you identify the real causes of the problem and understand the full effect of those causes.

Date:	Change Consultant:	Client:	Problem Category:

Stakeholders	**Process** What are the processes involved in the performance issue— jobs, roles, tasks, procedures, and so forth?	**People/Departments** Who are the people or departments affected by the performance issue?	**Picture of Ideal Environment** What would things look like if the problem did not exist? 1._____ 2._____ 3._____	**Value** What value does fixing the problem add to the bottom line?

Organizational Systems and Processes	**Lack of Solution Fit (Y/N)**	**Degree (high, medium, low)**	**Relationship to Problem/Issue**
Communication			
Training and Development			
Rewards and Recognition			
Performance Management			
Selection and Promotion			
Customer Input			
Employee Involvement			

© 1997, S. Cowan

95

Change Management Tactics

A dictionary might define "tactics" as maneuvers, procedures, or schemes—and all three apply within the context of change management. Tactics are the individual actions you use to ignite, maintain, and revitalize (if necessary) the change process. Listed below are some sample tactics you might consider using in your change efforts.

Meetings
- all-employee meetings—scheduled on a regular basis or as needed
- leadership meetings—scheduled on a regular basis or as needed
- quick focus sessions (for example, lesson-learned session after project completion or team intervention)
- department huddles (that is, impromptu, informal department gatherings for giving information, celebrating, or reinforcing morale)

Telephone Coaching
- performance, career, or process coaches can use
- potential coaches include human resources (HR) staff, internal subject matter experts (SMEs), and external consultant experts

On-Site Coaching
- performance, career, and process coaches can use this tactic with groups or individuals
- potential coaches include HR staff, internal SMEs, and external consultant experts

Communication Vehicles
- newsletters
- department bulletin boards
- intranet bulletin boards
- all-employee letters

Telephone Hot Line
- employees submit questions, share challenges and successes, and request information

Training
- classroom, on-the-job, or self-instructional (for example, workbook, video, CD-ROM-based) training for technical or behavioral issues
- knowledge/information partnerships
- learning contracts
- action plan for transferring learning
- peer teaching

Tools and Models
- help develop skills transfer knowledge and provide a means for applying learning (for example, a communication debrief and the Four Point Coaching Model presented later in this issue)

Nerve Center
- group containing key personnel, technology, and resources for deploying and coordinating change leadership tactics across the organization

Survival Kit
- application-oriented tips and resources for coping through an organizational change

Recognition Day/Week
- leadership and co-worker acknowledgement of employee contribution
- banners, certificates, and profiles in the organization's newsletter recognizing achievements
- non-monetary rewards such as flextime, compressed workweek, special assignment, resources or technology, and special partnerships

Being able to manage these types of activities well is why project leadership skills are beneficial in a change management position.

Operationalizing the Change Strategy

The change management strategy starts from the big picture view, which is very broad and incorporates a number of initiatives. Operationalizing the strategy simply means breaking down the broad and wide into action-oriented activities (for example, programs, processes, or events) that move the change forward. The change practitioner can embrace these activities and measure progress and success more easily.

While all of the tactics listed in the above sidebar are effective in facilitating change, a few deserve some additional attention:

- tools and models
- training and coaching

Tools and Models

The organization's employees are the bedrock of successful change tactics. As harbingers of the new culture, they must believe in the vision and use job behaviors that support realization of it. Obviously, changing performance or job behavior is not an exact science. It requires, among other factors, a way to perform the following:

- create common practices
- communicate those practices
- support application of those practices

One such way is developing or adopting appropriate performance tools and models. A performance tool is a logical, straightforward learning or application aid (such as the *Communications Debrief* on the next page). A performance model is a succinct, easily applied example of a process or procedure (see the *Four Point Coaching Model* sidebar for an example and design tips).

Both models and tools provide a mental picture, which provide a more assessable framework for analysis or discussion. They also present a structured way of digesting information and perform the triple duty of teaching, coaching, and reinforcing.

Teaching. The boxes in the Four Point Coaching Model—observe, individualize, encourage, and track—represent separate subject areas for training in the classroom. Organize activities or exercises around each area. You can also design each area as a mini, stand-alone training module (possibly 45-90 minutes).

Coaching. Use the coaching questions on the communication debrief to guide discussion, identify challenges, and determine development needs during individual coaching sessions.

Reinforcing. The call-outs in the communication debrief make it easy to review and reinforce the application tips.

The idea is to pass the knowledge along while creating a sense of independence. This act builds the change tactics infrastructure, which is an important part of transforming the culture.

Training and Coaching

Training and coaching are interrelated essential parts of the infrastructure. With the redesign of jobs, the reengineering of whole processes, and the introduction of new technology, a need definitely exists for training employees. Training can occur in the classroom or on the job, but it also includes self-instructional training and performance coaching. No matter how you decide to provide it, training should be *application oriented*. This means that the instructional strategy focuses on how to apply the classroom concepts on the job.

To ensure that training transfers to on-the-job application, include a process and worksheets on application planning in your training programs. Design your instruction to place less emphasis on conveying concepts and more emphasis on creating experiential learning opportunities (for example, simulations, role plays, learning games, and behavior modeling).

The *Leader as Change Facilitator* sidebar is an example of an application-oriented program. The theme of the program is "Be a change *instigator* not a change *spectator*." A segment from W. Mitchell's powerful book *It's Not What Happens to You, It's What You Do About It* is included as pre-reading. The program is a one-and-a-half-day classroom experience with follow-up coaching for the implementation activities. A pre-training survey is administered (preferably in person) to gather the following information from the leader:

- department's key customers
- methods for collecting customer data
- methods for communicating with staff

Both the survey and follow-up coaching, which can be in person, by telephone, or by email, help establish a partnership between you and your customers. Through activities like these, you increase your sensitivity to your customers' world (that is, their requirements, issues, and challenges).

Communication Debrief

Below is a sample of a communication debrief, which is a leader development tool. Use it as an example of how to learn from your meeting experience.

Briefly summarize the results of the meeting.

Base the debrief checklist on your task actions and use it to help you reflect on the way you conducted the meeting.

Whether or not you need to obtain information from the person depends on the nature of the meeting.

Action: Something you did—like not refocusing the group when it went on a tangent in the middle of the meeting. Unchecked tangents can kill the momentum and consume valuable time.

Statement: Something you said such as, "Ron, it's silly to feel anxious about the new job roles." Minimizing how someone feels makes that person defensive and less open to the message or purpose of the meeting.

Not all meetings require actions, resources, or deadlines as outcomes. For those that do, try to involve the group members (that is, solicit their input and ideas) in developing these items. When people are involved they are more receptive and feel ownership of the outcomes.

Date:	*Communication Topic:*	
How did the meeting go overall?	**What action or statement would I repeat? Why was the action or statement effective?**	**What action or statement would I *not* repeat?** **Why was the action or statement ineffective? How would I change it?**
Debrief Checklist		
☐ Did I begin by describing the **purpose** (for example, communicate a new policy) and desired **outcome?**		
☐ Did I **address questions** or concerns about the purpose or outcome (for example, whether or not the new policy being communicated would also be provided in writing)?		
☐ Did I **obtain information** needed to meet the purpose?		
☐ Did I **provide clarity** or background information on issues related to the purpose (for example, the criteria used to make a policy decision)?		
☐ Did I **deliver the complete message** or information? Did I verify whether the group understood the message?		
☐ Did I develop **next actions** (if required), with input from the group?		
☐ Did I identify **resources,** with input from the group?		
☐ Did I set **deadlines** for completion of actions, with input from the group?		
☐ Did I **restate** the outcomes at the end of the meeting?		
☐ Did I **check for unanswered questions** or concerns before concluding? Did I answer or make arrangements to get answers to the group later?		
☐ Did I **thank the group** for participating in the meeting?		

© *July 1998, S. Cowan*

Four Point Coaching Model

Observe and respond to coaching opportunities.

- Pay attention to behaviors, actions, and feedback that indicate a need for coaching (for example, customer or peer complaints, procrastination, or expression of uncertainty about handling project).

Individualize the coaching style based on who is being coached and the particular circumstances of the coaching opportunity.

- Consider the person's abilities, experience, willingness, work style, and confidence level—*the who*.

- Consider the deadline, resources, complexity of the task, impact of the task, logistics, organizational priority, and so forth—*the circumstances*.

Track performance and provide feedback.

- Reinforce desired performance.

- Identify ineffective performance and suggest alternative actions.

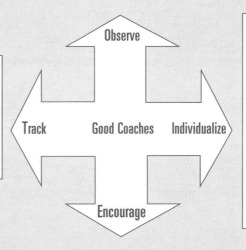

Encourage initiative and ownership, and offer support and guidance.

- Ask open-ended question to solicit input such as ideas, actions, and solutions.

- Provide expertise, experience, knowledge, and direction.

- Balance the "asking" and the "providing."

© July 1998, S. Cowan.

Implementation Roadblocks

Just because senior leadership has decided that the organization needs to change, it does not mean automatic success. Implementation roadblocks manifest themselves in many ways. No matter how well designed your overall strategy is or how skilled you are, you will likely confront some of the following roadblocks.

Lack of vision. When the corporate vision or specific business strategies are unclear, people are sometimes unsure about how they should interpret changes.

Lack of leadership support. The change manager is often the chief advocate of the change process. This role includes injecting the sense of advocacy into the rest of the organization—particularly leadership. Actions that are essential for success must first be present in leaders. They must model the behaviors needed to bring about change in both process and culture. Only top leadership can provide the sanctions of time and resources necessary for change. They must also remove obstacles to change that are out of the realm of direct reports. Problems occur when senior leadership says one thing, but their behaviors suggest the opposite.

Lack of HR systems alignment. Hiring people with the right abilities and attitude, rewarding people for the right behaviors and outputs, and training people in the right skills are all part of aligning the systems to provide what you need to redesign the culture.

History of poor implementation. When an organization has a history of poorly implemented strategic plans, people tend to expect very little when new change efforts are announced.

Insufficient time. If insufficient time is allocated for implementation, there will be large maintenance cost after the change.

Environment of low risk taking. Overly punishing errors or rewarding the mere absence of errors promotes an environment of low risk taking. High risk taking should be the desired behavior in an organization undergoing change.

Lack of clear communications. If information about change is allowed to filter down the organization in an unmanaged fashion, it becomes diffused, less specific, and interpreted in arbitrary ways.

Lack of resistance planning. All major changes, even ones that have positive implications, encounter resistance. People are not necessarily resisting change but rather the disruption caused by change.

Poor management of resistance. When resistance does not surface, it is often because it has been denied or quashed. When overt resistance is not acknowledged and managed properly, the resistance often goes "underground." The results are covert resistance:

- slowdowns
- malicious compliance
- outright sabotage

Lack of synergy. Forgetting that an organization's various operations are interdependent can lead to initiating changes in one place and encountering resistance from people and functions in another place.

Poor follow-through. Many organizations reward people with a lot of fanfare for starting big projects, but they fail to follow through to see that the project was finished or that it achieved the desired results.

Roadblocks like these just prove that the world of change management is unpredictable, exciting, and challenging. During change, addressing both the process needs *and* the people needs of your organization is a complex—but necessary—balancing act.

As the change manager, you and the committed, visible support of top leadership are the primary catalysts of this balancing act. Your ability to translate broad strategy into action-oriented tactics lays a pathway for creating real systems and behavioral change. Moreover, thriving on the excitement, enduring the challenges, and expecting the unpredictable are the hallmarks of a successful change manager.

Leader as Change Facilitator

Below is an example of the course design for an application-oriented program. The theme for this program was "Be a change *instigator* not a change *spectator*." Use this example to help you design your own application-oriented programs that facilitate change.

Section	Title	Content
Introduction/ Ice Breaker	**Change is like …**	Ask participants to stand beneath one of the four flipchart titles (listed below) that best describes their feelings about change. ● Change is like a roller coaster ride—*It is both exhilarating and frightening.* ● Change is like a new pair of shoes—*It is tight and uncomfortable until you break it in.* ● Change is like a hot fudge sundae—*It is delicious and satisfying and leaves you eagerly anticipating the next one.* ● Change is like a hailstorm—*It is fast and furious and you just have to ride it out.* Once participants are gathered beneath the flipcharts, ask them to chat for a minute about their reaction to recent changes in their lives. Next, ask them one-by-one to introduce themselves (for example, name, department, job/responsibility, and reason they stood beneath that particular flipchart) to the large group.
Opening Activity	**What, why, and how**	Through use of poster boards, summary information sheets, question and answer time, and an appearance from someone in senior leadership, address the following questions: ● What is changing? ● Why is it changing? ● How will it benefit the organization? ● How can it benefit the organization's employees?
Learning Outcomes	**Goals**	Asking these questions is critical in setting a framework for the learning and application process. Discuss the fact that a certain amount of ambiguity comes with dramatic organizational change—not all questions can be answered. ● Understand change in general. ● Understand implications of the change or transition for the organization. ● Understand leader's role in facilitating change or transition. ● Develop a plan for helping staff manage change or transition.
Department Environment Maps		Through an interactive exercise using the department environment maps that were created during pre-training sessions, participants should realize the following: ● They have similar challenges. ● They share customers, technology, and resources. ● They have common goals. ● They can be a resource to each other.
Supervisor's or Manager's Role	**Change— personal view**	Examine the personal view of change through an activity involving a three-part instrument: ● change grid (What does change look like? How does it affect me?) ● change pulse (How do I feel about the change? Where am I on the change Adaptation/Acceptance Spectrum?) ● change implementation (What can I do to adapt/accept this change? What can I do to facilitate the change?)
Management Behaviors	**Eight keys**	Examine the eight keys of management leadership (listed below), and, using an assessment process, determine development needs relative to the eight keys: ● listening ● collaborating ● recognizing/rewarding ● presenting information ● communicating one-on-one ● coaching ● supporting ● clearing the way
Action Planning		Complete a plan for transferring the learning to the job (for example, what will be done, when, who needs to be involved, resources, benefits, and so forth). The training department sets up a coaching schedule for continued support during implementation.

© July 1998, S. Cowan.

References & Resources

Articles

Barrier, Michael. "Managing Workers in a Time of Change." *Nation's Business,* May 1998, pp. 31-34.

Buchel, Mary. "Accelerating Change." *Training & Development,* April 1996, pp. 48-51.

Carrig, Ken. "Reshaping Human Resources for the Next Century—Lessons from a High Flying Airline." *Human Resource Management,* Summer 1997, pp. 277-289.

Caudron, Shari. "Rebuilding Employee Trust." *Training & Development,* August 1996, pp. 18-21.

Cook, Julie. "Tackling Large-Scale Change." *Human Resource Executive,* May 20, 1997, pp. 44-46.

Cutcher-Gershenfeld, Joel, et al. "Managing Concurrent Change Initiatives: Integrating Quality and Work/Family Strategies." *Organizational Dynamics,* Winter 1997, pp. 21-37.

Demers, Russ, et al. "Commitment to Change." *Training & Development,* August 1996, pp. 22-26.

Denton, D. Keith. "9 Ways to Create an Atmosphere for Change." *HRMagazine,* October 1996, pp. 76-81.

Frady, Marsha. "Get Personal to Communicate Coming Change." *Performance Improvement,* August 1997, pp. 32-33.

Kramlinger, Tom. "How to Deliver a Change Message." *Training & Development,* April 1998, pp. 44-47.

Orlikowski, Wanda J., and Debra J. Hofman. "An Improvisational Model for Change Management: the Case of Groupware Technologies." *Sloan Management Review,* Winter 1997, pp. 11-21.

Prickett, Ruth. "House Proud." *People Management,* November 12, 1998, pp. 43-45.

Rough, Jim. "Dynamic Facilitation and the Magic of Self-Organizing Change." *Journal for Quality and Participation,* June 1997, pp. 34-38.

Schneider, David M., and Charles Goldwasser. "Be a Model Leader of Change." *Management Review,* March 1998, pp. 41-45.

Smith, Dick. "Invigorating Change Initiatives." *Management Review,* May 1998, pp. 45-48.

Strebel, Paul. "Why Do Employees Resist Change?" *Harvard Business Review,* May/June 1996, pp. 86-92.

Topchik, Gary S. "Attacking the Negativity Virus." *Management Review,* September 1998, pp. 61-64.

Trahant, Bill, and Warner W. Burke. "Traveling Through Transitions." *Training & Development,* February 1996, pp. 37-41.

Books

Barger, Nancy J., and Linda K. Kirby. *The Challenge of Change in Organizations: Helping Employees Thrive in the New Frontier.* Palo Alto, CA: Davies-Black, 1995.

Carr, Clay. *Choice, Change & Organizational Change: Practical Insights from Evolution for Business Leaders & Thinkers.* New York: AMACOM, 1996.

Hambrick, Donald C., et al., eds. *Navigating Change: How CEOs, Top Teams, and Boards Steer Transformation.* Boston: Harvard Business School Press, 1998.

Jeffreys, J. Shep. *Coping with Workplace Change: Dealing with Loss and Grief.* Menlo Park, CA: Crisp Publications, 1995.

Maurer, Rick. *Beyond the Wall of Resistance: Unconventional Strategies that Build Support for Change.* Austin, TX: Bard Books, 1996.

Mitchell, W. *It's Not What Happens to You, It's What You Do About It.* Partners Publishers Group, 1997.

Smith, Douglas K. *Taking Charge of Change: 10 Principles for Managing People and Performance.* Reading, MA: Addison-Wesley, 1996.

Info-lines

Carr, Don Aaron. "How to Facilitate." No. 9406 (revised 1999).

Koehle, Deborah. "The Role of the Performance Change Manager." No. 9715.

Smith, Warren. "Managing Change: Implementation Skills." No. 8910 (out of print).

Titcomb, T. J. "Chaos and Complexity Theory." No. 9807.

Change Management Planning

This job aid has two parts. Part I provides descriptions of when particular change tactics are most appropriate. Part II provides space for you to list the various components of your program and to select the change management tactics you think best support each component. The purpose of the descriptions and the worksheet is to support designing the best overall strategy for a specific change-related problem.

Part I.

Tact	Application
Education	Appropriate when looking to close a **knowledge gap** or **skill deficiency** that requires college or technical education (such as the completion of a degree or certificate).
Training	Applies when **job processes** or **job technologies** have changed and internal training programs are available to meet the need. Local colleges and training firms offer technical, skills, and interpersonal training.
Coaching/ Counseling	There are four types of coaching or counseling: ● **Performance coaching** closes gaps in the quality or production of an individual's or a group's work outputs. It can involve reviewing examples of desired outputs, reinforcing strategies for producing desired outputs, and giving constructive feedback on outputs. ● **Career coaching** is useful during workforce transition situations (such as job transfer, elimination, or redesign). It can involve skills assessment, résumé writing, cover letter writing, job searching tips (internal or external), and education planning. ● **Process coaching** supports groups working on their flow-charting of processes, identifying redundancies, and recommending improvements or changes. It is also an appropriate analysis activity when reengineering organizational systems. ● **Human relations coaching** provides support, insight, or guidance in handling inter-group or team relations, change adaptability, or communication issues.
Interviewing	Useful if you are collecting sensitive information, if the questions are mainly open ended and less suited for a written survey, or if there is a need for the interviewer to interact with the interviewee during the interview. Can be done in person or by telephone. In-person is desirable when hearing the information and seeing the person providing the information is beneficial to the outcome (for example, better opportunity to establish rapport or build relations and to observe the interviewee's behavior).
Mentoring Program	Useful if you want to **impart leadership knowledge** and **experience** to the culture. Appropriate for addressing **diversity issues** around change by establishing special programs for underrepresented groups. Can be an informal or formal program.
Tool or Model	Helpful in situations where a **job aid** can contribute to improving performance or can provide support in applying a process. Can supplement formal training, be used as a guide when coaching, and is an effective method for enabling employees to perform independently.
Intervention	Involves using activities (such as team building, role clarification, or structured feedback) to influence behavior, stop certain behaviors, or increase awareness. The goal is to get a group back on track and can involve one activity or a series of activities designed to meet a specific need.
Assessment or Survey	Aids with **collecting employees' opinions** or **attitudes** about change (for example, change readiness survey or team participation survey).
Focus Group	Useful to **obtain sensitive information,** debrief after an incident to channel emotions, debrief after completion of a project for lessons learned, or assess employees' readiness for or adaptation to change. Can be intact or cross-functional groups.
Communication	Used to inform, educate, motivate, or influence. Newsletters, email, voicemail, all-employee letters, banners, and bulletin boards are examples of communication vehicles. Appropriate during change (for example, a merger) because **employees need and want to be informed** of what is happening and motivated to stay engaged. A communication vacuum leads to half-truths, innuendoes, and lies. Communication during all phases of change is necessary. Timeliness, honesty, and consistency are key.

(Job Aid continued on page 104)

Job Aid

Action Planning	Helpful in transferring classroom learning to the job, applying a process to a situation, and implementing individual or group performance development activities.
System Alignment	Involves changing systems (such as compensation, performance review, training, and selection/promotion) to support the type of culture the organization wants to build. For example, if your organization wants to create a culture of entrepreneurial thinkers, the design of its compensation system might include a reward (such as a bonus) for developing and successfully implementing ideas that grow the business. Elements like employee empowerment, risk-taking, and trust would have to be a part of this culture. You would also need an infrastructure of resources, tracking methods, and reporting. (This is actually more of a strategy than a tactic.)

Part II.

Project Components	Appropriate Change Management Tactic					
	Education	**Training**	**Coaching/ Counseling**	**Interviewing**	**Mentoring Programs**	**Tool or Model**

Project Components	Intervention	Assessment or Survey	Focus Group	Communi- cation	Action Planning	System Alignment

On-the-Job Training

Issue 9708

On-the-Job Training

AUTHOR

Charles I. Levine, Ph.D.
President, Instructional Design
Associates
P.O. Box 457
Sharon, MA 02067-0457
Tel. 781.784.5994
Fax. 781.784.2578

Dr. Levine, a nationally respected and active educator on the subject of OJT, has over 25 years experience as a trainer and consultant. He has held key management and training positions with Raytheon, Honeywell, and The University of Wisconsin. His clients include Toyota Motor Corporation, Michigan Bell, Illinois Bell, and Heinz, Inc.

Editor
Cat Sharpe

Associate Editor
Patrick McHugh

Designer
Steven M. Blackwood

Copy Editor
Kay Larson

ASTD Internal Consultant
Dr. Walter Gray

On-the-Job Training

On-the-job training (OJT) is one of the oldest forms of training; it was born when the first parent took his or her child aside and said, "Let me show you how to do that." OJT at its most fundamental level can be defined as two people working closely together so one person can learn from the other. Whether the person teaching is called trainer, mentor, or guide, the function is the same—to teach the student so that he or she can correctly and safely perform a task. OJT's strengths are in its flexibility and portability, all the while remaining an informal and human form of training.

There is no company, factory, or home business in the world where one person—the so-called expert—has not helped a fellow employee learn a new skill. This *Info-line* covers the essentials of OJT and just how you and your organization can best employ and enjoy OJT's far-reaching benefits. The concepts and advice presented apply to any organization, ranging from manufacturing to services and from government to education. Whenever and whereever employees need training in specific work-related tasks, OJT is the training method you'll want to consider.

Everyone has their own definition of what OJT means. Essentially, it is a just-in-time training delivery system that dispenses training to employees as and when they need it. An OJT system can be as small or as large as the needs and resources of an organization allow.

Whether they know it or not, all companies have OJT systems in place. There is always someone standing next to another worker who says the magic OJT words, "Let me show you how to do that," and then teaches the other how to run a machine or perform a task. This is called *unstructured OJT* because it occurs haphazardly—the employee-trainer (a.k.a. expert) teaches the tasks as he or she knows and remembers them. Because of time or other pressures, important steps may be forgotten or simply skipped. As an unstructured system, no criteria are established for the quality of training, nor are records of the training maintained.

Building a Structured OJT System

In response to quality, ISO 9000 (see *ISO 9000 and OJT* on the next page), and budget constraints, companies have been "organizing" the OJT process. Specific employees are designated OJT trainers, checklists of required skills are used to ensure that all employees receive the same training, and the training effort is tracked and recorded. Because an organizational structure supports the training, this is called *structured OJT*. Structured OJT is more efficient than unstructured OJT and in some reports, companies relate a 60 to 80 percent decrease in training time.

Most companies want to implement a structured OJT system, but few achieve this goal. What typically happens is that the already existing, but unstructured OJT system, also begins to fail. In unstructured OJT, all the training time is casual—untracked and therefore invisible. It never appears on a budget or time sheet. Structured OJT, on the other hand, makes this time visible and in many companies visibility is risky. Once training time becomes real, supervisors often move to eliminate or convert it into production time, since they, of course, are measured by production output. This explains how many organizations simply botch an existing unstructured OJT system when moving to a structured one.

Before making the transition, beware of the fact that structured OJT exists only with the assistance, support, and understanding of management and production supervisors. Training takes time; if supervisors do not allow enough time for preparation and training, they will thwart any structured OJT effort. If you cannot gain internal support from the organization's managers and supervisors, don't waste time trying to implement structured OJT. Instead, work to strengthen the existing training process.

Similar to quality programs and true ISO 9000 programs, a structured OJT system will change your production operation: Training assumes new importance—trainers are included when developing new production processes and are given time to carry out proper training. As with any system, trainers still need to be flexible when dealing with production and customer needs.

When to Use OJT

The use of OJT as a training method is determined by the following:

- safety considerations
- size of the training unit
- geographic distribution of the trainees

When safety is a major issue, some companies use simulators or spare machinery for OJT training. Though simulators are expensive, they allow trainees to experience potentially catastrophic circumstances without any danger to themselves or the facility. If you are going to use simulators or spare machinery for OJT training, be sure to have scripted scenarios so the training is useful, realistic, and consistent. In some companies, regulatory statutes require the use of simulators within the boundaries of a very structured OJT system.

ISO 9000 and OJT
....

ISO 9000 is a set of generic standards that provide quality management guidance and identify system elements necessary to assure quality. Each company decides how to implement the standards to meet its own and its customers' needs. Basically, the ISO 9000 standards require a company to document procedures, follow those procedures, review the process, and then change them when necessary.

Under ISO registration, training checklists and any other OJT documentation should become controlled documents that cannot be changed without appropriate approval. Trainers must become part of the procedure development and sign-off process, thus establishing a link from the OJT system to quality and engineering. As OJT systems grow, they become further intertwined into normal daily operations of the company. Wherever new employees need to learn specific skills or procedures in order to succeed on the job, the OJT concept is applicable.

For example, a company implementing an OJT system under mandate from their ISO 9000 registrar might devote more resources to the system due to requests from production supervisors. It is a fact of life that problems that threaten to close a facility or cause it to lose its certification will receive more attention than those having less impact. For more information on quality systems, see *Info-lines* No. 8805, "Training for Quality" and No. 9111, "Fundamentals of Quality."

If group interaction, interpersonal skills, or other personal communication objectives are part of the training, classroom instruction is probably the best delivery medium. OJT instruction cannot fulfill interpersonal skills objectives since **OJT, by definition, is one-on-one training.** If the trainer has the requisite skills in specific training techniques and there are sufficient controls in place over the training methods, OJT can be used for conceptual training in areas such as quality and customer satisfaction. In this scenario, trainers act as role models and instruct students through skills and behavior training. If a large number of employees need to be trained or if the potential trainees are geographically dispersed, other methods of training should be used.

OJT has one major drawback—it assumes that trainees are capable of learning and have the background skills, such as math and reading, necessary to perform the task. If prerequisite skills are not present, the OJT training will fail. Trainers should be educated to recognize these deficits and respond appropriately.

From Unstructured to Structured OJT

Building on the example of unstructured OJT where two people stand together and one person informally teaches the other, we can begin to construct a more structured system.

The next phase in the growth of an OJT system is to train the trainers in methods and techniques. Most OJT trainers have never been shown how to adapt to various student learning styles or how to most effectively present materials. This is one of the most critical and important steps in the growth of OJT within a company. Untrained trainers will surely cause an OJT system to fail.

Until now, we have been dealing with casual trainers, that is, employees who work in a production area and train when there is spare time. As the OJT system continues to grow, some companies will "bite the head count bullet" and assign full-time trainers to the OJT system. These trainers may have the responsibility to train new personnel, retrain existing employees who are changing jobs, or recertify staff on their current jobs. Full-time trainers do not need to be experts in all tasks; they may delegate some training tasks to part-time trainers who are experts in specific skill areas, but it is the full-time trainers' responsibility to ensure that all checklists are completed. At this time the company may assign an employee as an OJT system coordinator to track and record employee training progress.

Components of an OJT System

There are a number of components to an OJT system. Every OJT system contains all of the components, but the intensity of each varies significantly depending on the type of implementation.

Management Support

Management controls all of the resources you need and without their support you have little chance of success. This includes attention to the details of OJT training, review of tracking reports, support with supervisors and production managers, and specific allowances for your budget—both in terms of dollars and time. The budget is used for:

- OJT training materials
- computers
- software for tracking students
- training the OJT developers and trainers
- time for the training
- time to work on processes and procedures

It is important to note that management may approve these expenditures, but in the crush of production, may never actually get a chance to spend the money.

Unfortunately, production supervisors (in any type of company, from financial to manufacturing) are caught in the middle between two completely conflicting goals—training and production. If supervisors take people out of production and allow them to go into training, they lose production time and their numbers may be lower than those of other supervisors who do not allow for training time. Supervisors/line managers generally do not want to hear "let me have your workers today and I will give them back to you trained tomorrow." To a supervisor, that means a loss of production today, and he or she may not care about tomorrow.

OJT Myths

Management and supervisors find several basic OJT concepts confusing or hard to understand. Understand and work through these misconceptions before you implement an OJT system, otherwise there will be trouble and confusion later on.

■ *Myth # 1: OJT Is Free*
OJT systems take time, money, people, and energy. When finished, OJT may be as expensive as classroom training, but produces a much higher return-on-investment for specific skills training.

■ *Myth # 2: Training Time Is Production Time*
Production personnel who participate in OJT cannot produce at full capacity and trainers cannot perform in both positions at the same time.

■ *Myth # 3: OJT Is Simply Part of the Job*
OJT training is work and necessitates trainers who agree to perform the training and tracking activities. Workers should not be "volunteered" to become OJT trainers. OJT structures such as training procedures, lists of tasks, assigned personnel, training materials, and equipment are essential.

■ *Myth # 4: Anyone Can Be an OJT Trainer*
Trainers should be selected carefully and then schooled in OJT training techniques and the use of the OJT materials.

■ *Myth # 5: Once Implemented, OJT Is Forever*
OJT systems require continuous review of OJT checklists, OJT trainer decisions, return-on-investment, resource allocation, and so forth.

■ *Myth # 6: OJT Changes Organizational Development*
OJT does change the organization and increase communication and force power sharing, but it is implemented *on top* of existing systems, not in place of them.

©1997, I.D.A.

Formal Trainer Support Process

Supervisors are very busy people and are not always known for their problem-solving or people skills. Generally, first-line supervision is the weakest link in the management chain. Trainers need another person, outside their organization, to go to for support, help, and advice on sensitive personnel issues.

Successful systems appoint an OJT coordinator from a neutral organization (usually HR) who regularly interacts with the trainers. The trainers then work for the production area but have a dotted-line relationship with the support organization. In some systems, the trainers are transferred to the support organization and have a dotted-line relationship with the production organization.

Trainer protection is needed when the trainer does not think an employee is ready to be checked off on a task, but the supervisor insists that they be allowed to work and asks the trainer to check them off anyway. In this case, where does the trainer go for help and support? In other cases, when the trainer and the student have a conflict or when the trainer is asked to fix a nontraining problem, who supports the trainer? In extreme cases, the student may actually verbally attack the trainer and accuse him or her of not being a good trainer. Safeguards need to be in place to protect the trainer.

Checklists

To succeed over the long term, OJT must be linked to other plant or company systems. Usually OJT is linked to ISO 9000, pay-for-performance, procedure sign-off, or regulatory or mandated training systems. Linking the OJT system to another company system simply means that the OJT system cannot go away or be mortally wounded without also wounding the linked system. It provides some protection to the funding, time availability, and resource availability for the system and its trainers.

The basis of the linkage to any system is the checklist, which proves that the student is capable of performing a specific task at a specific competency level. OJT systems without checklists cannot be linked to others, and generally are not acceptable as a basis for ISO 9000 registration.

The checklist is the foundation of any OJT system. It lists the tasks that need to be trained along with administrative information such as the student name, training dates, and completion dates. It also has room for the signatures of the trainer and student for each task along with the supervisor signature when the entire checklist is completed. (See the *Sample Checklist* sidebar.)

Skills checklists also add structure to the process. With a list of specific skills that need to be taught, fewer tasks slip through the cracks and the employee is "checked off" as each task is successfully performed. While checklists decrease the variation in skills being taught, some will still exist. During training, some trainers will let the students operate the equipment, while others push the student to the side and show the student how to operate the equipment. Some trainers let students explore and make mistakes, while others make the students follow their exact directions step by step.

Important OJT Concepts

There are several important concepts to remember when implementing an OJT system:

■ *OJT Systems Are Not Implemented to Improve Training*
They are implemented to improve productivity, lower scrap, or to meet ISO 9000/quality requirements. The decision to implement an OJT system is a *business decision* not a training decision. Keep this in mind lest you get carried away with the training aspects of the system.

■ *OJT Systems Take Resources from Other Projects*
Energy, time, and personnel may be taken away from other projects, including production. Do not attempt to implement a system beyond the needs of your company.

■ *Good OJT Systems Grow*
Build the foundation carefully—checklists, trained trainers, and most important, buy-in from all stakeholders. Remember, OJT systems will change your organization and you cannot succeed without acceptance from those you seek to change.

■ *OJT Systems Are Nonexclusionary*
They are about training, helping, and ensuring that every employee has an equal opportunity to complete the tasks on his or her checklist and become a productive employee.

Characteristics of Good OJT Systems

The number of variations in OJT systems is staggering: Every company designs a slightly different system to solve its OJT training problems. Certain characteristics of OJT training are consistent across every system, however. Before implementing an OJT system, it is vital that you understand these characteristics. Unfortunately, like many concepts, these characteristics are subjective. This list does not comprise the "golden rules of OJT training"—what is successful in one company may prove disastrous in another. OJT systems should generally possess the following characteristics:

Structure

- OJT processes are written and part of your company's operating procedure.

- OJT materials and training guides are fully described and developed.

- Supervisors include performance checklists in performance (or new hire) reviews.

- Trainers are familiar with job and OJT training skills.

Objectives

- Students know what is expected of them on the job.

- Quality and quantity variables are clear and explicit.

- Skills are broken down into manageable segments and recorded in the OJT structure.

Accountability

- Standardized evaluations are established for all major tasks.

- Students are tested on job-related skills as called for in the OJT procedures.

- Skill/task is checked off from a list when performed to trainers' satisfaction.

Preparation

- Trainers are given adequate time to prepare their training, develop aids, and collect materials.

- Training activities, visual aids, and materials are completed ahead of time.

- Training time is scheduled.

Consistency

- Training does not vary by trainer, shift, or time of year.

- All students complete training with the *same* set of core skills.

Humanity

- Trainers are sensitive to learners' needs and can change instructional strategies as required by student, content, and time requirements.

- Students are coached until they can successfully perform the tasks.

- Training is a one-on-one, human-to-human activity.

Benchmarking Exercise

The objective of this exercise is to measure your company's current OJT system against an ideal system. It can serve as a convenient discussion tool with management as you explain the process of implementing an OJT system.

Instructions

Listed below are the six basic characteristics of an OJT system. Think about your company, analyze your current OJT system, and score each characteristic on a scale of 0 to 5 according to the following scale:

0 = this characteristic is totally absent from our OJT system
5 = our company devotes enormous amounts of time, energy, and money to this characteristic.

Scoring

Please note that this is an awareness—not a pass or fail—exercise to show where you stand in relation to other companies and the "perfect" OJT system.

Companies that score below 10, with no one score above three, tend to have disorganized and unstructured OJT systems. Most training is informal and uncontrolled with little management attention given to the OJT training area. Attention may be devoted to a training "problem," but requests for time, money, or personnel are inevitably turned down.

If your score is between 10 and 20, one or more characteristics may be scored highly while others are relatively low. This indicates a system in flux—growing and preparing for additional structure, or shrinking and becoming more informal. A score in this range calls for a more detailed investigation of each of the characteristics and the direction each is taking.

If you score above 20, congratulations! Your company has devoted resources to OJT and received buy-in from managers, supervisors, and workers. This is not an excuse to sit back and relax, however. OJT is ever-changing and you need constant vigilance to maintain your enviable standing.

Characteristics	Score	Comments
1. Structure		
2. Objectives		
3. Accountability		
4. Preparation		
5. Consistency		
6. Humanity		
(MAXIMUM = 30)		

In some companies, the checklists and other OJT documentation are "controlled" and cannot be changed without approval. In good OJT systems trainers are on the sign-off list for procedure changes and know about them far in advance. This gives trainers the chance to contribute to the decision-making process and ensure that procedures are realistic. It also gives them the opportunity to update training materials and evaluations before the change is implemented.

In the case of mandated training or in a pay-for-performance system, the checklist assumes increased importance. In both cases the checklist may become a legal document, either due to an accident or in connection with pay rates. Trainers should never take shortcuts or check off students until they can perform the task to specifications because they could be held responsible for any accidents or pay disputes.

OJT Training Materials

OJT trainers should not train "off the top of their heads." This is dangerous and invites mistakes. In addition to checklists, students should also receive procedures or other job aids. If students can take notes during training, they should be provided with a notebook or other organized method for writing. Students should not take notes on "little pieces of paper." These will quickly get lost and the effort will be wasted.

If students cannot take notes, or get copies of the procedures, they should be posted near the machine or work area. Many companies keep copies of procedure manuals in supervisors' offices, but rarely does anyone use them.

Some companies support trainers by giving them a room complete with computer equipment and printers where they can go to develop the handouts or procedures necessary for the training. For more information on training materials, see *Info-lines* No. 9707, "High Performance Training Manuals" and No. 9711 "Effective Job Aids."

The time, equipment, and resources necessary to develop OJT materials are also vital to trainers. One training scenario might go like this: "Here is a good widget [as the trainer picks up a widget from the line]. Notice how the edges meet and the color is even throughout the part. If the color is not uni-

form or if the edges do not meet, reject the piece." What do you think of that training? Is it sufficient? Will the student learn how to inspect the product properly? The answer is "no" to all of these questions. The student does not know what "uniform" or "edges meet" mean. Do they have to meet exactly, with absolutely no overlap, or is a little overlap OK? The student has not been told these criteria or have a context within which to learn them.

Train-the-Trainer Program

Do not assume that training comes naturally or that anyone can be an OJT trainer; selection and training must be carefully considered and may involve considerable effort and expense. But remember, poor trainers will kill OJT systems and, in the long run, will be more expensive. Good trainers increase acceptance of a program, perform the training faster, and increase the efficiency of the training process.

No one has a fail-safe method for selecting trainers. OJT trainers succeed or fail for several reasons including:

- lack of training skills
- lack of support
- an unstable political situation
- caught between supervisors and management
- blamed for employees' performance
- blamed for lower production numbers

A successful process consists of two parts: select the trainers and then train them.

Step 1: Trainer Selection

■ *Write a Job Description for the Position*
Define training goals, tasks to perform, and available support. Delineate how much time will be devoted to training, materials development, and other responsibilities. Also specify how training will be measured and the process by which trainers will be schooled—the train-the-trainer program.

Writing the job description forces management to think carefully about trainers, how they will be supported, and how they will fit into the organization. Having early answers to these kinds of questions eliminates unnecessary work later in the process when these questions typically are asked.

■ **Select Trainers**

Post the job description and ask if anybody wants to volunteer for the training position. Ask supervisors or others who already perform OJT to recommend well-respected employees (not necessarily the most proficient) for the positions.

■ **Enroll as Many People as Possible**

This may be the most expensive option, but it also produces the best results. Many employees do not want to be trainers because they don't know what the job entails, but people who consider themselves experts may want to be trainers and get upset when they are not chosen. By sending these experts through train-the-trainer programs, you allow them to decide whether they want to be trainers. This also lets those who are excited about training take the lead.

Step 2: Train-the-Trainer

Companies implement many different types of train-the-trainer programs, some successful and some not. It is important to decide what program objectives should be. Following are the three main objectives of an OJT trainer program:

Sample Checklist

Widget Task Training Checklist

Widget Inspection

Student Name: _____ Employee No. _____

Date Started: _____ Date Completed: _____

Widget Inspection Task

TASK	DATE	TRAINER	EMPLOYEE
1. Use of gloves and glasses			
2. Handling of widget			
3. Calibration of elevator			
4. Inspection product—color striation			
5. Inspection of product—edge alignment			

Completion Signatures

Supervisor _____ Student _____ Trainer _____

Date _____

■ **Ensure Trainer Buy-in**

For some trainers this involves a massive change in the way they conduct training. Most OJT trainers use a dump method—that is, they sit next to their student and dump out everything they know. It may be easy to teach specific OJT training techniques to trainers, but getting them to apply them is another task. Changing the behavior of an OJT trainer requires process activities in the train-the-trainer program rather than lecture or skills activities. They should be able to use alternative instructional strategies, checklists, and appropriate evaluation techniques.

■ **Teach Training and Learning Styles**

This enables trainers to know something about themselves and their style of training. Many have been training for years but have never learned about training styles or students' learning styles. These introspective activities help trainers understand how their style affects students' learning and also find ways to fine tune their training behavior. For more information, see *Info-line*s No. 9604, "How to Accommodate Different Learning Styles"; No. 8804, "Training and Learning Styles"; No. 9608, "Do's and Don'ts for New Trainers"; No. 8808, "Basic Training for Trainers"; and No. 9003, "How to Train Managers to Train."

■ **Teach One-on-One Training Techniques**

Use specific OJT training skills such as the four- step OJT training model, OJT-oriented instructional strategies, and appropriate evaluation techniques. If these skills are taught without the benefit of the process and behavior adjustment activities, then students will smile, nod, perform the class activities, leave the class, and generally go out on the floor and do what they want. **They do not learn.**

Experience shows that OJT trainers rarely conduct formal classroom group presentations, but rather perform one-on-one training by standing or sitting next to a student. Therefore, they do not need to use overhead projectors, give presentations, or use large group-training techniques. OJT train-the-trainer programs should concentrate on techniques best suited to one-on-one learning.

A word of caution here. The OJT training program described on the following page is a high-process class and contains many introspective activities designed to help students interpret, use, and place in context specific OJT skills. This class is closer to an intervention than to a traditional skills training program because the primary objective is to change the trainers' behaviors.

Most companies either design and run the trainer program in-house, purchase materials for a program to be run by an internal trainer, or bring in an external trainer to conduct the program. If you design and conduct an OJT trainer course with internal talent, make sure the personnel assigned to this task have experience in high-process training activities or organizational interventions. Typically, these employees have designed and trained management, supervisory, or career development classes and are comfortable in the role of facilitator. This class can not be taught as a lecture.

If you purchase an OJT trainer course or contract with an outside trainer, make sure the course meets the requirements discussed above. As an extra check, contact previous clients for references and make sure the contract trainer has conducted similar courses before. Sometimes local colleges offer to teach courses like this, but be prepared for an academic overview of adult learning taught by a person who has never worked in a factory. A little investigation at this point in the project can save enormous amounts of money and keep the OJT project on the right track. See *Info-line* No. 8610, "Find the Right Consultant," for more information on outsourcing training.

Tracking and Report Generation

It is important that an OJT system be able to track and report on its activities. Generally, these reports are statistical, providing numerical data on:

● number of students trained
● checklists completed
● number of training hours
● percentage of successful students
● cost of training (total and per student)
● return-on-investment of training

Some systems report on training development activities, test or evaluation results, and trainer effectiveness. Some systems also report on certification expiration and notify employees when they need retraining.

The administrator or coordinator who is responsible for the tracking system should also be prepared to produce reports supporting ISO 9000 audits, GMP audits, or annual budget reviews.

When checklists are created, you can decide if the checklist is valid forever or carries an expiration date. When students complete checklists, the expiration dates should be recorded and tracked within the system. In some cases, regulatory requirements will define retraining or recertification time intervals. Both students and trainers should be automatically notified when recertification training is required.

Some systems distribute "smile sheets" so students can evaluate their instructors. These student critiques are no more valid in this environment than in classroom training environments but are useful for detecting trends and highlighting areas for improvement or praise.

Sample Train-the-Trainer Program

This sample OJT trainer program is designed to meet each of the three objectives (see previous page) as well as provide a pleasant experience and some fun along the way. The course typically takes three days, although it can be taught in two if the class is small. A successful program should:

- build training skills and encourage buy-in to the OJT program and use of the OJT materials
- contain high-impact exercises to change trainer behavior from telling to coaching
- include modules on training skills, instructional strategies, practice training activities, and introspective activities

Typical outline for a three-day OJT training program

Day 1	Day 2	Day 3
Introduction/outline	Introspective exercise:	Videotaped OJT coaching sessions—10-minute coaching sessions that are videotaped, reviewed, and critiqued by the class and instructor
What is OJT training?	• Instructor styles inventory	
Learning curves	• Identifying types of students	
Four-step training model	• Instructional strategies for different types of students	
Lunch	**Lunch**	**Lunch**
Practice training exercise in groups of two	Practice training exercise in groups of three	Class wrap-up
Introspective exercise	Prep time for video coaching teaching sessions	Course critique
		Presentation of certificates

©1997, I.D.A.

Implementation

There are several techniques and procedures you may want to consider before and during the OJT implementation process. Take into account that OJT systems change the production environment and often require supervisors, management, and workers to change how they train and, in some cases, the way supervisors supervise. In hierarchical and authoritarian organizations, OJT systems often intrude on others' turf, and this can be risky, both to the OJT system and to individual career aspirations.

This is not a complete listing of techniques used to implement OJT systems, neither is it a full discussion of the ways in which you can change an organization. For that you will need several books on organization development and the help of several knowledgeable assistants. Think very hard about the effort required to implement the system and the support you really will receive. If you realistically will not receive any management or supervisory support, use the materials at the beginning of this *Info-line* to design a very low-level system, keep your head down, and go with the flow. If you really need help, find assistance within the company at the corporate level or go outside for a good OJT consultant. Think about these issues when making the decision:

■ *What Is Your Motivation?*
Is it your idea? Do you have the political and financial muscle to implement the system by yourself? Is this an assignment? If it is, can you negotiate a realistic effort level for the system?

■ *What Is in It for Them? (WIIFT)*
What will the rest of the people in the plant get for their efforts? People will not buy in to systems without first asking WIIFT and getting meaningful answers. An attempt to implement the system by edict may receive lip service, but as soon as you, the champion of the system, turn away it will be ignored and disappear.

■ *What Problems Does the System Solve?*
What will be better after the OJT system is implemented? You should be able to list specific problems and the ways OJT will solve them. Do not list training—everyone wants training to be better, but very few will expend the effort and resources to do it. Training must also solve a particular problem or help the organization achieve a goal. Problems should be specific and solutions should be directly connected to the OJT system. This forms a foundation for the WIIFT needed to implement the system.

After you answer these questions, you are ready to implement your OJT system. Successful techniques for bringing out the best of a company during the implementation process include:

■ *Hook to Another Project*
You usually cannot lose by hooking up with another project, especially if that project has some urgency about it. Projects like this include ISO 9000, quality, and customer satisfaction. The upside of this association is that you will receive more support and resources than you would if OJT were implemented alone. The downside is that you will have to share resources, power, and may lose some implementation authority. Usually this is a fair trade.

■ *Build on a Crisis*
Every company has its annual or semi-annual crisis. They usually revolve around production, late shipment, or similar "emergencies." If it makes sense, offer OJT as a partial solution. There are two downsides to this: You may end up as the scapegoat if the problem occurs again or, once the emergency is over, all of your support may disappear. The advantage of this strategy is that you—for a limited time—receive resources that may allow you to build a foundation for the system and keep it operating after the "emergency" is over.

■ *Start Small and Build*
Many successful OJT systems begin like this. The implementor recognizes the current support level, designs an appropriate system at that level, and produces a system that is useful to the corporation. Supervisors slowly buy in as they see the usefulness of the system. Problems such as additional staffing are answered over time and the system grows slowly, receives more support, and eventually becomes part of the corporate culture.

This approach does not work in all situations, especially when a fully implemented system is needed immediately. It may not work in situations where another OJT implementation has failed.

■ *Wait for the Right Time*

Let's say you have read everything so far and feel overwhelmed. You know you do not have much support and have lots of responsibilities besides setting up an OJT program. Sit tight, continue to talk about the program with supervisors and management, find people who will support you and the system, and most important, wait for the right time. Just remember, OJT implementation has components of both training and organizational development, and any successful implementor has experience in both of these skills.

Finally, implementing an OJT system is a major undertaking and may result in significant changes in your facility or factory. Don't fight the established informal OJT system and insist on starting from scratch. Instead, go with the OJT flow, investigate, improve, and begin to control the informal OJT system. Then harness OJT's considerable energy to help build better projects, customer satisfaction, and a better OJT system that will grow, adapt, and provide better training as time goes on. Good luck on your OJT system.

OJT Training Procedures

The OJT procedure calls out the functions, responsibilities, and interfaces of the OJT system. Located between the trainer, production requirements, and the supervisor, these interfaces are sources of potential conflict and misunderstanding. A complete procedure will govern the activities of the trainers and describe the process for solving misunderstandings.

Specific items that should be covered in the procedure include:

■ *Escalation Procedure*

What happens if the student fails the checklist—how many times will they be trained and what happens if the student asks for another trainer?

■ *Trainer Responsibilities*

What specifically are trainers' responsibilities with regard to procedures, development, and training?

■ *Supervisor Responsibilities*

What are the supervisors' specific responsibilities regarding signing checklists, releasing people from the line for training, and so forth?

■ *Checklist Sign-Off*

Should the supervisor conduct the final evaluation before checklist sign-off, or can the trainer conduct the evaluation? On what basis? Remember that the checklist could become a legal document for pay or regulatory purposes.

■ *Organizational Responsibilities*

What is the organization required to provide to the trainer and the training process?

■ *Procedure Interfaces*

Are trainers added to the sign-off list for procedure changes and revisions to production processes? How is this interface implemented?

■ *Conflict Resolution*

In the event of a conflict between training and production requirements, what procedures are followed to resolve it?

■ *Certification Expiration*

If the certification for an employee has expired, but production requirements do not allow release from the line for training, should the employee be allowed to work? What are the regulatory and liability issues? Can a temporary waiver be signed? What is the procedure for that?

Within any organization there are many other interfaces to be negotiated and resources to be assigned. Without clear procedures, turf issues will arise and, generally, trainers end up yielding. It is best for everyone concerned to sit down and draw up appropriate procedures during the development of the OJT system. See *Info-lines* No. 9706, "Basics of Instructional Systems Design," and No. 8909, "Coming to Agreement: How to Resolve Conflict," for information on setting up OJT procedures.

Articles

Al-Ali, Salahaldeen. "An Assessment of On-the-Job Training Programs in the Ministry of Finance (MOF): A Case Study of Kuwait." *Human Resource Planning,* June 1996, pp. 50-53.

Alexander, Steve. "Training You Can Build On: Fannie Mae's In-house Programs." *Computerworld,* January 15, 1996, p. 77.

Arjas, Bridget Kinsella. "Trainer Needs Company Support." *Graphic Arts Monthly,* August 1992, pp. 74-77.

Barron, Tom. "A Structured Comeback for OJT." *Technical & Skills Training,* April 1997, pp. 14-17.

Benson, George. "Informal Training Takes Off." *Training & Development,* May 1997, pp. 93-94.

Charney, Cy. "Self-Directed Peer Training in Teams." *Journal for Quality and Participation,* October/November 1996, pp. 34-37.

Filipczak, Bob. "Who Owns Your OJT?" *Training,* December 1996, pp. 44-49.

Fisher, Susan E. "Hands-on Training." *PC Week,* February 19, 1996, p. E1.

Grant, Linda. "A School for Success: Motorola's Ambitious Job-Training Program Generates Smart Profits." *U.S. News & World Report,* May 22, 1995, pp. 53-56.

"How to Get More Out of Training Workers on the Job." *Refrigeration News,* December 10, 1993, p. 28.

Hubbard, Andrew S. "Typical Training." *Mortgage Banking,* July 1995, pp. 105-106.

Kupanhy, Lumbidi. "Classification of JIT Techniques and Their Implications." *Industrial Engineering,* February 1995, pp. 62-66.

Levine, Charles. "Unraveling Five Myths of OJT." *Technical & Skills Training,* April 1996, pp. 14-17.

Lynch, Lisa M. "The Role of Off-the-Job vs. On-the Job Training for the Mobility of Women Workers." *American Economic Review,* May 1991, pp. 151-157.

McFarland, Bonnie. "Smart Training Means Getting Managers Involved." *Washington Business Journal,* January 5, 1996, p. 20.

Marsh, P.J. "On-the-Job Learning." *Technical & Skills Training,* August/September 1994, pp. 7-12.

———. "Training Trainers." *Technical & Skills Training,* October 1995, pp. 10-13.

Mont, Michael A. "Training Toll Collectors." *Technical & Skills Training,* April 1995, pp. 25-26.

Moore, Tony. "Training Tips for Managers." *Performance & Instruction,* May/June 1996, pp. 10-11.

Mullaney, Carol Ann, and Linda D. Trask. "Show Them the Ropes." *Technical & Skills Training,* October 1992, pp. 8-11.

Nemec, John. "Supervisor as Clerk Trainer." *Supervision,* January 1996, pp. 11-14.

Phipps, Polly A. "On-the-Job Training and Employee Productivity." *Monthly Labor Review,* March 1996, pp. 23-29.

Schriner, Jim. "Where Are the Quality Workers: Skills Shortages Proves Urgency of New Job-Training Approaches." *Industry Week,* September 2, 1996, p. 52.

Semb, George B. "On-the-Job Training: Prescriptions and Practice." *Performance Improvement Quarterly,* vol. 8, no. 3 (1995), pp. 19-37.

Stevens, Margaret. "A Theoretical Model of On-the-Job Training with Imperfect Competition." *Oxford Economic Papers,* October 1994, pp. 535-561.

Vickers, Margaret. "A New Take on On-the-Job Training." *Vocational Education Journal,* March 1994, pp. 22-23.

Walter, Diane. "A Model for Team-Driven OJT." *Technical & Skills Training,* October 1996, pp. 23-27.

Walter, K. "The MTA Travels Far with Its Future Managers Program." *Personnel Journal,* vol. 74, no. 3 (1995), pp. 68-72.

Yawn, David. "On-the-Job Training: Motorola Veterans Buy Service Center." *Memphis Business Journal,* May 20, 1996, pp. 58-63.

References & Resources

Books

Jacobs, R.L., and M.J. Jones. *Structured On-the-Job Training: Unleashing Expertise in the Workplace.* San Francisco: Berrett-Koehler, 1995.

Lawson, Karen. *Improving On-the-Job Training and Coaching.* Alexandria, VA: ASTD, 1997.

Rothwell, William J., and H.C. Kazanas. *Improving On-the-Job Training: How to Establish and Operate a Comprehensive OJT Program.* San Francisco: Jossey-Bass, 1994.

Info-lines

Darraugh, Barbara, ed. "Coaching and Feedback." No. 9006 (revised 1997).

Finn, Tom. "Valuing and Managing Diversity." No. 9305 (revised 1999).

Hodell, Chuck. "Basics of Instructional Systems Development." No. 9706.

Meyer, Kathy. "How to Train Managers to Train." No. 9003 (revised 1997).

Novak, Clare. "High Performance Training Manuals." No. 9707.

O'Neill, Mary. "Do's and Don'ts for New Trainers." No. 9608 (revised 1998).

Waagen, Alice. "Essentials for Evaluation." No. 9705.

Robinson, Dana Gaines, and James G. Robinson. "Measuring Affective and Behavioral Change." No. 9110 (revised 1997).

Internet Sites

American Society for Training & Development
http://www.astd.org

Department of Energy Technical Standards
http://www.osti.gov/html/techstds/standard/hdbk1074/hdb1074d.html

OJT
http://www.ojt.com/

OJT Process Steps

As you develop your OJT system, be sure to complete each of these steps:

1. Develop management support and secure resources.

Date completed_____

2. Create a formal trainer support process.

Date completed_____

3. Link your OJT to another system with checklists.

Date completed_____

4. Produce training materials.

Date completed_____

5. Implement a train-the-trainer program.

Date completed_____

6. Select trainers.

Date completed_____

7. Design tracking and report generation procedures.

Date completed_____

8. Develop OJT training procedures.

Date completed_____

9. Implement your system.

Date completed_____

10. Evaluate training.

Date completed_____

Supervisory Training

Issue 0008

Supervisory Training

AUTHORS

Annette M. Cremo
Performance Plus
Pa. Human Resources Advisors, LLC
1209 Redwood Hills Circle
Carlisle, PA 17013
Tel: 717.241.6600
Fax: 717.241.6700
Email: acs@epix.net

Amy B. Felix
Innovative Performance Solutions
PO Box 467
State College, PA 16804
Tel: 814.867.3557
Fax: 814.234.0143
Email: ips@vicon.net

Editor
Cat Sharpe Russo

Managing Editor
Sabrina E. Hicks

Production Design
Leah Cohen

Why Train Supervisors?

All organizations need leaders who can bring people together to accomplish extraordinary results. Because people and knowledge are scarce and valuable resources, you need dynamic leaders able to develop the potential of your most valuable asset: your employees. To do this, you must educate your supervisors.

Regardless of the industry or organization, supervisors must have the ability to manage resources and work effectively with others. High-performance workplaces require supervisors who are aware of their organization's big picture and are able to oversee employees' actual work—thereby, implementing the organizational vision. Your workplaces demand that supervisors be able to do the following:

● solve problems
● acquire and use new information
● master complex systems
● work with a variety of new technologies
● communicate effectively with all personnel

A special need exists for supervisory training because the supervisor represents the face of the organization: They communicate company initiatives, changes, and policies. They provide reinforcement and feedback related to performance, and they encourage employees to improve and grow. In addition, they complete their other, administrative job duties. If an organization does not develop its supervisors to meet the challenges of leadership as well as complete management responsibilities, they are, in fact, creating a weak point in the organization and not showing their best "face."

For the most part, employees are still promoted to the role of supervisor because of their technical expertise. They are good at what they do, so management believes assuming the role of supervisor will come naturally to them. But here is the problem: No one takes the time to teach these employees the skills necessary to do the job—which is, how to get things done through people.

At the heart of this necessary organizational change are some universal trends. These trends affect not only the supervisory position but also every job at every level—and present themselves in core competencies. These competencies directly influence supervisors and their development in the organization.

The skills and competencies presented in the chart on the following page reflect a move away from a mechanistic, bureaucratic model of organizations. This organizational model is flatter and centers on learning and continuous change. This new strategic business paradigm and the skills employees need in the 21st century have a strong emphasis on human relation skills in addition to technical skills. Training is an important part of the organization in this changing environment.

To support this changing environment, your supervisory training needs to provide staff with the knowledge and skills to adapt to changing conditions. Regardless of the state of your organization, upper management will require supervisors to perform the following tasks:

● solve problems quickly and effectively

● provide meaningful communication

● provide performance feedback

● encourage and grow employees through targeted development

While technology may assist supervisors in their administrative responsibilities, it poses a continuous learning curve as new changes are introduced almost daily. Supervisors are responsible not only for adapting to a changing environment but also for sharing knowledge and generating staff buy-in so that employees can be productive and successful.

This *Info-line* describes how to develop your supervisory training program step-by-step. After defining what it means to be a supervisor in your organization, you learn the importance of needs assessment and designing, developing, and evaluating your training program. Each of these steps is important in building a supervisory staff that is knowledgeable, skilled, and successful in a world of constant change. The benefit? Your supervisors will be able to develop their employees and help your organization reach the level of success necessary to stay competitive.

Skills and Competencies

This chart depicts the relationship between universal trends, implications for the supervisor, and required core competencies. The first column takes a broad look at what is happening in society and organizations. The second column explains how these changes affect supervisors. The third column lists core competencies that are universal to the job of a supervisor.

Universal Trends	Supervisory Implications	Core Competencies
Competition—Organizations vying for market share, mergers and acquisitions—organizations are searching globally for the right fit for effectiveness and profitability.	Greater awareness of trends and forces affecting the organization. Supervisors see the organizational big picture and how it translates into their span of control.	Communicating effectively with others in the organization. Working well as part of a team and developing a team.
Demographics—Dramatic changes in the nature of the family, the aging population, disparity in education levels, diversity of ethnic groups, values of the various generations.	Supervisors must know how to maximize the diversity of all human potential in their organization. They must realize that maximization of resources makes good business sense.	Problem-solving skills. Self-directed learning skills, improving one's own learning and performance.
Continuous learning—Learning does not stop with graduation. In many instances, that is where learning starts. Organizations are becoming increasingly responsible for "skilling" the workforce.	The knowledge worker is the most valuable asset in the organization. Because of the tremendous rate of change in the organization, learning never stops. Supervisors must embrace learning for themselves and their employees.	Technological competence. Team or group learning. Dealing effectively with change.
Technology—Not only affecting the way we do business but now intertwining with education and how we learn.	Supervisors must be open to new ways of doing business as well as new ways to learn. For example, Web-based self-directed team learning.	

Step 1: Define "Supervisor"

Before you begin to develop a training program, you must think about what it takes to be a supervisor in your organization.

In very structured organizations, supervisors are the conveyors of information and directives from upper management to employees. In organizations without layers, supervisors facilitate processes between all employees in an organization. Regardless of the type of organization, they are responsible for getting work done through people. Supervisors have basic roles in all organizations. As you review the following roles, think about your organization and the importance it places on each.

Coach

As coaches, supervisors develop plans for meeting performance outcomes and departmental and organizational goals. They must make daily tactical decisions that lead their staff closer to desired goals. Coaches keep track of employees' overall individual performance—both strengths and developmental needs. They can recognize talent and know who possesses what talent and skills. Supervisors are specifically concerned with creating an environment that nurtures professional growth. Strategically, the supervisor asks these questions:

● How does each individual fit in?
● What are each individual's strengths?

- What is each individual's potential?
- How do individuals fit in the big picture?

In addition, coach supervisors bear the following responsibilities:

- recruit and retain the best talent
- be consistent and fair
- listen to employees
- show concern
- focus on collaboration, not competition

Role Model

Supervisors are the message. Everything about them sends a clear message: what they say, how they say it, what they do, how they do it, and what they do not do. Employees look to role model supervisors for guidance on acceptable and unacceptable behavior. Supervisors must convey the organizational code of conduct in all they do.

The catch? Most supervisors were once a member of the group they now supervise. Some of the behavior a supervisor must admonish is behavior he or she may have been guilty of before becoming a supervisor. How does the supervisor satisfy this new responsibility and still feel authentic?

First, the supervisor must address the facts of the situation. Second, the supervisor must remember that while he or she may have committed the same behavior in the past, it still was not right. As the supervisor must now speak to former peers regarding the behavior, it is important that he or she do the following:

- Explain the desired behaviors.

- Identify the behavior's impact on the department or organization, and explain why it is not acceptable.

- Identify how he or she will assist in avoiding this type of actions or behavior in the future.

The supervisor must still maintain employee responsibility for his or her actions but also show encouragement and assistance. The key to working with former peers is demonstrating consistency in the new role.

Teacher

Knowing how to help people learn and encouraging that learning is an important tool in the age of the knowledge worker. The teacher supervisor aids the learning process by knowing these facts:

- when employees need information

- what delivery mechanisms are available for needed information

- how to develop each individual's potential for learning

The supervisor's experience is a valuable tool for assisting learners with understanding new information. Supervisors must know when to use their knowledge and when to refer to it to facilitate the learning of others.

Mentor

As mentors, supervisors think of themselves as walking alongside their employees. Mentoring involves teaching, doing, watching, and being watched—sometimes parenting, understanding, and providing empathy. Mentoring is helping people do what they never thought or believed they could do.

For more detail on mentoring, refer to *Info-line* No. 0004, "Mentoring."

Motivator

To be a good motivator, find out what stimulates others to act. Supervisors who are good motivators have a keen awareness and a deep understanding of others. For example, they know what each employee enjoys and the tasks that each employee excels at—they then use this knowledge to motivate. Supervisors as motivators realize that they do not have the power to motivate, but they can ignite the spark that leads employees to motivate themselves.

They also realize that knowledge motivates. When employees know what management expects of them, when they are aware of the process for completing tasks and why management has asked them to perform certain tasks, employees are more likely to stay motivated.

Team Developer

The supervisor's direct reports are the supervisor's team or work group. One individual cannot make success happen; it takes a group of people working together toward a common goal. To reach the common goal, supervisors must take time to inform their team about the organization's big picture. They must take time to tell employees how their work promotes the organization's mission. A team developer must communicate effectively and clearly, practice active listening skills, and be skilled at setting performance goals—as well as able to provide both constructive and positive performance feedback.

The Supervisor's Work

In addition to the many roles they assume, supervisors perform certain tasks and responsibilities on a daily basis. Following are descriptions of the basic work tasks of supervisors.

Educate Employees

One of a supervisor's most basic and important tasks is to let employees know what management expects of them. Most of us are familiar with the stress experienced when your boss assigns you a task but does not tell you what he or she expects of you. The following example is typical:

For years, Tom's position in field sales required that he do his work alone. His organization was in the midst of a structure change. It was reconfiguring to a team-based organization. One day, he received a memo from his supervisor stating that from now on, the sales force was required to work in self-directed work teams. In addition, their annual bonus would be based on successful completion of self-directed work team projects.

Tom never worked on a self-directed team before and had no idea what his supervisor expected of him. Tom asked for clarification but never received any training or other information about this initiative. Tom was confused and frustrated—and he was not alone: His teammates had the same concerns. After six months, the organization abolished the idea of self-directed teams.

What do you think happened? If you are not aware of expectations, it is like getting in a car and driving without a destination: You waste time and money and never get anywhere. Was this initiative salvageable? One thing obviously missing from this scenario is clear, consistent communication:

- What was the purpose of the initiative?

- What new skills would be required?

- What performance changes did the supervisor expect?

Supervisors have the responsibility to answer these questions when announcing an initiative. If the answers are not readily available, then supervisors must pursue the answers until found.

What was the other mistake in the above scenario? When an organization introduces a change of this magnitude, it should arrange to have someone deliver the news in person and provide employees the opportunity to ask questions. Such communication creates a framework for the informational and developmental needs of staff.

Monitor, Evaluate, and Review Performance

After informing employees of expectations, supervisors must let them know how they are doing. Formal yearly performance reviews are fine, but you should couple it with weekly checks on progress. Hold weekly, informal meetings (lunches, 15-minute "check-ups," email reports, and so forth) with individual employees to follow up on specific progress. This type of continuous communication and concern for the individual minimizes the opportunity for slips in performance and generates an appreciation from the employee's perspective.

Identify Talent

In addition to making employees aware of expectations, supervisors have another responsibility: identifying talent. But they must remember that sometimes observations about specific behavior are incorrect. Take the following example:

Jessie excels at assembling intricate machinery. In fact, she is so good that her manager "rewarded" her by promoting her to shift supervisor. After becoming the supervisor, Jessie's work started to slip. What Jessie really enjoyed—what she had a talent for—was doing very detailed work with her hands, not delegating that work to others.

Placing the right people in the right jobs and providing them with the tools to accomplish their jobs involves constant communication. It also requires the supervisor to be aware of the nontangible clues in the work environment, such as the example above. Was Jessie's work slipping because she was not capable? Or because she was not committed to the task? For a supervisor to be this aware of his or her employees' needs goes beyond the "cookie cutter" approach of traditional management and draws on acute observation skills.

Delegate

Supervisors often obtain their positions because of their outstanding ability to accomplish a task or because of their in-depth knowledge of a process. Once becoming supervisors, they must inspire others to perform that task—in other words, delegate responsibility. Delegation encompasses getting things done through people. But a common temptation many supervisors give in to is doing the task themselves. It sometimes seems easier and faster to "just do it yourself," as opposed to delegating responsibility and letting someone else do the job.

Plan

Supervisors have the unique position of seeing the totality of the organization. They should understand the vision and know what it takes to get the job done. Based on the organizational vision, the supervisor must perform the following tasks:

- set appropriate goals
- determine needed actions to achieve goals
- identify talent to accomplish desired actions
- set target dates for completion
- describe measures of success

Control

Controlling involves looking at the entire process; setting standards; and reviewing time, quality, costs, and material. The supervisor's unique position of knowing the organizational vision and being involved with the methodology for achieving that vision makes his or her job integral to the overall operation of the organization.

Lead

Leadership is the ability to get everyone working together to achieve the common goal. Writers on leadership agree that leadership is difficult to describe in one sentence because of its many elements. It involves setting direction, committing to goals, and communicating the vision. One thing is certain: Having followers is an essential part of leadership.

The Supervisor's Attitude

While you can teach supervisors skills that affect their success in the tasks described above, some things you just cannot teach, like how to be the following:

- responsible
- accountable
- trustworthy
- ethical
- action-oriented

Now, review all the possible roles and responsibilities of the supervisor and determine what it takes to be a supervisor in your organization. The training you design must get you to the goal of successfully developing these supervisors. The second step will tell you what you need to do to get to this goal.

Step 2: Assess Supervisor's Needs

At a basic level, needs assessment identifies gaps between current and desired conditions. You must link training assessment to core competencies, organizational goals, and other strategic initiatives to show a connection of support. Linking helps supervisors see the clear purpose of development and learning as an integrated approach toward organizational success. Such action provides a well-based training curriculum. The assessment results will help you identify the following:

- training topics that will grow the organization

- issues for other methods of process improvement

- situations that translate into training scenarios facilitating on-the-job transfer of learned skills

Be sure that any assessment you choose (whether off-the-shelf or developed in-house) measures the level of proficiency in the supervisory competencies standard for any organization. This baseline of measurement is a firm foundation toward achieving organizational and tactical goals. The fundamental elements of any assessment must include the following:

Ideals. When the supervisor is doing his or her job and things are working well, what is happening? Determine what specific behavior the supervisor performs.

Current snapshot. How is the supervisor doing his or her job at the present time? Again, what behavior does the supervisor show?

Gap. Where is the performance gap? What is the "problem"?

Cause. What is the cause of the gap between what the supervisor should be doing and what he or she is doing? What are the causes of the problem?

Solutions. What do you need to eliminate the gap? What do you need to fix the problem? Is training the answer? Is improving processes the solution?

How Do You Complete a Needs Assessment?

Prior to administering the assessment, be sure to communicate the intent of the assessment clearly to the intended audience. Explain what it *is* and what it is *not*. The "why" of any staff measurement is essential for their cooperation and buy-in to the process.

Using Existing Assessment Tools

Many supervisory assessment tools are on the market. Finding the one that suits your organizational needs will require you to examine your motives for training:

- Are you providing training to meet suspected needs of supervisor-employee relations?

- Are you examining the impact of supervisory decisions on the organizational strategy?

- Are you looking at training in response to supervisors' requests?

After you identify your primary purpose for training, consider the following points when selecting your assessment tool:

Ease of completion. How easy is the assessment to complete? Can you administer it with your own staff or do you need a firm or consultant who sells the assessment to administer it?

Staff administration and analysis requirements. Do you need a core group dedicated to the administration and analysis? Is the assessment relatively easy to analyze? Are special tools or software required? Are the results easy to report?

Time. What is the average time to complete the assessment? What amount of time is involved in the analysis?

Method. Is the assessment available only via paper and pencil? Is it available in other mediums, such as computer-based or Web-based? If you have a geographically diverse participant group and your Information Technology department's support is available, you may want a computer-based assessment for ease of administration.

Regardless of the selection you make, be sure it meets confidentiality requirements for your organization.

Reviewing Existing Data

In addition to the formal assessment, collect relevant data from existing resources. The purpose of your assessment and intended training will determine the type of data you choose to gather. Below are examples of existing information you should examine prior to developing your curriculum:

- exit interview information (why people leave)
- internal transfer data (who, how often)
- percent of turnover by level
- employee opinion survey data
- percent of performance appraisals completed

Use data gathered during the assessment phase to establish a baseline. (In step 6, you will evaluate against this baseline to determine improvement resulting from your training intervention.) For a different perspective, hold focus groups composed of participants from a sample of the target group and their employees. Focus groups need to include a mix of the following:

- new supervisors
- experienced supervisors
- employees of supervisors

After you complete all focus groups, collectively compare results and identify similarities and differences. The differences may help define gaps or the levels of training necessary. Or, you may find that you need to collect more information before you can draw a conclusion.

Step 3: Design Your Program

During the assessment phase, you identified the most critical knowledge and skill gaps and determined the desired impact of the training content on both the supervisors and organization. This assessment information helps you to determine the following:

- goal of the course
- starting and finishing points of the course
- desired outcomes of the course

With this information in hand, you can begin developing a supervisory training program that is specific to the needs of your organization. You will not waste time on objectives that you have not identified as a knowledge or skill gap for your employees.

Focus Group Questions

The types of questions you ask depend on the purpose of your training intervention. Before conducting focus groups, develop a list of questions addressing the information you need to obtain. Keep the questions consistent between all groups. The questions below are a sampling of what you might ask.

- Explain the most effective training you have received to date at this organization that has helped you prepare for your supervisory position.

- Describe the most effective training you have received (other than at this organization) that has helped you with your job.

- If you could name the best source of support for supervisors, who or what is it and why?

- What is the most difficult supervisory challenge you face today? That you will face in the future?

- What is the one thing you would change about your job? Why?

- Do you feel that your daily decisions influence the organization? Why or why not? If they do, how do they affect the organization?

- What is the most important role you fulfill as supervisor?

- What is the least important role you fulfill as supervisor?

Chunking

The first step in designing your training program is to "chunk" information into meaningful sections. Chunking serves as a building-block approach to the training program. Breaking down course design information provides an opportunity for participants to master each subsection before moving to the next level. This approach to training develops participants' confidence and increases the likelihood of transfer of new knowledge and skills to the job.

Developing Learning Objectives

The next task is to develop learning objectives from the information identified in the assessment. Objectives help you to perform the following:

- State, in terms of outcomes, what you want the participants to do.

- Organize chunked information in a meaningful manner.

Learning objectives define the specific behavior you hope supervisors will glean from the course. State objectives in action terms, using verbs such as "identify," "explain," "choose," "apply," "discriminate," "design," "perform," "generate," and "select." Choose your words based on the knowledge, skill, or desired behavior you expect participants to gain or practice. For example, if you want participants to be able to communicate performance feedback to their employees, an objective might be the following:

Given a sample employee performance meeting scenario, participant can apply the five steps of performance feedback.

Sequencing Information

Next, sequence your chunked information based on what is relevant to the course content. The following are examples of sequencing patterns:

- easiest information and skills to more complex

- general information to specific knowledge and skills

- time-based/sequential (for example, provide *setting performance standards* first because it falls before *performance review* on the annual calendar)

- long segments to short segments

Learning Styles/Delivery Methods

Three basic adult learning styles affect how you design the details of the training:

1. Aural: learning through hearing information in terms of lectures, music, and so forth.

2. Visual: learning through reading, charts, graphs, and so forth.

3. Kinesthetic: learning through hands-on practice.

Two additional elements to these basic styles include independent learning and group learning.

Be sure to include activities and training methods that incorporate all elements. While important to know which delivery methods your participants prefer, using a combination of the delivery methods increases the likelihood of learning transfer to the job. Consult the sidebar at right for more information on delivery methods.

As you design each segment of the training, ask yourself this question: "How will I know that the participant can do this?" The answer to that question will be how you test the participants. Your test does not need to be formal; it can be in the form of a classroom activity or small group feedback exercise.

Step 4: Develop Your Program

After determining your program's core content areas, add content specific material. Remember, your goals and objectives will drive the actual content. This material comes from a variety of places: text books, management and supervisory books, journal articles, professional associations, professionals in the field, supervisors, and online literature searches.

After finding sources for your information, begin to write your program. Remember the basic concepts of adult learning when you write your materials. Your learners will learn best when you incorporate the following elements into your instructional materials:

Overview of Delivery Methods

Integrate the following methods into your training session to create the variety adult learners need in a learning environment. By using all these techniques you provide a well-rounded session that incorporates group learning, individual learning, and opportunities to identify immediate application.

■ *Facilitator Lecture or Commentary*
Use this method to tie training together, introduce concepts, summarize, and transition from one major concept to the next. A facilitator can present the background necessary for learners to understand the topic; he or she can also provide examples of how learners apply the material.

■ *Active Training Techniques*
Incorporate all learner styles into a methodology that is active, has variety, and encompasses participation by the learners. Participants learn by doing, discussing, and applying.

■ *Small Group Discussion*
Participants discuss concepts in an environment that fosters more openness than a large group. Small groups allow all members to have a chance to participate and share ideas. Each small group can work on individual problems and share answers with the larger group through a reporting out process at the end of the discussion.

■ *Individual Activity*
Assessments, action planning, readings, or written exercises are examples of individual activities that allow participants to synthesize and process information on their own.

■ *Experiential Activities*
Case studies, role plays, scenarios, video vignettes, and problem-solving activities are examples of experiential activities. Such activities allow participants to test new information in a structured environment before going out into the workforce with their new skills.

■ *Pre-Reading*
Asking participants to read selected reprints, articles, or books prior to training sets the tone for the session. Pre-reading provides a frame of reference and prepares participants in advance for the training session.

■ *Modeling*
Participants model expected behaviors to witness skills management expects of them.

■ *Web-Based Training*
Web-based training is useful when you need just-in-time learning, but it is not a cure-all for every training need. Explore your options and weigh the pros and cons.

■ *Self-Directed Team Learning*
This technique allows a supervisory team to take pre-designed packets of information and learn by themselves. They take responsibility for their own learning and pace their learning based on decisions from the group.

■ *Action Planning/Supervisory Consultation*
This method requires supervisors to make a commitment to try something they have learned in class, look at all aspects of implementation, and set deadlines. When the supervisor has finished his or her action plan, he or she consults with another supervisor, who listens to the action plan and gives feedback. One of the first steps in having knowledge gel is to explain it to another person or to teach it to another person. This method synthesizes, applies, and explains the information.

Pre-Program Design Survey

The better you know your learners, the better acquainted you are with their individual needs—and the better you will be able to design a winning training program. This survey identifies items you need to consider before designing your program.

1. How many supervisors are familiar with the subject matter?
   __ Most   __ About half   __ Few   __ None

2. What is their vocabulary level of understanding?
   __ Technical   __ Nontechnical   __ Generally high   __ Generally low   __ Unknown

3. How willing are supervisors to accept the ideas you present?
   __ Eager   __ Receptive   __ Neutral   __ Slightly resistant   __ Strongly resistant   __ Unknown

4. How do you know your supervisors need to hear what you have to say?
   __ Contacted them   __ Your authority   __ Assessment   __ Performance review need identified
   __ General information   __ Don't know

5. Why do they need this information?
   __ To make decisions   __ To carry out decisions   __ Information   __ Promotion   __ Organizational changes

6. The training is: __ First thing in the morning   __ After lunch   __ Mid-morning or mid-afternoon   __ After lunch
   __ Mandatory   __ An obligation   __ Voluntary

7. Will they have materials to support the training you provide?   __ Yes   __ No

8. Will they have anything to divert their attention?   __ Yes   __ No   If so, what? _____

Specific Analysis of Audience Members

9. What is their knowledge of the subject matter?
   __ High   __ Moderate   __ Limited   __ None   __ Unknown

10. What are their opinions about the subject and about you or the organization?
    __ Very favorable   __ Positive   __ Neutral   __ Slightly hostile   __ Openly hostile   __ Unknown

11. You are an information source. How will the audience respond to you?
    __ As someone qualified in your field   __ As an expert in the subject   __ As a stranger   __ Someone who knows little
    __ Someone who cannot relate to the group

12. How will demographics affect the training session?
    __ Not at all   __ Somewhat   __ Extremely   __ Audience bias not an issue

13. List some advantages and disadvantages of the course objectives to the supervisors:
    Advantages: _____

    Disadvantages: _____

Information and Techniques

14. What types of information and techniques are most likely to gain the audience's attention?
    __ High-tech   __ Statistical comparisons   __ Cost-related/bottom line   __ Anecdotes   __ Demonstrations
    __ Research   __ Activities   __ Application

15. What information or techniques are most likely to get negative reactions from the members of this audience?

    _____

Need to know. What's in it for me—or *WIIFM*? Because learners need to know why you are presenting this information, do the following:

- Explain how this information or skill benefits the supervisor.

- Outline how this information will be useful back on the job.

- Ask supervisors how they feel this information benefits them.

Readiness to know. Have your learners mastered the basic information they need to know as a prerequisite to the supervisory program? Is your organization ready for them to learn? Keep these questions in mind when you perform the following:

- Write materials at the appropriate level.

- Provide all preliminary reading material or documents that support learning (for example, the organizational mission, vision, and goals).

- Secure buy-in from upper management.

Richness of experience. Your learners come to the learning event with a wide variety of experiences. The program will be a learning experience for you as well if you remind yourself of this and do the following:

- Value, respect, and use your learners' knowledge.

- Allow for learner input during sessions.

- Know what they do so you can talk their talk.

- Get supervisors involved with program development before the program start date.

- Incorporate workplace examples in the session materials.

Self-concept. Learners like to be in control of their own learning. Due to this desire for self-direction, follow these guidelines:

- Give them the opportunity to incorporate and apply new information in a way that applies to their specific situation back on the job.

- Allow them to experience, observe, reflect, and form new generalizations about the information as it applies to their situation, and apply it to their work.

Motivation. When they value what you teach, adults are motivated to learn. Perform the following tasks to help make your program a motivational success:

- Find out why the information is important to them and weave the importance throughout your material.

- Chunk the information into manageable pieces so they are not overwhelmed with new concepts or theories.

- Incorporate an element of fun in the learning experience.

- Reward learners for their accomplishments. Take a lesson from Socrates: You did not teach them, rather you have helped them find the knowledge within themselves.

Getting the Information Across

When developing the program content, think about how you are going to get the information across to participants. Keep in mind the various learning styles, as well as the diversity of your group. An active approach to supervisory training works well because of the nature of the training. You should encourage supervisors to do the following:

- try new skills
- interject their own experiences
- take risks to maximize learning by the group

Supervisors appreciate trying new skills and techniques in class in a nonthreatening environment. This method works especially well in practicing conflict resolution techniques and in applying techniques and strategies for dealing with difficult people.

In addition, research on team learning, or learning by a group, indicates that individuals learning from others in the group and offering their own experiences facilitate the transfer of new information and skills while developing the capacity of the team or group to create the results its members truly desire.

Because adults learn best when they can see a practical use of the training content, be sure to include the work examples you gathered during the assessment phase as you design activities and exercises. The more relevance they see to their immediate job duties, the more learners will use the knowledge and skills.

Do not be shy about using out-of-class activities. Have participants complete forms via email, fax, or standard paper and pencil; respond to posttraining questions online; or complete a group interview using online meeting tools. Use follow-up emails to continuously reinforce the key points of training after the close of the program.

Another element to consider in developing the curriculum is how to design assignments that will take the information out of the classroom and into the real world of supervision. If your curriculum extends over a period of weeks, have participants try new skills or apply the information learned during the session on the job. Ask participants to keep a journal of what they did, how it worked, and any suggestions they may have for making it more effective.

Whatever methods you choose, be sure you emphasize the "why" and the relevance of the training topic to the supervisor's daily job.

Step 5: Deliver Your Program

Presenting text on this step could fill up a number of separate *Info-lines*. In fact, it has. Please consult the following *Info-lines* for information about delivering your program: No. 8911, "Icebreakers"; No. 8606, "Make Every Presentation a Winner"; No. 9102, "How To Make a Large Group Presentation"; and No. 9406, "How to Facilitate."

In the meantime, use the sidebar at right to help you gather supplies and equipment for your training.

Step 6: Evaluate Your Program

As with needs assessment, it is important to determine the purpose of the evaluation. This includes identifying *who* wants the evaluation results and *what* they want to do with them. The audience for the evaluation affects what type of data you gather. Evaluators must take into account desired learning and organization outcomes and the level to which they are evaluating.

Donald Kirkpatrick's levels of evaluation are the standard gauge. The Kirkpatrick model discusses what you may want to evaluate and for whom.

Level 1: Reaction. Measures the participant's feelings about the training.

Level 2: Learning. Measures how well the instruction met the course goals.

Level 3: Behavior. Measures the transfer of learning to the job. By integrating with a competency-based performance review system, you gain insight into actual, on-the-job performance and application of learned knowledge and skills.

Level 4: Results. Measures return-on-investment toward meeting the original goals.

Building assessment data and metrics into the training and related activities makes it easier to evaluate the impact of training on supervisors' job duties and behaviors. By using data collected during the needs assessment phase as a baseline, you can measure any change related to training.

Types of Evaluation

Several training evaluation methods are available. The challenge lies in determining the most appropriate method or methods to use for the intended learning outcomes, evaluation level, and data audience.

The most common evaluation methods include surveys, interviews, observations, work samples, and document reviews. Evaluation is more effective when you collect data both before and after the training intervention. This provides you with data to show marked improvement as a result of the training.

Training Delivery Preparation

Listed below are some of the items and equipment you need for supervisory training. As you prepare, you will probably identify other items to add to this list. To be sure that you do not overlook anything, review the list; decide which items are appropriate for your situation; indicate who is responsible for specific tasks; and determine a target date for completion of each task. Once a task is completed, indicate that date in the "completed" column.

Course Title: _____

Date: _____ **Time:** _____ **Number of Participants:** _____

Task	Person Responsible	Target Date	Completed
Logistics			
Schedule room			
Set up room			
Beverages			
Scheduling with trainees			
Materials: Supervisors			
Develop handouts			
Duplicate handouts			
Name tents			
Name badges			
Pencils/pens			
Notepaper			
Materials: Trainers			
Handouts			
Lesson plan			
Evaluations			
Transparencies			
Presentation slides			
Video			
Newsprint/easel			
Overhead projector			
Computer with connectors			
Video player/monitor			
Trainer's Tool Box			
Markers			
Pencils/pens			
Candy/mints/gum			
Prizes			
Tape			
Toys			
Stapler/staples			
Extension cord			
Index cards			
Sticky pads			
Stickers			
Computer supplies (if needed)			
Electrical adapter plugs			
Glue			

Evaluation Methods

Review the following chart to help you understand the relationship between evaluation levels, assessment data, training curriculums, and evaluation types.

Evaluation Level	Assessment Data Examples	Training Content & Activities	Evaluation
Level 1: Reaction	• Focus group (opinion-based and attitude data)	• Training curriculum and content	• Reaction evaluation sheets • Verbal information
Level 2: Learning	• Pretest • Pretraining skill assessment	• Pretest from training interventions • Posttest from training interventions	• Reaction evaluation sheets with open comments and feedback • In-class test and exercises • Post-class test
Level 3: Behavior	• Employee opinion survey • Exit interview • Internal transfer • Interview data	• Training curriculum and content • Posttraining activities and assignments	• Integration into a competency-based performance review system • Employee interviews and feedback • Management surveys or interviews • Observations of participants
Level 4: Results	• Organization strategy • Strategic metrics • Tactical goals and metrics	• Action plans developed during training • Implementations and measurement plans	• Achievement of organizational and tactical goals • Measure of perceived value of impact on organization success • Dollar metrics that align with goals

To help in your evaluation method selection, use the chart above to establish the relationship between assessment data, training curriculum, and type of evaluation.

Leaders Growing Leaders

You want to design supervisory training that makes an impact on participants and the organization. By linking the assessment data, training design and delivery, and evaluation methods, you ensure a smooth, consistent flow of the training as well as increase the likelihood of transfer of learned knowledge and skills to the job.

Leaders control the future of their organizations. Supervisors not only lead, they also inspire up-and-coming leaders in the organization. Groom them, develop their core competencies, reinforce their behavior, and you will have a strong workforce today and for years to come.

References & Resources

Articles

Dyer, L. "Linking Human Resource and Business Strategies." *Human Resource Planning,* vol. 7, no. 2 (1984), pp. 79-84.

Grensing-Pophal, Lin. "Training Supervisors to Manage Teleworkers." *HRMagazine,* January 1999, pp. 67-72.

Merit, Don. "Supervising Versus Working." *American Printer,* September 1998, p. 106.

Reynolds, Angus. "The Basics: Evaluating Training." *Technical & Skills Training,* August/September 1990, p. 47.

Stanley, Jan. "The Map for the Seven Danger Zones of Supervision." *Training & Development,* June 1999, p. 54.

Books

Broadwell, Martin M., and Carol Broadwell Dietrich. *The New Supervisor: How to Thrive in Your First Year as a Manager.* Reading, MA: Addison-Wesley, 1998.

Chapman, Elwood N., and Cliff Goodwin. *Supervisor's Survival Kit: Your First Step Into Management.* Upper Saddle River, NJ: Prentice-Hall, 1999.

Felix, Amy. *Matching Evaluation Methods to Learning Outcomes and Evaluation Levels.* Unpublished manuscript. 1994.

Moglia, Tony. *Supervising for Success: A Guide for Supervisors.* Menlo Park, CA: Crisp Publications, 1997.

Office of Personnel Management (OPM), Human Resources Development Group, Office of Executive and Management Policy. *Leadership Effectiveness Framework and Inventory (descriptive materials).* Washington, DC: 1993, 1998.

Rothwell, William J., and Henry J. Sredl. *The ASTD Reference Guide to Professional Human Resource Development Roles and Competencies.* 2 volumes. 2nd edition. Amherst, MA: HRD Press, Inc., 1992.

Salmon, William A. *The New Supervisor's Survival Manual.* New York: AMACOM, 1999.

Silberman, Melvin L. *Active Training: A Handbook of Techniques, Designs, Case Examples, and Tips.* San Francisco: Jossey-Bass/Pfeiffer, 1997.

———. *101 Ways to Make Training Active.* San Francisco: Jossey-Bass/Pfeiffer, 1995.

Turner, David. *60 Role Plays for Management and Supervisory Training.* New York: McGraw-Hill, 1996.

Williamson, Bobette Hayes. *The ASTD Trainer's Sourcebook: Supervision.* New York: McGraw-Hill, 1996.

Info-lines

Bedrosian, Maggie. "How To Make a Large Group Presentation." No. 9102.

Carr, Don Aaron. "How to Facilitate." No. 9406 (revised 1999).

Kaye, Beverly, and Devon Scheef. "Mentoring." No. 0004.

Prezioso, Robert C. "Icebreakers." No. 8911 (revised 1999).

Sullivan, Richard L., and Jerry L. Wircenski. "Make Every Presentation a Winner." No. 8606 (revised 1998).

Job Aid

Competencies and Goals

This job aid features a sample assessment designed to measure the importance of aligning your leadership competencies with your organization's strategic goals. Ask participants to use the Importance Scale to rate the importance of each skill listed in the first column against identified strategic goals in the second and third columns. This exercise results in the overall perceived value of each skill on strategic goals.

On another sheet of paper, have participants rate how they perceive their skill in each of the competencies. This identifies each participant's skill development needs. These two assessments can lead to a discussion on how best to develop a supervisory curriculum that targets the development of skills that support your organizational strategic initiatives.

Importance Scale **4** = Very Important **3** = Important **2** = Somewhat Important **1** = Not Important	Strategic Goal 1 _____ _____	Strategic Goal 2 _____ _____
Skill Areas		
Conflict management: Anticipates and seeks to resolve confrontations, disagreements, and complaints in a constructive manner.		
Creative thinking: Develops insights and solutions; fosters innovation among others.		
Customer orientation: Seeks internal and external customer input actively; ensures customer needs are met; seeks continuously to improve quality of services, products, and processes.		
Decisiveness: Takes action and risks when needed; makes a difficult decision when necessary.		
External awareness: Stays informed on laws, policies, politics, trends, special interests, and other related issues; considers external impact of statements or actions; uses relevant information in decision making.		
Financial management: Prepares and justifies budget; monitors expenses; manages procurement and contracting.		
Flexibility: Adapts to change in the work environment; copes effectively with stress.		
Other: _____		

The material appearing on this page is not covered by copyright and may be reproduced at will.

Call Center Training

Call Center Training

AUTHOR

Nancy M. Giere
The Working Force, Inc.
2232 Edgewood Drive
Grafton, WI 53024
Tel: 262.376.2988
Fax: 262.376.2989
Email:
nancyg@theworkingforce.com
Web:
www.theworkingforce.com

Nancy Giere is president of The Working Force, Inc., a performance improvement consulting firm. She has worked extensively with service companies in the analysis, design, and development of their training programs for call center employees and service technicians.

Editor
Cat Sharpe Russo

Managing Editor
Sabrina E. Hicks

Production Design
Leah Cohen

Internal Consultant
Maria Capestany

Developing Call Center Agents

Want to set your organization apart from its competitors? Investing in a call center might be your answer. Possessing a well-run call center with the capacity to handle a large volume of customer transactions while maintaining a high level of service quality can give you that competitive edge. Because our everyday context for doing business has changed from over the counter, in person transactions to over the phone or Internet transactions, call centers have metamorphosed from a business cost to a competitive advantage. New and existing customers contact call centers worldwide to request service on business or personal equipment and to purchase new products and services for their homes or businesses.

The telephone, as a tool that both enhances and minimizes communication, allows us to reach people anywhere in the world. Yet, this technology is not enough. Because call center employees are unable to see the person with whom they are talking, they require highly developed communication skills. These skills are mandatory if agents are to provide a positive experience for the customer. A properly run call center, staffed with well-trained agents who are knowledgeable and effective communicators, builds customer loyalty and, ultimately, increases profitability and market share.

When customers call your organization to do business, they have already decided that they want your product or service. To build loyalty and keep them as customers, however, you need to meet their expectations for customer service. These expectations go beyond the product or service you sell and touch on the quality of the interaction they have with your agents.

If your customers do not experience a level of service that is in line with their expectations, they will find alternatives for your products or services. While the call center is only one part of your organization, to the customer it *is* the organization. Every contact with a customer is an opportunity for you to either increase or decrease customer loyalty.

Overall, your customers expect your agents to act in the following manner:

- Be polite and courteous.

- Be friendly and professional.

- Listen, and respond to their needs.

- Be interested and willing to help.

- Avoid jargon, and use language they understand.

- Be accessible, and provide prompt service.

- Be honest, and present themselves as believable and trustworthy.

- Set realistic expectations, and deliver what they promise.

- Have the knowledge and skills needed to complete the transaction.

To meet these expectations, you need to hire people who are service minded and enjoy working with people. Once you hire people who possess "call center characteristics," you can train them in your products, services, and software applications. You can further develop and refine their interpersonal communication and call management skills through training and coaching.

Your agents' confidence in their ability to do the job will improve the quality of their communication with the customer. While you cannot teach confidence, you can help employees gain it through product and systems training, as well as advanced interpersonal communication topics (such as call control, cross-selling, up-selling, and dealing with difficult customers).

This issue of *Info-line* provides instructions on how to develop measurement criteria for agent performance that coincide with the goals and objectives of your organization. You will learn how to hire for attitude and train for skill by finding service-minded individuals with the ability to learn your products, services, and systems. In addition, this issue provides guidance on how to retain your call center agents through ongoing learning opportunities, regular coaching, and clearly defined career opportunities. The job aid helps you ensure that your agent development plan is well rounded.

Components for Call Center Agent Training

Bemused by what elements to include in your call center agent training? No idea what to cover to develop successful agents? Listed below are the fundamental components you must include in your training.

Customers

- Who are they?
- What do they need, require, and expect?

Interpersonal Communication

- What types of questions should agents ask?
- How can agents learn to listen to customers?
- How can agents develop call control skills?

Written Communication

- Do you require agents to email customers and co-workers?
- Do you require agents to write business letters to customers and co-workers?

Product and Services

- What does your organization offer?
- What are the features, advantages, and benefits?

Business Processes, Procedures, and Applications

- How do you want your call center to handle calls?
- What is your complaint handling process?
- How do your systems and applications manage customer transactions?
- How do agents access information to complete customer transactions?

Step 1: Identify Measurement Criteria

At one point in Lewis Carroll's classic story *Alice in Wonderland*, Alice says, "If you don't know where you're going, anyplace will do." As you begin to look at your current call center to determine whom to hire, what and how to train them, and how to retain your new and existing agents, you need to begin by looking at what is important to your organization.

To determine what is important to your organization, perhaps it would be helpful to know what other organizations perceive as "most important." AchieveGlobal (a division of The Times Mirror Company and combination of Kaset International, Learning International, and Zenger Miller training and consulting organizations) and the National Investment Company Service Association (NICSA) surveyed investment organization call centers. They surveyed managers on the criteria they use to measure agent performance, including the following:

- attitude
- accuracy
- teamwork
- business knowledge
- attendance
- customer satisfaction
- team productivity
- occupancy
- average number of calls per day
- average talk time
- employee satisfaction
- rate of call escalation to supervisor
- average call handling time
- average wait time

Of the items on this list, call center managers ranked the following as most critical to the agent's job:

- accuracy
- attitude
- teamwork
- business knowledge
- attendance
- customer satisfaction

Ranked at 90 percent, accuracy, attitude, and teamwork were the most important; followed by business knowledge, attendance, and customer satisfaction—ranked between 79 and 89 percent. What you find important on this list is what is important to your organization.

If you know what is important to your organization and why, you can target your hiring, training, and employee development efforts. This information is a good starting point for the development or improvement of your programs. It also provides criteria for your Human Resources department to incorporate into the performance appraisal system, as well as coaching criteria for managers and supervisors.

Step 2: Hire for Attitude

Hiring people with the right skills is critical to the success of any organization. One of the things that Jim Bohn, Director of Integrated Customer Solutions at Johnson Controls (an automotive systems, and facility management and controls company headquartered in Milwaukee, Wisconsin), looks for in his Customer Success Center Agents is the "customer service gene": an innate desire to help others. This factor is consistent among his most successful agents.

A review of your call center employees will undoubtedly reveal a few star performers. As you examine what makes them successful, you will discover that they share common attitudes and characteristics. Identifying what makes them different from the rest of your agents uncovers the attitudes and characteristics you need to use as the foundation for hiring and job performance requirements.

Your criteria may include some of the following:

☐ possesses a service attitude—a genuine concern for other people

☐ learns quickly and has a commitment to life-long learning

☐ adapts to a rapidly changing environment

☐ possesses outstanding verbal and written communication skills

☐ pays attention to detail and quality

☐ is able to conduct business and be cordial

☐ appears genuine and interested during phone conversations

☐ listens and captures essential customer information

☐ has keyboarding skills

☐ has education and experience in a particular field

If you have a clear picture of what you are looking for, you have a better chance of finding it as you evaluate job candidates. Once you find people with the right personality and service attitude, you can train them in your products, services, and systems.

Hiring Process

After defining your criteria, examine your hiring process. What information do you need to make the best decisions about job candidates? One way to evaluate people is to observe them in a setting that simulates the work environment. More and more companies are using simulations as part of the hiring process. Because your agents spend most of their time working with customers on the telephone, it is important to assess how they sound and act under these conditions.

At Johnson Controls, personnel responsible for hiring interview all of their candidates by telephone. This gives them the opportunity to judge the quality of the candidates in a comparable work environment. Interviewers evaluate the candidates overall telephone demeanor, including vocal quality, listening skills, and ability to ask questions.

Many of your candidates will have outstanding verbal communication skills, but they may have difficulty communicating effectively in writing. If your agents need to send email or other written correspondence to customers and co-workers, consider developing a test that requires candidates to gather information concerning customer needs over the phone, and then have candidates provide a summary of the conversation. This task provides you with a basis to judge each candidate's writing and keyboarding skills.

Telephone Interview Checklist

Because call center agents work mostly on the telephone, many organizations conduct telephone interviews of job candidates. Interviewing prospective call center agents over the telephone provides insight into how each individual will perform on the job. Use the checklist below to identify key traits of successful call center agents:

☐ How does his or her voice sound?

☐ Is the person clear and articulate?

☐ What is the pitch and tone of his or her voice?

☐ Does the person use vocabulary appropriate to the situation?

☐ Does he or she sound genuinely interested in the conversation?

☐ Is he or she a good listener?

☐ Does the person appear interested in what the interviewer has to say?

☐ Does he or she seem to enjoy talking with people?

☐ Is the person polite and professional?

☐ Does he or she ask questions that are thought-out and appropriate?

☐ Did he or she provide examples of past performance that demonstrate a service focus?

☐ Can the person accurately summarize key points of the conversation?

☐ Is the person able to explain what skills he or she possesses, as well as what he or she would like to do?

New Employee Orientation

From day one, you should strive to make your employees feel welcome and a part of your organization. Offering organization tours, providing department overviews, and explaining the life cycle of an order are just a few ways you can help new agents get the feel of the organization. Emphasize where new agents fit in the big picture and how they contribute to the goals, objectives, and mission of the organization. Let employees know that they are part of something important.

At Pleasant Company (the makers of the American Girl dolls, books, and accessories), call center trainers accomplish this by showing a video of a little girl receiving her first American Girl Doll. The expression of pure joy on the child's face sends a very clear message about how important each call is to their customers. An agent may take hundreds of calls, but a child may only receive one American Girl Doll—so it is vital that every order is correct.

Step 3: Train for Skill

In her article "The Impact of Technology on Call Center Training," Linda Gherardi states: "Turnover in call centers has long exceeded levels found in other professions or other areas of companies. The Olsten Survey [a survey sponsored by Olsten Staffing that included more than 400 call center managers representing North American companies] found that there is a direct correlation between the amount of training and the type of turnover a company experiences. The average training program is about three weeks in length. Those companies with minimal levels of training (three days or less) tend to report annual turnover rates averaging 55 percent. By comparison, for companies with training that extends over a month, the rate drops to 25 percent." This survey makes it clear that an investment in training call center agents will increase employee retention and, ultimately, reduce your overall cost of doing business.

Agent training usually begins in a classroom setting. Employees spend time learning the organization's mission, products, processes, and systems. The most successful programs concentrate on how to manage the customer relationship. They focus their attention on further developing each agent's interpersonal communications skills.

Interpersonal Communication Skills

Customers naturally assume that employees who work in the call center are knowledgeable about the organization and will be able to handle their requests for products or services. The quality of the conversation, however, is what will build the customer relationship and, ultimately, customer loyalty. Quality conversation is rooted in a strategic communication model, such as AchieveGlobal's SERVE model:

> **SERVE** is an acronym:
>
> **S**ee the "big picture" and how customer service fits into it.
>
> **E**stablish an authentic human connection with each customer.
>
> **R**ender timely, accurate, and thorough service.
>
> **V**alue and respond to unique customer needs.
>
> **E**xtend a hand to repair and strengthen relationships with customers who are upset or angry.

This type of structured communication model provides employees with a foundation upon which to build their abilities. It addresses core interpersonal communication skills and requires employees to look at how customer service contributes to the overall success of the organization.

Once they are able to apply the basic communication model, agents can expand their interpersonal skills to include the following:

- handling irate customers
- using appropriate questioning techniques
- using active listening skills
- cross-selling
- up-selling

They accomplish this by listening to what the customer says, responding appropriately, and entering the correct information into the system.

As agents gain more product knowledge and build their data entry skills, introduce role playing as a learning method that will help them put everything together. Here, you move new agents through a series of customer situations of increasing complexity. Build the complexity of the call around different types of orders and customer behaviors. Working with an angry customer or increasing the quantity of information the agent needs to manage heightens the complexity of the situation.

The most successful role plays simulate the work environment in terms of the systems, types of calls, and customer behaviors. To collect information and build realistic situations, do the following:

- Spend time out on the call center floor observing your best agents at work. Pay close attention to how they handle each situation.

- Observe your less experienced agents at work, and capture areas that they have not yet mastered.

- Listen to recorded calls, especially those that are not up to your organization's standards. These point to potential gaps in your training.

- Look at your complaint history to identify additional gaps in your training.

- Listen to your agents. What do they complain about? This could also be a source of identifying gaps in your training.

Once you collect this information, you are well on your way to building quality simulations.

Call Control

Call control is an important concept that involves asking the appropriate questions for each customer's situation to find out what that customer needs. Using this technique, agents really listen to customers to ensure that they clearly understand the customer. Such comprehension enables the agent to guide conversation toward a solution that satisfies the customer.

For example, at Pleasant Company, agents must be able to respond to different types of people. Their customers range anywhere from the "gushy grandma," who desires to learn all about the doll's features, to "frantic aunt," who is in a rush and wants to get her order completed quickly. Each of these customers has different purchasing requirements, and the agent must respond to these needs accordingly. In both instances, the agent must come across as genuinely interested and provide the customer with a positive purchasing experience.

Scripting

A script is a document that identifies the kinds of information agents must solicit from the customer to help satisfy the customer's request. An experienced agent, like an "improv" actor, will not need a set script: He or she needs only a few key words or cues to work. To a certain extent, your new call center agents are like novice actors following a very specific script. Any deviation can change the meaning or intent of the call.

Call centers use scripting as a tool to build the skill level of their new agents. Most managers expect their employees to rely heavily on scripts when they are starting out. As agents become more confident, managers encourage them to personalize their scripts. Personalization helps make the agent's conversation sound more genuine. Depending on the type of industry, however, managers may require agents to read a particular sentence or phrase word-for-word to ensure legal compliance.

Written Communication

In addition to call control, you may need to address written communication skills in your training program. Depending on your call center requirements, agents may provide customers with a written response in the form of an email or business letter to better clarify what the customer wants and determine the best course of action. Often, an agent handles the initial call and then forwards service request information to a service technician. The service technician will conduct further diagnosis and troubleshooting. In both cases, the agent must write a clear, concise written response to provide the appropriate level of service required to successfully complete the transaction.

Product and Systems Training

Even with good call control and writing skills, if agents do not possess a fundamental understanding of your products and systems, they cannot be successful. The extent of product training agents need depends on the type of calls handled. Some call center managers expect agents to handle a call from start to finish. Other call centers consist of a core group of agents who take the initial call, identify the problem, and then, based on this information, queue the call to a technician who has the expertise required to solve the customer's problem.

The skill sets are very different: One person's area of focus is on identification; the other's focus is troubleshooting and repair. Due to these differences, you should target product and systems training toward distinct job requirements.

Product Training

When thinking about your organizational needs for product training, consider your suite of products:

- What information (features, benefits, and so forth) does the agent need to learn in training?

- What information can you provide to agents through documentation on the job?

- What are the most efficient ways to access information?

- What do your agents need to know about your competitors?

- Are agents information gatherers, troubleshooters, or both?

- What questions are your customers most likely to ask? Do your role plays or simulations address these questions?

Call Center Simulation Checklist

If you want to observe job candidates in a comparable setting to your work environment, conduct a simulation as part of your hiring process. Assess how candidates sound and act under work conditions. This will help you staff a successful call center. Use the following checklist as a guide:

☐ Observe your best agents to get a picture of the job requirements.

☐ Listen to call monitoring tapes to determine the range of customer transactions.

☐ Conduct a focus group with lead agents to determine the frequency, criticality, and difficulty of the different types of calls.

☐ Interview call center managers to determine their performance expectations.

☐ Review customer satisfaction requirements to establish performance objectives, standards, and criteria.

☐ Look at the whole job and then break it into separate parts. Parts should include communication, products, customers, and transactions.

☐ Prepare draft scenarios.

☐ Sequence the scenarios from simple to complex.

☐ Start with a simple request for a product or service.

☐ Introduce scripts, and encourage personalization where appropriate.

☐ Add customer contact, so the agent is on the telephone and entering information into the system.

☐ Require agent trainees to use your communication model.

☐ Add transactional variations to introduce the first level of complexity.

☐ Add customer variations: in a hurry, overly talkative, or angry.

☐ Set up scenarios that will test questioning and active listening techniques.

☐ Add cross-selling and up-selling situations.

☐ Increase customer relationship skills through call management techniques.

☐ Add the element of time pressure.

☐ Require agents to search for information to complete the transaction.

☐ Provide an opportunity for agents to observe experienced agents.

☐ Set up an approach that takes the agents from guided to unguided simulations.

☐ Work on similar transactions, products, and customers at the beginning.

☐ Randomize the scenarios toward the end of the training.

☐ Consider setting up new agents with a mentor or create a bridge training component to ease the transition from training room to the call center.

10 Mentoring Characteristics of Call Agents

A mentor can be the lifeline for new agents. This person helps new hires make a smooth transition from the training room to the call center floor. Select agents with the following characteristics to act as mentors:

1. Has a broad range of call handling experience.

2. Meets or exceeds performance expectations consistently.

3. Is patient.

4. Demonstrates leadership ability by a willingness to help other agents.

5. Is a good listener.

6. Is enthusiastic and has a positive attitude toward work and the organization.

7. Is capable of explaining how to perform the required tasks.

8. Provides consistent and sound feedback.

9. Transforms difficult situations into positive learning experiences.

10. Is well-respected by other agents.

Systems Training

When looking at your organizational systems and applications training, make sure your training provides new agents with all the knowledge and skills required to complete customer transactions:

- What information do your agents need to learn in training?

- Have you addressed the most critical and frequent procedures?

- Have you given them the tools they need to access information about more unusual transactions or problems?

You can build on the complexity of your role playing activities by requiring agents to search for product or procedural information to complete a transaction. This task further develops their questioning and listening skills while adding to their skill set the ability to access information.

Customer Information

As employees develop their communication, product, and technical skills and knowledge, you want to link these activities to your customer's expectations. This provides an overall context and relevance to the agent's learning experience. Here are some key success factors to consider:

- Develop realistic simulations.

- Base simulations on what your customers need, want, and expect.

- Build customer questions and model answers into your simulations.

- Be aware of changes to products, services, and processes that may affect your customers.

Step 4: Make the Transition

The shift from the training room to the call center floor is often difficult. The introduction of real customers with real needs and concerns often makes new agents nervous. They are so concerned about doing the job well that their confidence level goes down. To ease this transition, many organizations add mentoring and bridge training programs to their overall agent development strategy.

Mentoring Programs

In many instances, new agents are assigned a coach or mentor who helps them make a successful shift from classroom to call center. A mentor becomes a new agent's lifeline by providing the following guidance:

- demonstrating call taking procedures in the actual environment

- observing new agent's performance and providing positive corrective feedback

- answering questions

- introducing new agents to the other members of their team and helping them become a part of their new work group

Today's Merchandising Inc., a retail outlet for manufacturers in Peoria, Illinois, has an effective training program. This program, "New Employee Partners," works because it capitalizes on the natural tendency of call center agents to want to help others.

During their four-week training program, new agents spend five to 10 hours a week working with their mentors. New agents can observe and handle calls as they are learning the products, processes, and systems. This approach allows them to practice newly learned communication and sales skills with real customers early in their development process.

Training programs that include an on-the-job component are very successful because new agents receive just-in-time assistance while handling initial customer calls. Such teamwork creates a bond between the call center employees and decreases the time new agents need to adjust to the call center environment. Why? Because new agents know that someone will always be around to help out. Programs like New Employee Partners benefit the organization as well as the employees by improving employee morale and reducing turnovers.

Bridge Training

While the goal of new hire training is to quickly turn new employees into productive agents, often the transition is difficult. Even the most confident trainees can lose their nerve and forget everything they learned when faced with real customers and systems.

Bridge training is a technique that creates a smooth transition from training room to call center. Here, new hires have the opportunity to observe their supervisor or a more experienced agent take calls before they begin taking customer calls under the guidance of the supervisor or experienced agent. New hires can begin to apply their newly acquired knowledge and skills to actual customer situations. Because the agent-to-supervisor ratio is quite low during bridge training (an average of 6:1), new hires have the opportunity to ask more questions and receive more regular feedback on their performance. This higher level of support helps new agents quickly build their confidence and level of readiness to become successful agents.

Step 5: Retain Call Center Agents

Many organizations consider the call center agent an entry-level position. In this role, employees learn quite a bit about your organization's products, services, and customer needs. Because of this, it is important that you look at ways to retain your agents as a part of your overall employee development strategy. Four strategies contribute to agent retention:

1. Employee involvement.

2. Continuous learning.

3. Coaching.

4. Career development.

Employee Involvement

Agents are your best resource for continuous improvement activities. Include them in special projects, such as developing training programs, call monitoring criteria, script development, business application upgrades, and online help systems. Your agents will feel appreciated if you value and implement their suggestions. This results in a more highly motivated employee. Your agents have the potential to contribute to your company in the following ways:

- Because they talk and listen to your customers every day, agents can contribute to your overall call monitoring criteria.

- You can adapt scripts for new hires by listening to recordings of your best agents at work. This will result in a more natural and realistic sounding script.

- For your systems and applications to really work, your agents need to be a part of the process. Simple things like the sequence of fields on a screen can make a big difference if you are trying to build an efficient application.

- Help systems need to be driven by the way an agent receives information or thinks about a problem.

Keep in mind that employee involvement in the development of any new product, process, or idea can reduce implementation time. If a team of agents who worked on the project is positive about the change, they will be a positive influence during the deployment.

Continuous Learning

Learning no longer occurs as a single event at a fixed point in time. The dynamic world of work requires ongoing learning for agents to stay current and continue meeting customer needs. Keeping up with an organization's products and services is becoming increasingly difficult. Due to technological advances, time to market for new products and services is getting shorter and shorter. Agents need the knowledge and skills to deal with multiple versions of equipment. New-hire training captures an organization's products and services at one moment in time. To be successful, agents need to continuously add to their knowledge base.

The current norm is to use the classroom or training room setting to get new agents started. Many organizations use self-instructional methods to provide training on new products and processes, as well as to reinforce key communication principles and practices. An additional component of classroom training is the use of online learning via the organizational intranet, CD-ROM, broadcast email messages, and service bulletins. The depth of knowledge you require of your agents depends on the type and level of service the agent performs.

But away from the classroom, what can agents use to keep abreast of the latest products and services? Easy-to-access, online help systems that use key words and user-friendly indexes are important when agents are faced with unusual situations. Then, agents can quickly access the information

necessary to address the customers' needs and complete the call while maintaining the expected level of service. For example, an organization may use codes to classify different types of service problems. If agents are not sure of the correct code, they can access a pop up window and select the correct one while never breaking conversation with the customer.

Scripting is another good way to introduce new products or services. After briefing experienced agents on a new product or service, supervisors provide them with a script to use until they are comfortable with the new information. It is also important to expand your agents' knowledge of the business. At Pleasant Company, experts from other departments talk to call center agents. Topics may include how a book is written and printed, magazine publication, market research, and product development.

At Strong Capital Management Inc., a mutual funds investment firm located near Milwaukee, Wisconsin, agents have the opportunity to participate in a conference call with a portfolio manager every other Monday morning. Participants can email questions to the portfolio manager. This gives everyone the opportunity to stay current on the different mutual funds offered by the organization.

Strong Capital Management Inc. has established a corporate university as another means to encourage learning. Strong's Corporate University has a speaker series that provides employees with an opportunity to learn more about the world around them. These sessions occur before and after work and have included such speakers as Margaret Thatcher and Ron Chernow, the President of Yahoo. Access to this type of information increases employee morale and improves job performance.

Coaching

Training new agents to perform their jobs is not enough. You also need to train your managers and supervisors to be effective coaches. Managers need to be aware of what new hires learn in their training, so they can reinforce positive performance on the job. You can do this through a series of meetings that provide managers with an overview of the course content and behavioral measures. At the end of the session, provide each manager with a job aid that lists the top 10 new competencies and coaching tips for each item.

To be effective coaches, managers and supervisors need coaching development opportunities to learn how to identify performance problems and provide positive, timely feedback. This helps them to reinforce the skills agents learned in training.

Call Monitoring

Call monitoring provides supervisors with another coaching opportunity. Most call centers use this evaluation method to asses the overall quality of the customer's experience. A good program begins by looking at the organization's business measures. This tells you what is most important to your organization.

From here, you define your coaching criteria. The more specific the criteria, the easier it is to measure the agent's performance and provide feedback to improve performance. For example, the more specific the content of the agent's greeting at the beginning of the call, the easier it is determine how well the agent met the criteria.

The most successful programs include agents in criteria definition. Agents provide insight into customer issues and successes. This data helps you define areas that may need additional training and support. Here are some things to consider:

- If you are measuring attitude, how do you define it? What are you looking for? This could include tone of voice and the overall quality of the conversation. Did the agent sound genuine or scripted?

- What is your requirement for accuracy of information—100 percent or 90 percent? Are you looking at accuracy in data entry as well as the information that the agent communicated? Did the agent capture all the required information?

- If teamwork is important, what qualities are you looking for? This could include call transfer to the right party or assistance with difficult situations. Are team members able to understand and work with the information?

Case Study: Pleasant Company

If you have ever needed to buy a doll for a little child, you probably have heard of Pleasant Company, the makers of American Girl dolls, books, and accessories. And it should come as no surprise that Pleasant Company's busiest time is during Christmas. This peak season provides the company an opportunity for an innovative approach to succession planning.

To meet customer expectations during this time of increased call center calls, Pleasant Company increases the number call center agents from 350 to 1850. It hires seasonal agents between June and the week before Thanksgiving. Approximately 30 percent of this seasonal workforce consists of returning workers. Pleasant Company implements a seasonal support team to help new agents learn the call center procedures quickly and ensure consistent service quality for the customers.

The seasonal support team consists of a group of experienced agents who move out of their daily routine and take on new challenges as trainers, coaches, and supervisors. In addition to supporting the influx of seasonal workers, experienced Pleasant Company agents have the opportunity to take on new challenges and opportunities, which ultimately facilitate their long-range career planning. Many agents set a career goal of moving into management or training after completing their work on the seasonal support team or returning to their existing job.

The more experienced agents on the seasonal support team act as the training component and conduct classes using a training database. This database allows them to guide the seasonal workforce through the company's processes using its proprietary system. New agents begin training by receiving a basic script and working on simple transactions. The support team heightens the learning process by folding in more and more complex customer situations. New agents complete the formal classroom training in three weeks.

Upon completion of the formal training, new agents start taking calls in small groups under the guidance of a seasonal support team member. This period bridges the gap between training time in the classroom and working independently. Pleasant Company has found that using a seasonal support team reduces the transition time from training room to call floor for seasonal agents without negatively affecting customer service.

Using Call Monitoring to Benefit Coaching

Your organization's call monitoring program can provide you with a wealth of information to build a coaching program. While reviewing your call transcripts, look for the following to help you develop a performance improvement plan:

Attitude

- Did the agent meet your standards for tone of voice and overall quality of conversation?
- Did the agent sound genuine or scripted?
- Did the agent lack confidence, experience, or another issue?

Accuracy of Information

- Did the agent capture all the required customer information and process the transaction correctly? If no, is there a pattern that points to a particular skill deficiency?
- Are you looking at accuracy in data entry as well as the information communicated by the agent?

Teamwork

- Did the agent transfer calls properly?
- Is there rapport between team members?
- Do agents help each other with difficult situations?

Customer Satisfaction

- Did the agent control the call without appearing to rush the call?
- Did the agent uncover the customer's needs and offer an appropriate solution?
- Do these variables include average wait time, number of transfers, or difficulty getting through?
- Did customers feel confident in the agent's information, or did they feel it necessary to call back to verify information?
- Is the agent's number of calls per day and average talk time in line with the organization's expectations?
- Are the numbers reasonable given the nature and content of the calls?

- What elements of the call indicate customer satisfaction? Did the agent control the call without appearing to rush the call? Did he or she uncover the customer's needs and offer an appropriate solution? Do these variables include average wait time, number of transfers, or difficulty getting through? Did any of these issues affect the customer's perception of the interaction with the agent? Did the customer feel confident, or did he or she feel it necessary to call back to verify information?

- Is the agent's number of calls per day and average talk time in line with the organization's expectations? Are the numbers reasonable given the nature and content of the calls?

- How many calls can the agent handle without having to escalate to a supervisor? Is this reasonable given the nature and content of the calls as well as the agent's experience?

Once you define criteria, you must communicate expectations to your agents—and you must remember to coach supervisors on how to coach. Conduct the coach training experience so that it provides corrective feedback in a positive way that is specific and timely. If you treat your employees well, they will treat your customers well because they know what they do is important to the success of the organization.

Career Development

A formal career path is important to the success of an operation. In many instances, agent positions are entry-level positions, so it is important to make your agents aware of your organization's career options. The benefits of career development programs include the following:

- distinguishes your organization from its competitors during the hiring process, as well as acts as an ongoing performance incentive

- increases productivity and quality of work as employees build their knowledge of products and systems and develop the ability to handle more complex customer situations

- increases length of service and improves employee retention rates

- increases lateral movement across the organization and develops greater overall business understanding

- improves leadership

- provides more training opportunities

- promotes more frequent and detailed career planning discussions and updated competency profiles

- produces better informed, more proactive employees

Program and Trainer Development

Often, the best call center agents are asked to move into training. They have experience to draw on but may lack the knowledge and skills required to develop effective materials. This can be an effective strategy if you are willing to invest in their professional development in adult learning facilitation and instructional design. Applying these principles and practices will result in training materials that focus on what your agents need to know. You should also make sure to present these materials in a logical sequence that is consistent and supports long-term retention.

For more information on the topics of career development and subject matter experts as trainers, refer to *Info-line*s No. 9410, "Career Systems Development," and No. 9911, "Teaching SMEs to Train."

Another option is to use instructional designers to work with your agents to analyze training needs and design and develop program content. This gives your agents the opportunity to be involved in the development of the content. By bringing in an instructional designer, you develop a more effective program in a shorter period of time by leveraging the professional expertise of both agent and designer.

Start Taking Calls

The information presented in this *Info-line* should have you feeling more comfortable about building or improving your call center. If you are still a little nervous, see if you can answer the following questions with ease:

☐ What are your agent measurement criteria?

☐ Do you have a hiring plan that addresses knowledge, skills, and, most important, attitude?

☐ Does your training program include skill development as well as a transition plan?

☐ What are your strategies for employee retention?

☐ How do you plan to use call monitoring data as a positive coaching tool?

References & Resources

Articles

Armitage, Kathy, and Trish Lambrecht. "Media Reviews." *Training & Development,* April 1999, p. 63.

Berrey, Boone, Murray, Russ-Eft and Winkle. "When Caring Is Not Enough: The Service Providers Evolving Strategic Role." Achieve Global publication.

Davis, Roy. "Smoother Operators." *People Management,* May 6, 1999, pp. 56-57.

Doyle, John C., and Mary D. Carolan. "Calling All Trainers." *Training & Development,* January 1998, pp. 58-67.

Fishman, Charles. "How Can I Help You?" *Fast Company,* October/November 1997, pp. 107-124.

Ganci, Joe. "Case Study: Call Center Training on CD-ROM." *Multimedia & Internet Training Newsletter,* February 1998, pp. 4-5.

George, Michael, and Gary Lowe. "The Right Mix." *Human Resource Executive,* October 4, 1999, pp. 47-50.

Lambrecht, Trish. "Hiring Wizard for CSRs." *Training & Development,* May 1999, p. 96.

Lowe, Dan. "Ensuring New-Hire Success Via 'Transition Training.'" *CCM Review,* September 1999.

Maxwell, Jill Hecht. "The Way Training Should Be." *Inside Technology Training,* September 1999, pp. 14-17.

Mayben, Julia. "1-800-Flowers 'Televersity' Provides Top Notch Training." *CCM Review,* August 1999.

Patton, Carol. "Answering the Call." *Human Resource Executive,* December 1998, p. 31-33.

Stuller, Jay. "Making Call-Center Voices Smile." *Training,* April 1999, p. 26-32.

Thaler-Carter, Ruth. "Why Sit and Answer the Phone All Day?" *HRMagazine,* March 1999, pp. 98-104.

Vartabedian, Matthew. "State-of-the-Art." *Call Center Solutions,* March 1999, pp. 48-54.

Whitehead, Mark. "Churning Questions." *People Management,* September 30, 1999, pp. 46-48.

Internet Articles

Alesys, Marnie Feasel. "Training Can Produce Better Reps." *TMCnet.com, Call Center CRM Solutions.* October 1998. www.tmcnet.com/articles/ccsmag/1098/alesys.htm

Cleveland, Brad. "Polishing Your Act, Getting the Most From Quality Monitoring." *TeleProfessional Magazine.* October 1999. www.teleprofessional.com/issues/9910/9910 polish.htm

Coen, Dan. "The Latest Learning Curve: Recognizing How New Agents View Customer Contact Technologies." *TeleProfessional Magazine.* www.teleprofessional.com/issues/9909/9909_latestlearning.htm

Gherrardi, Linda. "The Impact of Technology on Call Center Training." *TMCnet.com, Call Center Solutions.* August 1999. www.tmcnet.com/articles/ccsmag/0899/0899olsten.htm

Karr, Angela. "Building Balanced Training." *TeleProfessional Magazine.* October 1999. www.teleprofessional.com/issues/9910/9910_build.htm

Mayben, Julia. "Agent Partners Tackle Training Challenges At Today's Merchandising's Call Centers." Call Center Review.

McKee, Judy. "Take Control of the Call." *TeleProfessional Magazine.* 1999. www.teleprofessional.com

Porter, Dianne. "Scripting vs. Training." *TeleProfessional Magazine.* 1999. www.teleprofessional.com

Books

Anderson, Kristin, and Ron Zemke. *Delivering Knock Your Socks Off Service.* New York: AMACOM, 1991.

Cheney, Scott, ed. *Excellence in Practice, Volume 2.* Alexandria, VA: ASTD, 1998.

Fast Company. *How To Find and Hire Stars.* Boston: Fast Company, 1998.

Zeithaml, Valeria A., et al. *Delivering Quality Service: Balancing Customer Perceptions and Expectations.* New York: The Free Press, 1990.

Interviews

Beck, Todd. AchieveGlobal. Portfolio Manager. December 1999.

Bohn, Jim. Johnson Controls, Inc. Director of Integrated Customer Solutions. November 22, 1999.

Fowler, Donna. Strong Mutual Funds. Strong University Specialist. January 2000.

Hay, Carol. Pleasant Company, Director of Call Center Operations. January 6, 2000.

Janssen, Ginny. Pleasant Company, VP of Customer Sales and Service. January 6, 2000.

Checklist for Call Center Agent Development

Use this checklist to ensure that you have a well-rounded agent development plan. If you answer "no" to any of the following questions, you need to create a plan to address those areas.

Agent Development Requirements	Yes	No
1. Have you defined the tasks your agents need to perform?		
2. Have you documented how these tasks are carried out?		
3. Have you established measurement criteria?		
4. Are your measurement criteria linked to your organization's business measures?		

Hiring New Agents		
1. Have you identified your star performers and determined what makes them successful?		
2. Are your hiring criteria based on the attitudes and characteristics of star performers?		
3. Does your hiring process capture the information needed to make the best decisions about job candidates?		
4. Would the use of simulations or performance-based tests improve your selection process?		

New Hire Training		
1. Is the program based on your agent development requirements?		
2. Have you addressed all the required tasks in the most efficient and effective way (for example, formal training, scripting, online help, documentation, and so forth)?		
3. Do delivery methods support your material and development timeframe (for example, class room training, multimedia, online learning, and so forth)?		
4. Do you provide realistic simulations?		
5. Does the interpersonal communication skills component of your program support customer satisfaction requirements?		
6. Does the program address your business processes and applications?		
7. Do you provide agents with sufficient training in your products and services?		
8. Do you provide agents with information about your customers' needs?		

(Job Aid continued on page 158)

Job Aid

Transition Plan	Yes	No
1. Do you have a successful bridge training program that supports an agent's transition from training room to call center floor?		
2. Do you use mentors to support an agent's transition to the job?		

Employee Retention	Yes	No
1. Are agents involved in special projects such as the development of the following: • training programs • call monitoring criteria • script development • business application upgrades • online help systems		
2. Do you provide continuous learning opportunities for agents to further develop their knowledge and skills?		
3. Do call center managers provide adequate agent coaching?		
4. Do you use call monitoring data to identify areas for additional training or coaching?		
5. Do you have a formal plan for career development?		

Sexual Harassment

Sexual Harassment

AUTHORS

Annette M. Cremo, M.Ed.
Performance Plus
Pa. Human Resources Advisors, LLC
1209 Redwood Hills Circle
Carlisle, PA 17013
Tel.: 717.241.6600
Fax: 717.241.6700
Email: acs@epix.net
Web: www.perform-plus.com

Richard C. Gaffney, M.B.A., Esq.
Pa. Human Resource Advisors, LLC
P.O. Box 627
Boiling Springs, PA 17007
Tel.: 717.249.2525
Fax: 717.249.5141
Email: rcglaw@aol.com

Editor
Cat Sharpe Russo

Managing Editor
Sabrina E. Hicks

Contributing Editor
Ann Bruen

Production Design
Anne Morgan
Leah Cohen

What Trainers Need to Know

Sam, a supervisor, asks one of his employees, Debby, to go out with him on a date. Debby refuses, but Sam continues to ask her out.

George, the maintenance man, has pictures of scantily clad women pasted on his locker door. No one has complained to management—yet.

A high school principal gives a student after-school detention for leaving a sexually inappropriate note in a girl's locker and for "accidentally" bumping into her in the hallway.

An admittedly gay employee complains to his foreman that fellow employees are taunting him for being homosexual.

Sandi, a secretary who dates the region manager, has just received a promotion to office manager. She is delighted, but her co-workers are jealous.

Can you identify which, if any, of the above scenarios are actionable sexual harassment? Could you properly investigate a case of alleged sexual harassment? Could you mediate or arbitrate a dispute concerning sexual harassment in the workplace?

Does your organization have in place an effective policy on sexual harassment that includes a complaint procedure? Is management aware that the organization can be held strictly liable for the conduct of its supervisory personnel? Are managers and supervisors aware that they may be held personally liable for conduct that constitutes sexual harassment?

Could you develop and conduct a training course to raise management, supervisory, and employee awareness of sexual harassment? This issue, based on *Info-line* No. 9202, "Sexual Harassment: What Trainers Need to Know," provides the information you need to answer these questions and prepare you to educate and train your workforce on this rapidly evolving area of law. When it comes to sexual harassment, what you (and your organization) don't know can hurt you.

Trainers need to be familiar with all laws and policies that pertain to sexual harassment in the workplace. In the past few years, the public's awareness of workplace sexual harassment has grown greatly. Not surprisingly, the number of sexual harassment lawsuits also has exploded. This has often resulted in expensive and protracted litigation, which could otherwise have been avoided through effective training and development. The following pages contain detailed information regarding the laws and court decisions that affect the field of sexual harassment training, as well as an extensive discussion of the trainer's role and responsibility, plus guidelines for conducting training sessions.

Defining Sexual Harassment

What exactly is "sexual harassment"? What behavior crosses the line? And who exactly decides what conduct rises to the level of being actionable sexual harassment?

The U.S. Congress enacted Title VII of the Civil Rights Act of 1964 to make clear that discrimination on the basis of sex is unlawful. The federal judiciary has found that sexual harassment is a form of sex discrimination and therefore a violation of Sections 703-704 of Title VII of the Civil Rights Act of 1964 *as amended*. These court cases further define what behavior constitutes sexual harassment and what elements a plaintiff must prove for the harassment to be actionable.

EEOC Guidelines

The Equal Employment Opportunity Commission (EEOC) is the federal administrative agency charged with responsibility for investigating filed complaints of sexual harassment. The EEOC has defined the following behavior as constituting sexual harassment:

"Unwelcome sexual advances, requests for sexual favors, and other verbal or physical conduct of sexual nature constitutes sexual harassment when:

1. Submission to such conduct is made either explicitly or implicitly a term or condition of an individual's employment.

2. Submission to or rejection of such conduct by an individual is used as a basis for employment decisions affecting the individual.

3. Such conduct has the purpose or effect of unreasonably interfering with an individual's work performance or creating an intimidating, hostile, or offensive working environment."

In determining whether alleged conduct constitutes sexual harassment, the EEOC will look at the record as a whole and at the *totality of the circumstances,* such as the nature of the sexual advances and the context in which the alleged incidents occurred. The determination of the legality of a particular action will be made from the facts, on a case-by-case basis.

Applying Title VII principles, an employer, employment agency, joint apprenticeship committee, or labor organization (hereinafter "employer") is responsible for its acts, those of its agents, and supervisory employees with respect to sexual harassment, *regardless of whether the specific acts complained of were authorized or even forbidden by the employer and regardless of whether the employer knew or should have known of their occurrences.* The EEOC will examine the circumstances of the particular employment relationship, and the job functions performed, to determine whether a person acts in either a *supervisory or an agency capacity.*

Fellow Employees

With respect to conduct *between fellow employees,* an employer is responsible for acts of sexual harassment in the workplace where the employer, its agents, or supervisory employees, knows or should have known of the conduct—unless the employer can show that it took immediate and appropriate corrective (or remedial) action.

Nonemployees

An employer also may be responsible for the *acts of nonemployees,* with respect to sexual harassment of employees in the workplace, where the employer, its agents, or supervisory employees, knows or should have known of the conduct and fails to take immediate and appropriate corrective action. When examining these cases, the EEOC considers the extent of the employer's control and any other legal responsibility that the employer may have with respect to the conduct of nonemployees.

In other related practices, where employment opportunities or benefits are granted because of an individual's submission to the employer's sexual advances or requests for sexual favors, the employer may be held liable for unlawful sex discrimination against *other persons who were qualified but were denied that employment opportunity or benefit.*

In light of the extensive categories of employer liability for unlawful conduct, prevention is the best tool for elimination of sexual harassment. An employer should take all steps necessary to prevent sexual harassment from occurring by:

● raising the subject affirmatively

● expressing strong disapproval

● developing appropriate sanctions

● informing employees of the right to raise and how to raise the issue of harassment under Title VII

● developing methods to sensitize all employees through training

Workplace Rights and Responsibilities

The sexual harassment cases that have been decided in court have set out clear guidelines for the workplace. The following sections cover the terminology applicable to sexual harassment lawsuits, recent developments, implications for trainers, and the specific rights and responsibilities of employees, supervisors, and organizations.

Terminology

In 1986, the U.S. Supreme Court made clear that Title VII prohibits sexual harassment in the workplace. Since then, numerous cases have defined—and redefined—what constitutes sexual harassment, who may be held liable, and what damages are recoverable in a sexual harassment lawsuit. Traditionally, the law has focused on two main categories of actionable sexual harassment:

1. *Quid pro quo* harassment, in which sexual considerations are demanded in exchange for job benefits.

2. Hostile environment harassment that unreasonably interferes with an individual's job performance, or creates an intimidating, hostile, or offensive work environment, whether or not the harassment is linked to economic job consequences.

Quid pro quo harassment is unwelcome sexual conduct that causes or threatens to cause a tangible job detriment (for example, where an employer extracts or attempts to extract sexual favors either in exchange for favorable job action or under the threat of taking adverse job action).

To establish a *prima facie* case of sexual harassment, a plaintiff must generally demonstrate the following circumstances:

- She or he is a member of the protected class.

- She or he was subjected to unwelcome sexual advances or requests for sexual favors.

- The harassment was based on sex.

- Submission to the unwelcome advances was an expressed or implied condition for receiving a job benefit or avoiding a job detriment.

Plaintiffs alleging **hostile environment** harassment do not need to establish deprivation of a job benefit (the fourth element described above). Instead, a claim is established by proof of unwelcome sexual conduct of such a severe or pervasive nature that it alters the victim's conditions of employment through the creation of an abusive work environment or hostile workplace. Although a single incident can be enough, it will generally be considered "trivial" and therefore not actionable. A key legal issue in establishing a prima facie case of sexual harassment under Title VII is whether the perpetrator's actions were unwelcome.

The Supreme Court made clear in *Meritor Savings Bank v. Vinson* that voluntary compliance with a sexual overture does not prove that the overture itself was welcomed. The court recognized that a solicitation might be unwelcome even when an employee voluntarily participates in a

Glossary

Hostile environment: one of two types of sexual harassment claims; requires showing of frequent, nontrivial acts of a sexual nature that create the effect of a hostile, offensive, or intimidating working environment.

Prima facie: legally sufficient to establish a fact or a case unless disproved.

Quid pro quo: unwelcome activity of a sexual nature in exchange for tangible job benefits or the loss of tangible job benefits because of the rejection of such activity.

Reasonable person/woman: a mythical judicial construct of an individual who thinks and responds the way an ordinary person would under such circumstances.

Sex discrimination: the favoring of one individual or group over another on the basis of gender or stereotypical assumptions associated with gender.

Sexual harassment: a cause of action grounded in sex discrimination; the imposition of unwelcome sexual conduct on an employee in the workplace.

Strict liability: the automatic imposition of liability, regardless of extenuating circumstances or intent.

Unwelcome conduct: behavior that is considered offensive to and undesirable by its recipient; behavior that is not encouraged or incited by its recipient.

Vicarious liability: indirect legal responsibility; for example, liability of an employer for the acts of an employee.

Landmark Sexual Harassment Court Cases

Although Congress enacted Title VII of the Civil Rights Act of 1964, the federal and state courts have breathed life into the concept of sexual harassment. Through thousands of cases, the courts have placed their judicial gloss on the definition of sexual harassment. Here are some of the major cases that outline the courts' evolving definition of the concept.

- *Griggs v. Duke Power* (1971) was one of the first major rulings in the sexual harassment area, establishing that women have a right to compete for all jobs. *Griggs* mandated equal employment opportunity for both men and women.

- *General Electric Company v. Gilbert* (1976) established the illegality of sexual harassment. The court defined sexual harassment as submission to conduct [unwelcome sexual behavior] that is made explicitly or implicitly a term or condition of an individual's employment, a basis for employment decisions affecting the individual, or conduct that unreasonably interferes with an individual's work performance by creating an intimidating, hostile, or offensive environment.

- *Barns v. Costle* (1977) ruled that sexual harassment becomes unlawful only when it is unwelcome, thus clarifying when sexual harassment is illegal.

- *Henson v. City of Dundee* (1982) held that, for harassment to violate Title VII, it must be "sufficiently severe or pervasive" to create an abusive environment and alter the conditions of the victim's employment. *Henson* established that creating a hostile environment by sexual harassment violates Title VII of the Civil Rights Act.

- *Zabowicz v. West Bend Company* (1984) established the "reasonable person" standard. The standard states that the objective standpoint of a "reasonable person" determines whether challenged conduct is of a sexual nature. On the other hand, Title VII does not serve as a vehicle for "vindicating the petty slights suffered by the hypersensitive."

- *Meritor Savings Bank v. Vinson* (1986) determined that employers are liable for the creation of a hostile environment. The court also ruled that voluntary (not forced) submission to sexual activities does not necessarily indicate "welcomeness."

- *Yates v. Avco Corporation* (1987) also expanded the court's position on the liability of the organization. Yates stated that an employer is liable when it has "known, or upon reasonably diligent inquiry should have known," of the alleged harassment.

- *Fields v. Horizon* (1987) defined the "scope of employment." The court found that a supervisor's actions are generally viewed as being within the scope of his or her employment if the actions represent the exercise of authority actually vested in him or her.

- *Kyriazi v. Western Electric* (1981) established the precedent that individual employees or co-workers may be personally liable for acts of sexual harassment.

- *Swentek v. USAir, Inc.* (1987) expanded the definition of "unwelcomeness." The court found that any past conduct of the charging party that is offered to show "unwelcomeness" must relate to the alleged perpetrator of the harassment.

- *King v. Board of Regents of Univ. of Wis.* (7th Cir. 1990) instructed that "although a single act (of harassment) can be enough, … generally, repeated incidents create a stronger claim of hostile work environment with the strength of the claim depending on the number of incidents and the intensity of each incident."

- *Robinson v. Jacksonville Shipyards* (1991) added the "reasonable woman" clause to the "reasonable person" standard. The new standard was necessary because the courts found that women and men often have differing opinions about what sexual harassment is. An action may be considered sexual harassment if a reasonable woman considers it to be sexual harassment.

- *Faragher v. City of Boca Raton* (1998) and *Burlington Industries, Inc. v. Ellerth* (1998) changed the court's focus of inquiry concerning employer vicarious liability for actions of its supervisors and employees. The court's traditional analysis classifies complaints of sexual harassment as being either quid pro quo harassment or hostile environment harassment. In *Faragher* and *Ellerth*, however, the Supreme Court held that where a supervisor's sexual harassment of an employee results in a "tangible employment action," the employer is strictly liable for the harassment regardless of whether the employer knew or should have known about the harassment and regardless of whether the employer took remedial steps to end the harassment after learning of it. Going one step further, the Court said that even when a supervisor's sexual harassment does not result in a "tangible employment action," an employer may still be vicariously liable for the hostile environment created by its supervisor. The Court did allow for an employer defense. To avoid liability in the second class of cases, an employer must show by a preponderance of the evidence that (1) the employer exercised reasonable care to prevent and correct promptly any sexually harassing behavior, and (2) the employee "unreasonably failed to take advantage of any preventive or corrective opportunities provided by the employer to avoid harm."

- *Oncale v. Sundowner Offshore Services, Inc.* (1998) teaches that Title VII covers same-sex sexual harassment. Three federal district courts (in Maine, Minnesota, and New York), however, have been careful to note since then that discrimination based on sexual orientation is not discrimination "based on sex" under Title VII of the Civil Rights Act. Thus, at least in those districts, *Oncale* cannot be read to open the door to claims based on mistreatment of homosexuals in the workplace.

- In *Davis v. Monroe County Board of Education* (1999), the Court held in a 5-4 decision that students harassed by fellow students may sue schools for money damages under Title IX of the 1972 Education Amendments.

Adapted from Info-line *No. 9202, February 1992.*

sexual act, where the threat of adverse employment consequences exists. The correct inquiry, the court explained, "is whether (the plaintiff) by her conduct indicated that the alleged *sexual advances* were unwelcome, not whether her *actual participation* was voluntary." The unwelcome nature of a sexual advance is demonstrated by evidence "that the employee did not solicit or incite it, and the employee regarded the conduct as undesirable or offensive."

Recent Developments

When a plaintiff successfully establishes a prima facie case of sexual harassment, the case is treated as a sex discrimination case under Title VII, and the burden of proof shifts to the defendant.

Employers are held strictly liable for conduct of supervisory personnel that constitutes quid pro quo harassment. An employer's liability for hostile environment harassment depends on the answer to two questions:

1. Can the actions of the harassing supervisor(s) or co-worker(s) be imputed to the employer?

2. Did the employer take prompt and effective remedial action once it received notice of the harassment?

Two important Supreme Court decisions have clarified and redefined the way in which courts will treat vicarious liability of employers for employee claims of sexual harassment in the workplace (see *Faragher v. City of Boca Raton,* and *Burlington Industries, Inc. v. Ellerth,* in *Landmark Sexual Harassment Court Cases* at left).

Implications for Trainers

The *Faragher* and *Ellerth* cases imply that, to avoid liability, employers must not only implement sexual harassment policies but they must also inquire into the harassing behavior of their employees and provide a reasonable mechanism by which employees can report claims of workplace sexual harassment. This enables the employer to take action to prevent and correct promptly any sexually harassing behavior.

Handling Harassment

While it is not legally necessary to take any of the following actions, they may be valuable when dealing with harassment.

- Tell the person you do not like what he or she is doing and ask them to stop. Be specific and be firm.

- Document what is happening in the workplace. Get as much information as you can: who, what, where, when, witnesses, others who were harassed, if you asked the person to stop, what they said or did, and so forth. Always keep copies of your performance appraisals.

- Get support from a friend.

- Let your organization handle the problem through proper channels. Tell someone the harassment is happening—your supervisor or any other supervisor or manager in your organization, or go directly to the Human Resources Department.

- If you need to go outside the organization, other channels include the EEOC or your state agency.

Sexual Harassment Charge Process

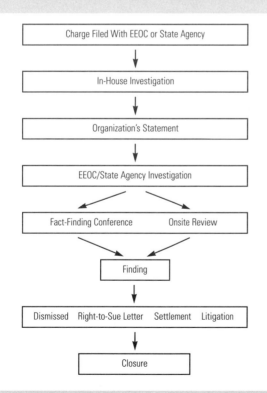

Charge Filed With EEOC or State Agency

↓

In-House Investigation

↓

Organization's Statement

↓

EEOC/State Agency Investigation

↓

Fact-Finding Conference   Onsite Review

↓

Finding

↓

Dismissed   Right-to-Sue Letter   Settlement   Litigation

↓

Closure

Courts will no longer mechanically focus on the existence of a formal sexual harassment policy, and such policies will no longer be an absolute defense to a hostile work environment claim. Indeed, the courts are now rejecting the traditional distinction of quid pro quo and hostile environment claims in favor of an inquiry into whether the alleged perpetrator of the harassment is in a supervisory or non-supervisory position.

These changes in the law imply that employers should reexamine their policies on sexual harassment, actively implement the policies, carefully train supervisory employees (because the employer's vicarious liability for actions of supervisory employees is nearly absolute), and provide a workable mechanism by which employees can report claims of workplace sexual harassment.

Employee Rights and Responsibilities

Employees have a right to work in an environment that is free from sexual harassment and sexual discrimination. So it follows that employees also have a responsibility to conduct their behavior so that they do not sexually harass or intimidate other employees, supervisors, managers, customers, or vendors—or contribute to a hostile, offensive, or intimidating work environment. All employees should understand the following things:

- the organization's policy concerning sexual harassment

- what behavior constitutes sexual harassment

- the procedures to follow if they feel that they have been sexually harassed

- the procedures to follow if they wish to file a complaint of sexual harassment with the state or federal administrative agency (EEOC)

Conducting a Workplace Investigation

When an employee complains that he or she has been the victim of discrimination or harassment, it is imperative that the employer take prompt, effective remedial action. Many organizations outsource workplace investigations to ensure an impartial and unbiased investigation.

A critical part of any investigation is for the employer to generate and maintain solid documentation of the investigation, the employer's conclusions, and the employer's actions taken in response. Before creating any notes, it is important that investigators carefully consider that they are creating a record that may later be reviewed by an administrative agency (like the EEOC), a plaintiff, a plaintiff's attorney, judge, or a jury. Accordingly, a few simple guidelines must be followed:

- Place on paper only the facts received. Avoid editorial comments at all costs.

- Review all notes promptly after creation to check for factual errors, spelling, and grammar.

- Once created, never destroy documents except for working drafts.

Investigation Steps

To conduct an orderly investigation, follow these steps:

1. Begin by recording the facts that you already have.

2. Write down which facts you need to discover.

3. Review the organization's policy on sexual harassment and procedures for handling complaints.

4. Consult with inside or outside counsel to review and update yourself on developments in the law.

5. Engage the services of an independent, "objective" investigator.

6. Outline a plan of who will investigate; what steps will be taken; where you need to go to gather information; when the steps will be completed; and how you will proceed.

7. Ensure that senior management will support the investigation, its objectivity, and its confidentiality and that they are committed to following through on the disciplinary process.

Conducting Interviews

Interviewing techniques are critical to the success of any investigation. Follow these guidelines:

1. Always prepare a list of questions in advance of the interview.

2. Begin by explaining the purpose of the interview to the interviewee.

3. Use the "funnel" technique of questioning. Begin with open-ended and broad-based questions. First ask what the person knows. Then move to specific questions that focus on information you have already obtained.

4. Keep questions simple and direct.

5. Employ "active listening." Paraphrase answers. Reflect information back onto the speaker. Use silence to create subtle pressure to talk.

6. Always ask whether the person has anything to add to what they have already said.

7. Before concluding, review initial questions and notes. Summarize the witnesses' testimony and obtain the witnesses' declaration that the information they have given is true, complete, and accurate.

Writing a Sexual Harassment Policy

It is important for employers to communicate a clear policy on sexual harassment. This policy should include these elements:

- The organization's **values statement** (if one exists) affirming that employees are entitled to a workplace that is free from sexual harassment.

- A citation to currently applicable **federal and state laws** and regulations governing sexual harassment.

- A **working definition** of sexual harassment.

- Specific **complaint procedures,** including alternative channels through which employees can complain.

- Assurances of **confidentiality** throughout the complaint process.

- An **investigative process** that is prompt, impartial, and confidential.

- An **adjudication process,** including who will hear the complaint and how the hearing will proceed following the investigation.

- An **appeal process** for parties who feel aggrieved by the results of the adjudication process.

- A **disciplinary process** that clearly delineates the disciplinary measures that will be administered if there is a sufficient finding of sexual harassment. These measures should allow sufficient flexibility to address proceedings on a case-by-case basis.

- **Procedural rules,** including a timetable for progress through the process. It is important to complete this process thoroughly, but promptly, to preserve employee's legal rights and remedies.

- Clear, consistent **documentation procedures** for the following: the complaint, investigative, adjudication, appeal, and disciplinary processes; record retention; personnel file documentation or expungement; internal management communications; and communications with counsel.

©Annette M. Cremo. Used with permission.

Supervisor Rights and Responsibilities

In addition to the rights and responsibilities they have as employees, supervisors need to understand that their behavior can result in personal liability and in liability for the organization. All supervisors should:

- thoroughly understand what behavior constitutes quid pro quo sexual harassment

- be sensitive to their own behavior and the behavior of the employees around them

- thoroughly understand what conditions might lead to a charge of hostile environment sexual harassment

- take affirmative steps to ensure that all employees understand the organization's policy on sexual harassment

Before harassment happens, supervisors should address their own behavior and awareness level. They should be role models, for their employees will look to their behavior for guidance. Moreover, they should know what is going on in their environment. There are no secrets in the workplace. Indicators that something is not right with a work group include the following:

- absenteeism
- fighting
- people not talking
- increased number of accidents
- poor morale
- low productivity
- increased number of mistakes

If harassment happens, supervisors should take action immediately. They should listen carefully, asking questions that will help put all the information together, but avoid criticism or judgments. Supervisors should inform the appropriate individuals and then conduct an investigation in accordance with the proper investigative and documentation procedures set up by the organization.

Organization Responsibility

A checklist of an organization's responsibility should include the following items:

☐ Adopt a no-harassment, zero-tolerance stance.

☐ Issue a policy and post it in many places in the organization.

☐ Distribute the policy to all employees.

☐ Train the entire workforce about the laws on sexual harassment as well as the policy.

☐ Be sure all new hires are trained.

☐ Provide managers and supervisors with additional training in communication skills, listening skills, negotiation skills, dealing with conflict, and the performance management systems. This ensures they are equipped with the tools they need to handle situations as they arise.

☐ Reinforce the information whenever possible. This could be done during organization meetings, during supervisory meetings, or as updates in memos.

☐ Reward appropriate behaviors.

☐ Practice what is taught. Be sure all management and supervisory personnel live the policy through their actions and words. A proactive supervisor or manager can put an end to inappropriate behavior and set the tone for the organization.

☐ Take action immediately should any complaints of sexual harassment arise.

Trainer Role and Responsibility

News coverage of sexual harassment and inappropriate behavior abounds. This coverage presents landmark decisions regarding what is appropriate and not appropriate in the workplace. It also tells of the huge awards victims receive due to certain workplace behavior that is prohibited by law.

What inappropriate behaviors occur in organizations that we know about, yet choose to ignore? How much goes on that we are unaware of? To restrict such inappropriate behavior, trainers must be the eyes and ears of the organization. They should work in tandem with management and human resources to help make the workforce aware of laws, policies, and the prevention of sexual harassment.

Many things that we do are subject to guidelines. Fishing rules and regulations, hunting rules, and guidelines for using equipment all exist so we know what we can do in that environment and what we should and should not do. Sometimes these rules are self-explanatory, and sometimes we need help in understanding them.

The guidelines for preventing sexual harassment in the workplace are no different. They tell us what we can and cannot do to maintain a harassment-free environment. Some rules are easy to understand, and some are a bit confusing. Yet, some organizations do nothing more than place a policy in the employee handbook—and hope the law will be followed.

Trainers help translate that law into appropriate behaviors in the workplace. They are integral to this process because their role requires them to do the following things:

● know what the laws are

● assist in the change process

● inform all employees (through a well-designed training process)

Content Trainers Need to Know

When teaching about sexual harassment, trainers need to be very familiar with all laws and policies that pertain to sexual harassment in the workplace. For example, there are federal laws, state laws, and organizational policies. State laws vary, and some states hold supervisors and managers personally liable for "aiding and abetting in an act of discrimination." In essence, if they themselves harass someone, or if they knew or had reason to know of such behavior in the workplace, they can be held personally liable.

Frequently Asked Questions

Training participants often ask similar questions to clarify acceptable behavior. Here are some of them—as well as the answers.

Where is the line? There is no line to cross that will make your behavior suddenly harassing. Harassment is something we do not like. What is harassment for one person may not be harassment for another.

Why can't people just leave if they don't like my jokes? People have jobs that require them to work at specific places. Leaving would adversely affect their job performance. They have a right to a job environment free from unlawful harassment.

Why are supervisors and managers liable for sexual harassment charges? According to some state statutes and some state common law, supervisors act as agents for the organization and can be liable for their own harassing behavior and for behavior they are aware of and choose to ignore.

What is my responsibility if I see one of my employees or another supervisor acting inappropriately? You must take action immediately. Remember your job as a supervisor is to maintain a harassment-free environment.

As an employee, if I see inappropriate behavior occurring, what is my responsibility? Legally you are not responsible for reporting such activity. But we all should help prevent harassment in the workplace. Tell your supervisor or any member of management immediately.

Can men be sexually harassed? Yes. While 91 percent of reported cases are filed by women, men can also be victims of sexual harassment. Men do not report incidents of sexual harassment for fear of ridicule or fear that some co-workers will make it more difficult on them if they tell.

We have 20 employees; are we covered by the law? Yes, you are covered under federal law. Organizations with fewer than 15 employees may be covered under another law applicable to their specific state, industry, or occupation. If you are unsure, consult legal counsel.

Must I tell the harasser I am offended by his or her behavior? It is not a legal requirement that you tell the harasser you are offended by the behavior for the behavior to be considered sexual harassment.

Remember that every new court case shapes the law. It is imperative that trainers partner with the human resources department or have a legal contact to keep abreast of how laws are changing. Trainers also must be thoroughly aware of the organization's policy prohibiting sexual harassment. Some of these policies are more inclusive than federal and state law, incorporating legal rulings prohibiting age and disability discrimination (ADEA—Age Discrimination in Employment Act, and ADA—Americans with Disabilities Act).

Facilitating the Change

The face of the workplace has changed, laws have changed, and our workplace and employees must adapt if they are to survive and thrive. We all have a right to work in an environment that is free from unlawful harassment. To that end, the government has stepped in and given organizations guidelines for appropriate workplace behavior. Just as there is a code of conduct where we shop, where we socialize after work, and in our own homes, so is there a code of conduct in the workplace. Federal and state laws as well as organizational policies describe that code of conduct.

In some cases, we are asking our workforce to change the way they conduct themselves at work. Long-held patterns of behavior are no longer acceptable. Greater numbers of women and employees of diverse ethnicity have entered the workforce. Each of us has our own sensitivities, and we must respect one another's differences. Training teaches people what behavior is inappropriate, what behavior could be viewed as harassment, and which situations constitute sexual harassment.

Because change is uncomfortable for some people, they will be more amenable if they know why they are changing and what benefits they will achieve. Training must facilitate that change process in a nonthreatening way. Be firm about your stance on the laws and about what is appropriate and inappropriate in the workplace. Nevertheless, be cognizant of how the participants perceive and accept this information, understanding that there might be resistance at first. Overcome resistance by listening to participants' concerns and modeling behaviors that you expect of them.

Assure participants that adhering to laws and organization policy will help the workplace become one that is healthy and harassment free.

Uncertainty about personal behavior is disconcerting to some. All training sessions include such questions as: "Where is the line?" or "How much can I do before I'm harassing someone?" That clear-cut line, in some instances, does not exist. Certainly, standards for appropriate and inappropriate behavior are clear. The line that tells a person when harassment starts is not as clear, however. What is harassment for one person, may not be harassment for another. Tell participants to stop and think before they engage in a questionable behavior, asking themselves, "What would my significant other (spouse, children, parents) think if they saw me behaving in this way?" To assist you in your training, see the sidebar opposite for a list of frequently asked questions and their answers.

Designing and Delivering the Training

Ideally, a male-female team should deliver the training. This helps break down any communication barriers between men and women in the audience. Of course this is not always possible. Therefore, it is important that you be sensitive and impartial. In many cases, training participants think sexual harassment is a male-versus-female issue. It is not. It is an individual issue, and it is about treating one another with respect.

Set up the training room to encourage participation and discussion. Be sure that you can interact with participants, and that participants can interact with one another. This training session might be the first opportunity members of the opposite sex have to talk honestly to one another.

In designing and conducting the training, break the content into digestible "chunks." Be sure to continually check for understanding after each chunk of information. For example, ask questions about the material, develop scenarios or case studies, or design short quizzes.

Introduction

Begin the training by giving an overview about harassment in the workplace—how prevalent it is, how it affects organizations, and how it can affect their lives or the lives of individuals they care about. Next, give participants an overview of what you will accomplish during the training session as well as the sequence of events. Review session goals and objectives for a clear understanding of what will be accomplished during the training.

If time permits, begin the training with an icebreaker—one that can be done in pairs. A good example is: "I'd like you and your partner to think of one question or piece of information you would like to know about sexual harassment. You can present this verbally or write it on an index card." At the conclusion of the icebreaker, ask each pair to share their response to your request. Post the answers where everyone can see them, and be sure to answer each concern by the end of the class. This activity gives you a gauge of their thoughts and concerns on the subject matter.

Give participants a pretest to open dialogue in the subject matter (see the job aid at the end of this issue). Encourage them to challenge anything they might find confusing or to seek clarification in areas where they need information. The pretest is designed to provide an overview of the material to be covered in the session, and the test results will give the trainer a flavor for the general knowledge of participants as well as their attitudes.

Core Content

The next part of the training focuses on a historical perspective of the law, both federal and state. Explain how it began, and take it to the point where it is today. During this time, explain the provisions of the law. For example, go over in detail both quid pro quo and hostile environment harassment and give detailed examples of both types. After explaining the law, read the organization's policy to explain and clarify its content—and to ensure that everyone has heard (not just read) it.

Examples provide a vivid picture of acceptable and unacceptable behavior. As you read or hear stories of actual occurrences in the workplace, make note of the general issues surrounding the examples and use them for future training. Nothing hits home harder than situations people can relate to.

Scenarios provide a check for understanding and give participants opportunities to apply analytical skills. They provide situations in which participants must decide if the described behavior is or is not sexual harassment. In addition, they must identify the rationale for their decision. A video may be included at this point to help reinforce learning through a different medium. The following is a sample scenario:

Dru was the only woman in the crew. All of the men on the crew really did not want her there because she was awarded the job over one of their friends. Besides, the work they did they thought was a "man's" job. Dru did the job quite well— sometimes even better than her male counterparts. While there were no sexual jokes or pressuring for dates, the men would flatten the tires on her truck, put sugar in the gas tank, change the locks on the locker, or put petroleum jelly on the steering wheel. She did not like what was happening and complained to the supervisor. His response was, "They are just initiating you into the crew; you got to take it like one of the guys."

Was the supervisor right in what he said? What is your rationale?

Is this a case of harassment?

The next segment of the training session reviews the rights and responsibilities of employees and supervisors and the consequences organizations face when harassment occurs. A segment follows detailing steps to take if an employee is sexually harassed. When conducting supervisory training,

be sure to detail specific supervisor responsibilities and liabilities. Supervisors and managers should then be given a chance to practice skills associated with handling claims of sexual harassment. Practicing in this nonthreatening environment allows participants to make and correct mistakes during the training session—not when they return to the work environment.

Summary

The session ends with an examination of case studies specific to the organization. Make the examples real to the participants by incorporating organizational terminology and situations that are potentially possible. During the debriefing of the scenarios, allow participants to explore "what if" situations. Although they will look to the trainer for the "correct" answers, encourage participants to explore options themselves and discover the appropriate determination.

In conclusion, explore what an organization free from unlawful harassment and discrimination looks like. How do people communicate? How do they interact? Allow participants to envision such a future for their own organization.

Putting It All Together

No two situations are alike. No two people are alike. What is right in one case does not apply to another. What trainers give participants is a guidebook or the rules of the road. In driving we know it is illegal to speed, yet how many of us go over the speed limit, watching at every turn for the flashing red lights. Some of us get caught; some of us do not. The same is true with the laws surrounding sexual harassment. Trainees will know the laws and the policy of the organization. They will know what is right and what is inappropriate. If they choose to break the laws, they know the consequence of their action.

Sample Curriculum

Session Objectives

At the conclusion of this workshop, participants will be able to do the following things:
- thoroughly understand and apply the organization's nonharassment policy
- discuss and apply federal laws, specifically Title VII, to workplace situations
- understand the applicable state laws
- define sexual harassment
- define discrimination
- identify sexual harassment in the workplace
- distinguish what is, what is not, and what could be sexual harassment
- understand implications of noncompliance
- describe supervisors' responsibilities in preventing sexual harassment
- deal effectively with and use proper procedures and organizational channels for complaints of sexual harassment
- identify appropriate and inappropriate behaviors in the workplace

Session Outline

I. Introduction
   A. Brief icebreaker and introductions.
   B. Reality check—what do we really know? Pretraining quiz (small group and discussion).
   C. Session objectives, outline, and logistics.
   D. The organization's policy.
II. Definitions and Provisions
   A. Definitions and terminology.
   B. Title VII.
   C. State law.
   D. Definition of sexual harassment as related to the law.
   - Quid pro quo.
   - Hostile environment.
   - What type of harassment it is (group exercise).
   E. Appropriate and inappropriate behavior.
   F. Scenarios (a small group activity to check for understanding).
VIDEO
BREAK
III. Roles and Responsibilities
   A. Employee responsibilities.
   B. Supervisor responsibilities.
   C. Procedures.
   D. Organizational responsibilities in maintaining a harassment-free environment.
   E. Case studies (to check for understanding of sexual harassment and of the methods for handling complaints).
   F. Debrief case studies "question-and-answer" session.
   G. Evaluation.

©Annette M. Cremo. Used with permission.

References & Resources

Articles

Baridon, Andrea P., and David R. Eyler. "Workplace Etiquette for Men and Women." *Training,* December 1994, pp. 31-37.

Barrier, Michael. "Sexual Harassment." *Nation's Business,* December 1998, pp. 14-19.

Bloch, Gerald D. "Avoiding Liability for Sexual Harassment." *HRMagazine,* April 1995, pp. 91-97.

Carmell, William. "Another Look at Sexual Harassment: Implications of the 1998 Supreme Court Decisions." *Diversity Facto,* Spring 1999, pp. 34-38.

Clark, Kathryn F. "Hands-Off Training." *Human Resource Executive,* January 1999, pp. 77-78.

Cole, Joanne. "Sexual Harassment: New Rules, New Behavior." *HRFocus,* March 1999, p. 1.

Crawford, Susan. "A Brief History of Sexual Harassment Law." *Training,* August 1994, pp. 46-49.

Fisher, Anne B. "After All This Time, Why Don't People Know What Sexual Harassment Means?" *Fortune,* January 12, 1998, p. 156.

Gallagher, Maureen M. "EEOC Speaks Plainly About Sexual Harassment." *HRFocus,* May 1994, p. 19.

Ganzel, Rebecca. "What Sexual Harassment Training Really Prevents." *Training,* October 1998, pp. 86-94.

Garland, Susan. "Finally, a Corporate Tip Sheet on Sexual Harassment." *Business Week,* July 13, 1998, p. 39.

Garvin, Stacey J. "Employer Liability for Sexual Harassment." *HRMagazine,* June 1991, p. 6.

Harris, Gloria G., and David A. Tansey. "Relearning Relationships." *HRMagazine,* September 1997, pp. 116-120.

Kirshenberg, Seth. "Sexual Harassment: What You Need to Know." *Training & Development,* September 1997, pp. 54-55.

Laabs, Jennifer. "What You're Liable for Now." *Workforce,* October 1998, pp. 34-42.

Mallery, Michael P. "The Answers to Your Questions About Sexual Harassment." *Workforce Tools,* (Supplement), November 1997, pp. 7-9.

Moore, Herff L., Rebecca W. Gatlin-Watts, and Joe Cangelosi. "Eight Steps to a Sexual-Harassment-Free Workplace." *Training & Development,* April 1998, pp. 12-13.

Parliman, Gregory. "The Evolving Case Law of Sexual Harassment." *Employee Relations Law Journal,* Winter 1995/1996, pp. 77-87.

Payson, Martin F. "Avoiding the High Costs of Sexual Harassment: Beyond Sexual Harassment." *Supervisory Management,* January 1994, p. 10.

Pope, Barbara Spyridon. "Handling Sexual Harassment." *Across the Board,* March 1996, p. 57.

Raphan, Melissa, and Max Heerman. "Eight Steps to Harassment-Proof Your Office." *HRFocus,* August 1997, pp. 11-12.

Reynolds, Sana. "Confronting Sexual Harassment." *US Banker,* July 1996, pp. 79-81.

Risser, Rita. "Sexual Harassment Training: Truth and Consequences." *Training & Development,* August 1999, pp. 21-23.

Solomon, Charlene Marmer. "Don't Forget the Emotional Stakes." *Workforce,* October 1998, pp. 52-58.

Books

Baridon, Andrea P., and David R. Eyler. *Sexual Harassment Awareness Training: 60 Practical Activities for Trainers.* New York: McGraw-Hill, 1996.

Cornish, Tony, ed. *Zero Tolerance: An Employer's Guide to Preventing Sexual Harassment and Healing the Workplace.* Rockville, MD: BNA Communications, 1997.

Fitzwater, Terry. *The Manager's Pocket Guide to Preventing Sexual Harassment.* Amherst, MA: HRD Press, 1998.

Orlov, Darlene, and Michael T. Roumell. *What Every Manager Needs to Know About Sexual Harassment.* New York: AMACOM, 1999.

Info-line

Talley, B.D., and M.L. Waller. "Sexual Harassment: What Trainers Need to Know." No. 9202 (out of print).

Other

9 to 5, The National Organization for Working Women. 1430 W. Peachtree St., Ste. 610, Atlanta, GA 30309. Tel.: 800.522.0925.

Pretraining Assessment

Administer this questionnaire to participants prior to sexual harassment awareness training. Have them read each of the statements below and mark the appropriate box. The answer code follows on the next page.

	True	False
1. According to recent Supreme Court decisions, once an organization issues a policy prohibiting sexual harassment, distributes the policy, and conducts training, it can no longer be held liable for sexual harassment in the workplace.	☐	☐
2. If a supervisor asks an employee for sexual favors in return for job benefits, it is all right as long as both parties agree.	☐	☐
3. In the workplace, it is all right to tell a person they look nice.	☐	☐
4. Supervisors have no power in preventing sexual harassment.	☐	☐
5. Some states have laws preventing harassment in the workplace.	☐	☐
6. Sexual harassment is a form of discrimination.	☐	☐
7. We must treat alleged harassers fairly in the workplace. Therefore, we must tell them we don't like their behavior and give them a chance to stop before filing a complaint.	☐	☐
8. Criminal charges can be filed along with charges of sexual harassment.	☐	☐
9. Today's dress and behavior norms are causes of sexual harassment.	☐	☐
10. Organizations should allow supervisors to always conduct sexual harassment investigations because their employees feel most comfortable talking with them.	☐	☐
11. It is difficult for individuals to come forward with a complaint because they feel it is embarrassing, they fear retaliation, or the organization just will not do anything about the complaint.	☐	☐
12. Once there is proof of harassment, organizations must take a firm stance and apply appropriate disciplinary action, which may include termination.	☐	☐
13. There are very few cases of men filing sexual harassment charges because few things are harassing to men.	☐	☐
14. According to federal law, there are four types of sexual harassment: hostile environment, criminal acts, quid pro quo, and inappropriate dress.	☐	☐
15. Some organizations are using external investigators to investigate claims of sexual harassment because of their expertise in that specific area.	☐	☐

(Job Aid continued on page 176)

Job Aid

Answer Code

1. False. Organizations are ultimately liable for what happens in the workplace.

2. False. This could be considered quid pro quo type of harassment.

3. True. We don't want to take the humanness out of the workplace. Simply telling a person they look nice is all right.

4. False. Supervisors can prevent harassment in the workplace. They can tell employees about the policy, reinforce it at meetings, post the policy where employees can see it, and most important, model appropriate behavior.

5. True.

6. True. According to Title VII of the Civil Rights Act as amended.

7. False. You can file a complaint without telling someone you do not like what they are doing. You are not legally required to tell them, and telling them does not guarantee they will stop.

8. True.

9. False. Just because someone dresses inappropriately does not give us cause to harass him or her. We are in control of what we say and what we do at all times.

10. False. Sometimes it is supervisor who is doing the harassing.

11. True.

12. True.

13. False. While it is true men have a higher tolerance for certain behaviors, they do not file charges because they fear what others might say, or because if they do tell someone, it is brushed off.

14. False. Only hostile environment and quid pro quo.

15. True.

Customer Service Management

Customer Service Management

Issue 9901

AUTHOR

Karl Albrecht
Karl Albrecht International
3120 Old Bridgeport Way, #100
San Diego, CA 92111
Tel: 619.576.3535
Fax: 619.576.3536
Email: karl@albrechtintl.com
Web: www.albrechtintl.com

Karl Albrecht is a management consultant, futurist, speaker, and author—having written more than 20 books on business performance, including the best-seller *Service America!: Doing Business in the New Economy.* He has lectured and provided consulting to executives worldwide.

Editor
Cat Sharpe

Associate Editor
Sabrina E. Hicks

Production Design
Anne Morgan

ASTD Internal Consultant
Pam Schmidt

Customer Service Management

What Is Service Management?

Service management is a total organizational approach that makes *customer-perceived value* the number one driving force for the operation of the business. It involves a new competitive focus, a new organizing paradigm, and a new vocabulary. It manifests its influence in an intense focus on winning and keeping the customer's business by delivering a *superior experience of value* to every customer. It has nothing to do with slogans, platitudes, motivational campaigns, or advertising promises. It tests all behaviors, practices, systems, and strategies against one overarching question: Does this enable us to build and sustain a competitive advantage?

Many outstanding service businesses use this model (such as Federal Express, British Airways, Disney, Ritz Carlton Hotels, Beth Israel Hospital, and the Japan National Railway). Each of these companies expresses the principles in its own particular language, and each uses its own unique means for achieving the core objective of *strategic customer focus.* But all of them subscribe to a set of core beliefs, values, principles, and practices that enable them to stay in the lead in their particular industry.

What makes service management distinctly different from traditional industrial management is the way in which the concept of *customer value,* as a priority, dominates all aspects of the organization's operation. In a typical industrially managed organization, the focus of attention is inward, on the compartmentalized systems and processes that produce the "output." In a service managed organization, the focus of attention is outward. The value delivery priorities do not stop at the boundaries between various internal units; instead, they cross over the boundaries and serve as a unifying focus of attention for everyone in the business.

Service management does not treat cost-efficient management practices as antagonistic to strategic customer focus. Instead it treats them as two sides of the same coin. There may be necessary trade-offs to be made in various cases, but in general, profit and customer value are treated as two factors to be co-optimized.

This *Info-line* explains how this process for strategic customer focus gives service businesses a competitive edge. After pointing out the importance of changing the organization's mindset and describing how service management works, this issue provides you with models, such as the *service triangle* and the *customer value model,* to guide you in making your organization more customer focused. The glossary on the next page defines any unfamiliar terms associated with this change model, and the job aid located at the end of this issue helps you view your organization from the customer's perspective.

Why Is Service Management Important?

Revolutionizing the culture and the thinking processes of a sizable corporation, government agency, university, or any other such organizational creature is no small challenge. Many intelligent and capable executives have tried and failed. Researchers who study the process of change management report astonishingly low rates of success for major "campaign"-type efforts to shift organizations out of their comfortable patterns of operation. The long-term impact of the majority of such campaigns is nearly nil.

Any experienced organizational consultant can tell more stories of big internal campaigns that failed than of ones that succeeded and delivered lasting results. It is hard to find any large organization—whether bank, brokerage organization, insurance company, hospital, telephone company, or airline—that has not launched an ambitious "customer service" program only to see it arc across the sky, burn brightly for a few months (or weeks), and then flame out and fall to earth. After six months, nobody mentions it any more, and, after a year, half of the people cannot remember what it was supposed to do. Many large-company cultures are characterized by cynicism about top management's "next big program," and this adds to the effect of the usual level of apathy and inertia.

Fizzle Factor

This "fizzle factor"—the tendency of organizational change efforts to stall out and die in the face of monolithic, inertial resistance by the population of the organization—has dogged the steps of every major new management theory that has claimed to revolutionize some aspect of business operations.

Glossary

A new paradigm requires a new language, a concise vocabulary for conveying its important concepts. Service management incorporates a special vocabulary that signals its focus on value creation. Following are some of the more important terms in the lexicon of service management:

Service triangle: the model that portrays strategic customer focus as a matter of aligning the organization's strategy, people, and systems around the needs of its customers.

Customer value package: the special combination of things and experiences that go together to create value for the customer.

Strategic value hierarchy: a progression of stages for delivering customer value, ranging from simple products through transactions, solutions, relationships, and shared successes.

Differentiation: a state of affairs in which the customer can recognize a significant and valuable difference between the value packages offered by various competitors.

Value proposition: the core benefit premise that gives your customer value package its competitive appeal.

Customer value model: a set of critical criteria or attributes of the service experience that define the customer's perception of value received.

Moments of truth: the many individual episodes or points of perception in which customers come into contact with the organization and make judgments about the value they receive.

Cycles of service: a series of moments of truth that go together in a natural sequence to create an experience of value for one customer.

Service blueprint: a time-flow diagram that portrays the interaction during a cycle of service between one customer and the various people or functions that deliver the service experience.

Critical practices: simple but effective procedures that can be used by employees to reinforce the customers' perceptions of value received. Also called **protocols.**

Total Quality Service (TQS): a set of five change-management methodologies aimed at strategic customer focus, ranging from market and customer research, through strategy formulation, communication and training, process improvement, and scorekeeping.

Management by Objectives (MBO), Total Quality Management (TQM), reengineering, and other change models (such as ISO 9000) fell below the expectations of executives in service businesses, not because their tools and methods were flawed but because they were typically applied with the manufacturing mindset—not the service management mindset. An organization is a living thing, with a culture, a sociology, a way of thinking, an ethos, a set of values, a history, and a tradition. Any change model, and its supporting mindset, that views an organization as an apparatus to be "reengineered" is doomed to fail. The only plausible hope is that it does as little damage as possible.

Changing the Mindset

These various theories were basically attempts to do the same thing, only harder. All were basically sideshows to the fundamental shift in the management paradigm that is taking place. They were rooted in the "factory" mindset (that is, the world view that sees people, processes, and machinery as simply "resources" to be moved about, used, and adjusted so that the whole "machine" works properly).

As the so-called "customer revolution" was gathering steam in the late 1980s and early 1990s, advocates of TQM, reengineering, and even ISO 9000 became keenly interested in applying those models to the problems of "customer service." After all, they reasoned, if service is 70 percent of the U.S. economy and a large part of most other developed economies, why not go where the opportunities are? This led to a number of attempts to "systematize" service, complete with specifications for smiling a determined number of times while talking with the customer, reciting the customer's name in conversation, and answering the telephone within three rings. These kinds of episodes still occur frequently in large companies—reminding us that the industrial mindset is very difficult for many people to relinquish.

Service Management at Work

This system works by guiding the thought processes —and consequently the behavior—of everyone who embraces it, helping them to align their energies toward the overall strategic objective of delivering superior value to the organization's customers. It creates meaning and focus. That is the short answer.

The long answer involves a set of conceptual models that enable leaders to decide the following:

- what the organization's particular brand of customer focus should look like

- how it should organize and operate to achieve that focus

- how the people in the organization can define and carry out the critical practices that actually deliver that value

- how to accurately evaluate the success of the organization's practices in creating preference in the minds of its customers

The Service Triangle

Service management demands careful attention to all levels of the business operation—from the highest levels of strategy formulation, to the various organizational levels and structures, to the delivery of the customer experience at the front line. It

The Service Triangle

The *service triangle* enables an organization's leaders to bring together the critical truths of its business strategy, the needs of its culture, and the design of its infrastructure into a unified concept for competitive success. By placing the customer at the center of the triangle, they are declaring that the *customer value model* (that is, the set of critical attributes of the service experience that drive the customer's buying behavior) will guide the decisions about how the organization operates.

The *business strategy,* at the top of the triangle, spells out the organization's unique way of winning and keeping the customer's business, with its particular *customer value package* (that is, the combination of things and experiences it offers the customer). This customer value package is based on a carefully chosen *value proposition* (that is, the fundamental benefit premise that gives the organization's offering its competitive appeal).

The *people* part of the service triangle refers to the entire culture of the organization, not just to the front-line "service delivery" people. In a service culture, people think of their personal success as connected to the success of the enterprise, and they treat one another with the same respect, cooperation, and added-value spirit they offer to the paying customers. The various departments in the organization treat one another as customers as well—concentrating more on contribution than competition. An organization's culture can be one of its best competitive weapons, or it can be a competitive handicap. Ultimately, the way your employees feel is the way your customers will feel.

The *systems* part of the triangle refers to the entire infrastructure of the organization. All organizational structures, functional relationships, physical facilities, information systems, procedures, rules, and regulations should be *customer friendly* in their design. They should make it as easy as possible for the people in the organization to implement the strategic customer focus and deliver an outstanding experience to the customers at the many *moments of truth,* (that is, the individual episodes or points of perception at which the customers come into contact with various aspects of the organization and make judgments about the value it offers).

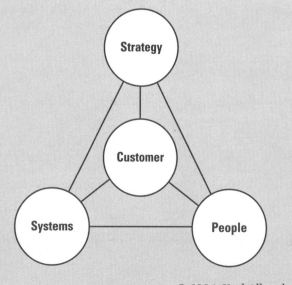

© 1984, Karl Albrecht.

requires an enormous breadth of attention on the part of the organization's leaders and the ability to think on many levels, a challenge for most executives. It requires a person with this breadth of vision to make it work, as well as the energy to implement it in every dimension of the operation.

The one model that spans this full range of thinking, from the strategic level to the tactical level, is the *service triangle* (see previous page). It forms the core of the service management concept and provides the conceptual "checklist" for evaluating the organization's progress toward its goal of strategic customer focus.

The real power of the service triangle as a thinking model for running a service business is the way it *integrates* the key components of customer value, business strategy, people, and systems into a unified concept. The strategy must be connected to the customer value model. The people must understand and implement the strategy. The systems must support the people in creating value. Each of the connecting lines defines a crucial dimension of the total concept of strategic customer focus.

Customer Value Model

The following is a customer value model for a typical hospital stay. Understanding what the customer (that is, the patient) sees as the basic and critical appeal of his or her hospitalization helps hospital executives discuss with customers the critical elements of a hospital stay.

The customer values the following during his or her hospital stay:

- empowerment as a customer
- trust in systems, continuity, and teamwork
- quality of clinical results
- comfort—physical and emotional
- respect for family and friends
- information and education
- coordination with other caregivers
- costs of treatment

Customer Value Model

One of the key starting points for adopting a strategic customer focus is finding out what the customer is really trying to buy when he or she confronts the business. People do not buy "products" or "services"; they buy *value.* They buy solutions to their problems, answers to their needs, and improvements in their lives. The first critical skill of service management is learning to think in customer-value terms. The customer value model enables you to accomplish this.

Discovering and defining the customer's value model is the first step in learning how to deliver it. How can you win the customer's business if you do not know what he or she really wants and does not want? Modern customer research methods focus on helping the customer tell you, in his or her own language and perspective, what the real value proposition is. What is the most basic and critical appeal of the service experience to the customer? Once you clearly understand this value proposition, you can engage in a dialogue with the customer that will help you discover the critical elements of the service experience that make it real. The sidebar at left shows a typical customer value model for a hospital stay.

Another critical skill of service management is *customer-experience thinking.* You need to help everyone in the organization understand what the service experience actually looks and feels like to the customer. This is where the traditional industrial model of management has failed so completely—it insists on describing events from the organization's point of view, not from the customer's point of view.

People working in an organization tend to think in terms of their individual departments and their local functional specialties and procedures. Their picture of the customer experience is a never-ending sequence of repeating encounters, as the individual customers come and go. The customer, however, tends to view the service experience as a unified sequence of events—the "moments of truth"—all connected into a single chain of experience, or a *cycle of service,* as shown on the following page.

For example, one person in a hospital may draw blood from the arm of the customer (formerly referred to as a "patient"), with no knowledge or concern for the person's previous or next experience. However, the customer who is undergoing a complete physical examination sees the experience as part of a total package. Similarly, the typical department store presents itself to the customer as a disconnected set of unrelated shopping areas, which the customer must visit one at a time. The customer, however, who is shopping for a complete set of clothes, including accessories, thinks in terms of the entire experience of acquiring what he or she wants. If the individual service person understands the customer's entire cycle of service, he or she can do more to make the entire experience a success.

The Business Strategy

Defining the competitive business strategy in terms of customer focus means deciding what kind of a total value package to offer. Different kinds of businesses have different kinds of challenges, and, therefore, different possibilities in designing the value package.

Some service businesses have simple value packages that require little skill, knowledge, or style to deliver. Fast food businesses, for example, typically provide a convenient, low-priced meal experience with little embellishment. Their customers typically expect no more of them. However, an enterprise with a more complex value proposition (such as a stock brokerage, university, or airline) has more challenges and more options for building customer preference.

Think of the organization's way of doing business with its customers as involving a set of possible choices along a spectrum, or a *strategic value hierarchy*, as illustrated on the following page.

In the service management way of thinking, organizational leaders must find the highest level on the strategic value hierarchy that makes sense for their line of business and focus on competing effectively at that level of value delivery. For example, if you place your business on both the product and transaction levels, speed, convenience, and low price are the critical value factors for you—and everyone in the organization must learn how to perform within that particular set of requirements. If you place your business on the levels of solutions and relationships, then information, advice, expertise, and special knowledge are

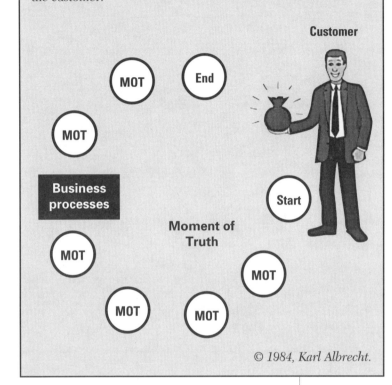

The Cycle of Service

The customer views the service experience as a unified sequence of events in which each moment of truth (MOT) connects to form a single chain of experience. Understanding this *cycle of service* helps service people provide a successful experience for the customer.

© 1984, Karl Albrecht.

required—and everyone must learn how to deliver those as cost-effectively as possible.

The People Involved

For people to make their best individual and collective contributions to the success of the organization, they must be Ready, Willing, and Able.

■ *Ready*
They need to have the resources—the tools, information, and methods necessary—to do their jobs effectively. They need to have clear direction, good leadership, and effective support from their supervisors. They need the support of an infrastructure, which is often information-driven, that helps them create value for their external paying customers and for their internal customers as well.

Strategic Value Hierarchy

At the simplest level, the customer buys only a *product*, such as an item of food, a pair of shoes, or a magazine subscription. There might be a simple transaction connected with the purchase, but it is involved only as a matter of necessity. Typically, this moment of truth stands alone in time; it has no history and no future. Neither the customer nor the server expects anything further of the other.

The *transaction* level is somewhat more complex—but still typically limited in time and scope. Opening a new bank account may take a bit longer and involve more discussion and assistance on the part of the server than buying a meal. It may also offer more opportunities for the server to enhance the customer's perception of value received. Once it is finished, however, it also passes into history. It will probably not be remembered by either party unless there was some mistake or the customer has a change of mind.

The *solution* level offers some extra possibilities for adding value to the customer's experience and possibly paves the way for future business. At the product or transaction level, the customer buys a computer system and takes it home or to the office. But at the solution level, the person selling the system helps the customer select a system and the related software and materials that will best meet his

or her needs. Doctors, lawyers, accountants, and consultants often operate at this level. Many businesses that see themselves as selling products and transactions could benefit by increasing their emphasis on the solution level.

As the customer value package becomes more complex and more diversified, it can move to the level where the *relationship* between customer and provider is more significant than the products, transactions, or even solutions. People like stockbrokers, real estate brokers, accountants, and consultants can capitalize on this possibility for long-term added value relationships. Years ago, the family doctor was the icon for the relationship-based service experience.

In some cases, it even makes sense for the customer and the service provider to think of themselves as engaged in some kind of mutually supporting partnership, based on *shared success*. Outstanding stockbrokers and investment professionals develop this sense of shared success with their clients, realizing that they succeed to the extent that they help the clients build their assets. Run-of-the-mill brokers and advisers tend to focus on products and transactions (that is, encouraging clients to buy and sell assets to generate commissions for themselves). Obviously, each level of the hierarchy can include the levels preceding it.

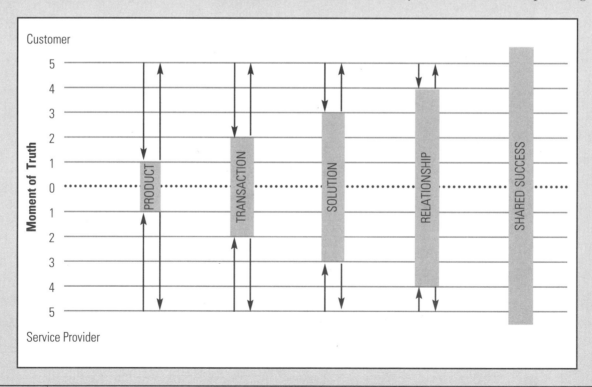

■ *Willing*

They have to believe in what they are being asked to do. One of the toughest and most important missions for leaders of any organization is to create meaning. Without a clear focus of attention, human energy gets scattered, dissipated, and squandered on internal political processes. Top management has to create, share, and promote a vision and mission for the organization that makes sense to people—one they can accept and support as a basis for managing their everyday work lives.

■ *Able*

They need the skills, knowledge, and personal maturity to contribute value in whatever jobs they do. The development of these qualifications is a never-ending management responsibility—one that can pay off enormously in the overall competitive capability of the organization.

Critical Practices

One effective way to focus the talents and energies of employees on the objective of customer value—both internal and external—is to adopt an inventory of specific *critical practices,* or *protocols,* which are simple procedures known to have high value for customers. For example, the hotel desk clerk who carries on a conversation with another staff member behind the counter while handling the guest's check-in formalities is signaling that the guest is not especially important or respected. The critical practice, sometimes called a "five-star protocol" in top hotels, is for the clerk to give his or her undivided attention to the guest until the transaction is complete.

In a hospital that operates with five-star practices, any staff member unknown to the patient is expected to introduce him- or herself upon entering the patient's room and to explain the purpose of the visit. Organizations should have such well-defined critical practices. For example, when handling situations that disappoint the customers (such as a canceled airline flight), employees need to know how to manage trouble situations gracefully. Employees and supervisors must learn how to apologize to a customer effectively.

These five-star practices can be a source of great pride and self-confidence for employees, especially when they make their jobs more pleasant and give them a feeling of empowerment. Of course, they must be natural, authentic, and effective—not just a set of procedures to be slavishly followed. They should create value for the employees as well as the customers.

★ ★ ★ ★ ★

Five-Star Practices

A "five-star" service operation, in any type of business, follows certain *critical practices* or *protocols* that impress the customer and contribute to a perception of superior value received.

■ *Nordstrom*

In Nordstrom department stores each sales associate is allowed to cross over departmental boundaries if it involves selling more goods to a customer. While most department stores require the customer to make separate stops and separate purchases at the various departments, a Nordstrom salesperson can escort customers anywhere in the store, helping them choose merchandise from any department.

■ *Volvo*

A Volvo dealer in California's Orange County uses a variety of five-star protocols that relate to the typical Volvo owner's perception of the car as a durable asset to be owned and cared for over many years. At most dealerships, when the owner comes to pick up the car after a repair, the cashier takes the payment and hands over the keys. The owner is then expected to wander around the parking lot and find his or her car. At this dealership, the cashier gives the keys to a lot attendant—well before the payment transaction is finished. When the customer steps outside, the lot attendant has the just-washed car waiting. The dealership's employees call this a "valet presentation," and they consider it a very important way to communicate that they respect and share the customers' feelings about the product.

■ *Ritz Carlton Hotels*

At Ritz Carlton Hotels, every employee is expected to be a problem solver. Each employee carries a small plastic pocket card, describing 20 important themes and protocols. One protocol requires that any employee who is approached by a customer for assistance is "glued" to that customer until the problem is solved or until someone else relieves him or her of the mission. This means that a customer who asks for directions to some place in the hotel does not hear, "Go up to the third floor, turn left, and go past the ballroom." The employee must personally escort the customer at least as far as necessary to be sure he or she is satisfied. No one tells the customer, "The concierge can help you with that." They escort the customer to the concierge desk, even if it is only a few steps away.

The Systems

Customer-hostile systems tend to be more the rule than the exception in most large businesses. Unreasonable refund policies, customer-contact employees with no authority to think or act on their own, "nuisance" paperwork, forms, red tape, and arbitrary "rules" for customer behavior all tend to alienate people and destroy their perceptions of value in the service experience. For example, many people perceive banks and other mortgage lenders as pompous and condescending in the ways they withhold information, demand personal data from prospective borrowers, and impose arbitrary rules and requirements. Similarly, many people perceive hospitals as places that care more about pushing people around than helping them get well.

The vast majority of "processing" systems (that is, systems set up by businesses to manage transactions with their customers) are designed with the organization's priorities in mind, with little or no attention to the possibilities for creating value for customers. The attitude seems to be "We make the rules here, and we expect you to abide by them." "After all," the employees unconsciously reason, "the customer may only go through this procedure once, but we do it thousands of times. Why not set it up for our own convenience, rather than theirs?"

Many service workers are so accustomed to their rules and procedures that they do not have the faintest idea how they appear to customers. It can be a humbling experience for the CEO or any senior executive to pose as a customer and anonymously partake of the service experience. That event has caused many senior management teams to seriously rethink the design of their service delivery systems.

One useful tool for helping people think about the service delivery process from the customer's point of view is the *service blueprint*. This simple diagram relates the customer's experience at the moments of truth to the structure and processes in the organization that create the experience.

By starting with the cycle of service model explained previously, and stretching it out into a chain of events, you can make it part of an activity flow diagram, with the customer as one participant and the various organizational units as co-participants. The illustration at right is a simple service blueprint.

The service blueprint has many practical uses. For one, it quickly identifies service systems that are unnecessarily complex, repetitive, slow, wasteful of resources, and toxic to the customer.

Service blueprinting is also for measuring the cost of service delivery. Many service organizations have little or no reliable information about their *cycle costs* (that is, the total cost of completing one cycle of service). Cycle cost in a service operation is equivalent to the "cost of goods" in the sale of a tangible product. What does it really cost to open a new bank account? What does it really cost to perform an appendectomy? What does it cost to install a new telephone line or replace a defective part on a car under warranty? Cycle costing can be an important tool in redesigning service delivery systems.

In addition, service blueprinting helps you understand the impact on customers of failed service delivery. What is the cost to the customer of bringing a new car into the dealership for warranty repairs several times? The dealer's invoice may show zero as the amount paid by the customer, but it does not show the cost to the customer in time and inconvenience. There may be actual direct financial costs as well.

Service blueprinting works as an excellent "radar" for identifying areas of opportunity, both for the organization and the customer, and it can pinpoint the most cost-effective areas for change or redesign of the service delivery system.

The Service Blueprint

This service blueprint relates the *cycle of service* instigated when a hotel customer decides to order room service.

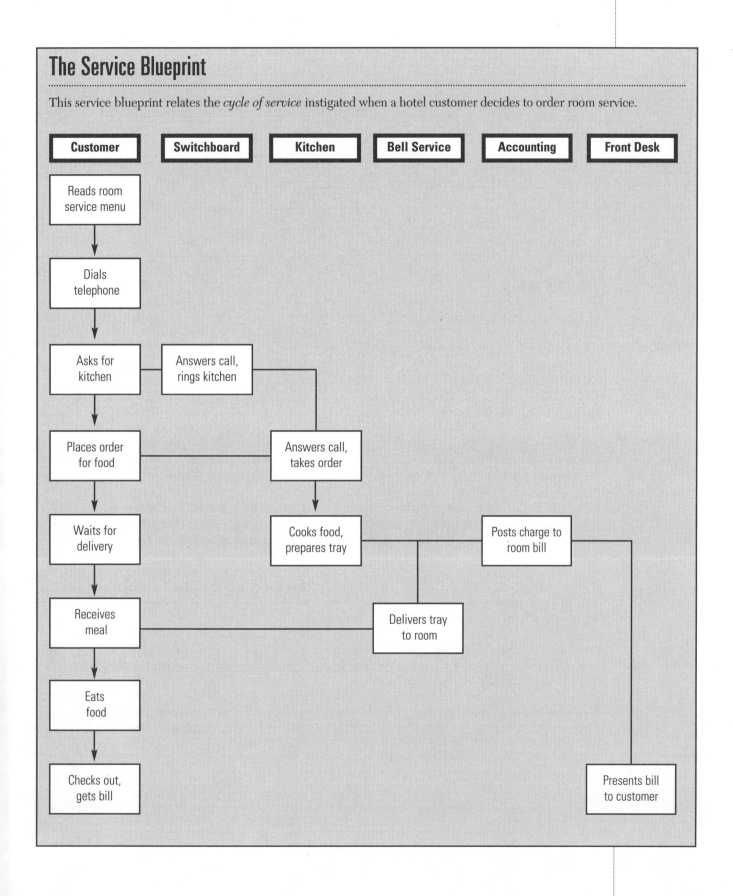

Implementing Service Management

Five closely related methodologies make up the primary base of resources and practices for implementing service management in a typical business:

1. Market and customer research.

2. Strategy formulation.

3. Communication and training.

4. Process improvement.

5. Scorekeeping.

The TQS Model

The five methodologies listed above go together in a model referred to as Total Quality Service (TQS), located at right. The following describes each part of the TQS Model.

Market and Customer Research

The TQS process involves two main kinds of research: *market research* and *customer perception research*. Market research is the investigation of structure and dynamics of the marketplace the organization chooses to serve. This includes the following well-established methods:

- segmentation analysis
- demographic analysis
- niche analysis
- product-customer match analysis
- analysis of competitors and competitive forces

Customer perception research goes at least one step further than conventional market research. It seeks to understand the thoughts and feelings of the customer toward the service product and the service provider in hopes of discovering critical factors in the customer's perception of value. This type of research can give invaluable information about how the customer sees the service experience as presented and what he or she is really trying to buy.

Strategy Formulation

At times it may be necessary for the organization's executives to review various aspects of the competitive strategy or possibly even to re-think the mission, strategy, and basic direction of the organization. Indeed, it may be difficult for executives to do the things necessary to build service quality until they have a clear definition of the following:

- what the service product actually is

- whom the service product is designed for

- what level of performance is required to compete effectively

Communication and Training

It is critical that everyone in the organization understand the following:

- customer value model
- competitive strategy
- service philosophy
- service product
- service performance standards

Some of the methods for building this knowledge and commitment are organization-wide, serving to create awareness and commitment. Others target specific aspects of service delivery. Still others are aimed at helping various employees acquire the specific skills and knowledge they need to handle their jobs well.

Communication and training methods range from new-employee orientation programs, to wall-to-wall training programs that share the vision and direction, to job-specific training programs, to the complete redesign of the messages and "signal systems"—elements that communicate the real values and priorities that dominate the culture, such as rules and regulations, people experience every day.

TQS Model

This graphic illustrates how each part of the Total Quality Service (TQS) Model relies upon the previous step to implement strategic customer focus successfully.

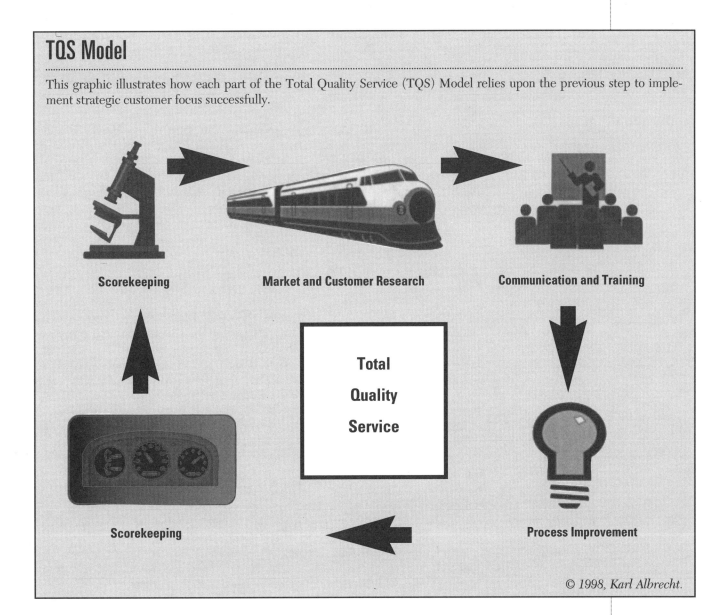

Scorekeeping

Market and Customer Research

Communication and Training

Total

Quality

Service

Scorekeeping

Process Improvement

© 1998, Karl Albrecht.

Process Improvement

A key part of any service quality program is a means for grassroots efforts to improve the various processes, systems, methods, tools, policies, and procedures involved in the delivery of service. This includes internal service functions as well as those dealing directly with the paying customers.

These process improvements can originate with management analysis of the organization or from the initiative of frontline people who want to improve the work processes with which they are involved. Often a high-level task force can play an important role in catalyzing and guiding those efforts. In many cases, special teams of employees work on specific issues and opportunities for improving the work processes they control. Models like the cycle of service and the service blueprint can serve as useful tools in process improvement.

Scorekeeping

Many organizations measure the wrong things. They often keep track of variables that are easy to measure but tell little about the competitive posture of the organization. They often fail to measure the most obvious variables, such as the customers' perceptions of their performance against the value model, process performance, cycle costs, and customer perceptions of their standing relative to competitors.

In any strategic customer focus program, the customer value model must be a basic tool for the following:

- measuring performance at the outset

- setting improvement targets

- evaluating the payoffs of various quality improvement initiatives

Steps to Take

Because every organization faces a set of challenges, issues, and opportunities unique to its own circumstances, defining a model plan for implementing a strategic customer focus must be done in general terms. The timing and sequence of events may be different from one organization to another, and the specific interventions certainly must be tailored to each organization's agenda for change. There is no one starting point for all programs or all organizations. Where you start depends on where you are.

For example, in an organization that has a strong tradition of measurement and analysis, it may be most comfortable to start right out with service audits, standards development, and the installation of a service quality measurement and monitoring system. The following steps in the program would flow from the learning process and insights gained in this assessment.

On the other hand, if the organization has typically done little measurement and analysis of its past activities and its leaders tend to "ride to the sound of the guns," they might feel more comfortable

starting with market and customer research as a way to get a clearer fix on the organization's image and positioning. They may want to deal with matters of mission and strategy before trying to measure service quality or set standards.

In yet another situation, the executives may feel that awareness and commitment at all levels are crucial—possibly because of a history of failed big programs or because of a "routinized" manufacturing type of culture that lacks an external focus. They might choose communication and training techniques to start managers and employees thinking about the implications of strategic customer focus.

The appropriate starting point for the process, sequence and timing of activities, and choice of methods all depend heavily on the organization's current state and the orientation of the executives who lead it. This is one reason why so many service programs fizzle or run aground: *The choice of methodologies is often not appropriate to the needs of the situation.*

The overall flow of events in a strategic customer focus initiative involves the following major steps.

Step 1: Assessment

Assessment involves evaluating the organization's current status, capabilities, possibilities, and competitive standing. Using the service triangle as a model, the executives need to answer a few critical questions, such as the following:

- How well do they understand the customer's value model?

- How clear is the competitive strategy, and how closely focused is it on the value proposition?

- How well prepared is the culture to deliver on the strategy?

- How well suited is the infrastructure to delivering a superior experience of customer value?

Step 2: Gap Analysis

This step defines the difference between what is and what needs to be. The executives need to identify the major dimensions of change or improvement necessary to achieve the state of strategic focus they consider essential to the success of the business. This process may involve the following tasks:

- learning more about customer value

- rethinking the basic competitive strategy

- refocusing the energy in the workforce

- realigning the organizational structure

- changing systems or technology

- learning to measure competitive performance in new ways

Step 3: Change Planning

This step involves three tasks:

- selecting the highest-priority initiatives for launching the effort

- setting the timetable and committing resources

- developing a strategy for dealing with resistance to change and ensuring the success of the effort

Step 4: Change Management

In this step, you choose and implement the various *change vectors* or micro-initiatives that you need to achieve the following:

- start the necessary changes

- sustain the energy

- achieve "early wins" that people can recognize and appreciate

- anchor the changes so they become permanent

This part of the program must be unique to the individual organization. It requires the following:

- careful thought

- consideration of the needs and reactions of the culture

- ability to create and dramatize a simple and compelling message

- ability to keep up the pressure for change over a long time

Success Is Never Final

Service management will take its place slowly, as the primary paradigm for the management of service businesses. It is an evolution, not a revolution. It will incorporate the new global realities that are driving the "deconstruction" of corporate organizations. It will incorporate the concepts of strategic partnering, with customers and partner-providers all involved in the co-creation of value. And it will continue to involve an emphasis on the micro-scale as well as the macro-scale (that is, on the individual, local practices that create value for one customer at one moment of truth).

However, lack of top management impetus will sooner or later sink just about any customer focus initiative. No matter how excited or enthusiastic the advocates are, whether they are middle managers, line people, task force members, or individual executives—they are not likely to be able to organize the energy and resources for a big enough attack on the problem. The hand of the chief executive must be at the helm if it is to have a good chance of success.

References & Resources

Articles

Albrecht. Karl. "Customer Value." *Executive Excellence,* September 1994, p. 16.

———. "Evaluating the Customer Loyalty Myth." *Quality Digest,* April 1998, p. 63.

———. "Terroristas de la Calidad. (Quality Terrorism)." *Noticias* (Argentina), September 1995, p. 105.

Berry, Leonard L., and A. Parasuraman. "Listening to the Customer: The Concept of a Service-Quality Information System." *Sloan Management Review,* Spring 1997, pp. 65-76.

Breen, Patrick, and Joe Liddy. "The Ramada Revolution: The Birth of a Service Culture in a Franchise Organization." *National Productivity Review,* Summer 1998, pp. 45-52.

Cheney, Scott, and Lisa L. Jarrett. "Up-Front Excellence for Sustainable Competitive Advantage." *Training & Development,* June 1998, pp. 45-47.

Cramb, Jennifer, and Ian Cunningham. "Face Value." *People Management,* August 13, 1998, pp. 48-52.

Fonvielle, William. "How to Know What Customers Really Want." *Training & Development,* September 1997, pp. 40-44.

Harari, Oren. "Thank Heavens for Complainers." *Management Review,* March 1997, pp. 25-29.

Kasanoff, Bruce. "Are You Ready for Mass Customization?" *Training,* May 1998, pp. 70-78.

Kohnke, Luane. "A Balanced Set of Measures Points the Way to Customer Satisfactions at Prudential." *National Productivity Review,* Summer 1997, pp. 19-27.

Margulies, Bob. "Using Competitive Intelligence to Bolster Customer Satisfaction at Douglas Aircraft Company." *National Productivity Review,* Summer 1997, pp. 75-80.

Rucci, Anthony J., et al. "The Employee-Customer-Profit Chain at Sears." *Harvard Business Review,* January/February 1998, pp. 82-97.

Specter, Robert. "The Nordstrom Way." *Corporate University Review,* May/June 1997, pp. 24-25.

Stewart, Thomas A. "A Satisfied Customer Isn't Enough." *Fortune,* July 21, 1997, pp. 112-113.

Wilhelm, Wayne R. "Expanding the Customer Care Frontier." *National Productivity Review,* Spring 1997, pp. 91-95.

Books

Albrecht, Karl. *At America's Service.* Homewood, IL: Dow Jones-Irwin, 1988.

———. *The Northbound Train: Finding the Purpose, Setting the Direction, Shaping the Destiny of Your Organization.* New York: AMACOM, 1994.

———. *The Only Thing That Matters.* New York: HarperCollins, 1992.

———. *Service Within: Solving the Middle Management Leadership Problem.* Homewood, IL: Business One Irwin, 1990.

Albrecht, Karl, and Ron Zemke. *Service America! Doing Business in the New Economy.* Homewood, IL: Dow Jones-Irwin, 1985.

Albrecht, Steven. *Service, Service, Service: The Growing Business' Secret Weapon.* Holbrook, MA: Bob Adams Inc., 1994.

Anderson, Kristin, and Ron Zemke. *Delivering Knock Your Socks Off Service.* New York: AMACOM, 1998.

Barlow, Jenelle, and Claus Moller. *A Complaint is a Gift: Using Customer Feedback as a Strategic Tool.* San Francisco: Berrett-Koehler Publishers, 1996.

Connellan, Thomas K. *Inside the Magic Kingdom: Seven Keys to Disney's Success.* Austin, TX: Bard Books, 1997.

Hiebeler, Robert. *Best Practices: Building Your Business With Customer-Focused Solutions.* New York: Simon & Schuster, 1998.

Lefevre, Henry L. *Quality Service Pays: Six Keys to Success.* Milwaukee: Quality Press, 1989.

Lele, Milind M., and Jagdish N. Sheth. *The Customer Is Key: Gaining an Unbeatable Advantage Through Customer Satisfaction.* New York: Wiley & Sons, Inc., 1991.

Schaff, Richard. *Keeping the Edge.* New York: HarperBusiness, 1995.

Shelton, Ken, ed. *Best of Class: Building a Customer Service Organization.* Provo, UT: Executive Excellence, 1998.

Whiteley, Richard C. *The Customer-Driven Company: Moving from Talk to Action.* Reading, MA: Addison-Wesley, 1991.

Info-lines

Cocheu, Ted. "Training for Quality." No. 8805.

Darraugh, Barbara, ed. "How to Provide First-Rate Customer Service." No. 9301.

Kaye, Beverly, and Devon Scheef. "Mentoring." No. 0004.

"Moment of Truth" Chart

Use this chart to analyze a single "moment of truth" (that is, a specific episode in which the customer interacts with your organization and makes a judgment about the service you provide).

Choose any typical moment of truth you like, or select one from the following list:

- Customer asks sales clerk to help him or her select a complete outfit of clothes.
- Customer (formerly known as "patient") arrives at emergency room with a painful injury.
- Customer calls telephone company to question a charge on his or her bill.
- Customer arrives at hotel desk and discovers reservation does not exist.
- Bank lending officer informs customer that bank has *not* approved his or her loan application.
- Customer visits a city department to apply for a building permit.

Step 1

Itemize the elements of the moment of truth by describing each of the following components:

1. The **environment** in which the encounter takes place.

_____

_____

_____

2. The interpersonal **interactions** the customer experiences.

_____

_____

_____

3. The **procedures** the customer must follow or participate in.

_____

_____

_____

4. The **deliverables** (that is, anything the customer physically receives).

_____

_____

_____

(Job Aid continued on page 194)

Job Aid

5. The **information** involved in the transaction.

_____

_____

_____

6. The **physical experience** (that is, what happens, if anything, to the customer—such as sights, sounds, sensations, pain, discomfort, excitement, and so forth).

_____

_____

_____

7. The **financial** transaction: What does the customer pay, and how?

_____

_____

_____

Step 2

List the typical customer irritants (that is, experiences that could disappoint, frustrate, irritate, or anger the customer).

_____

_____

_____

_____

_____

Step 3

List some value-builders (that is, things the service person can do or things the organization can offer that create the perception of unusual value on the part of the customer).

_____

_____

_____

_____

_____

Managing the Strategic Planning Process

Issue 9710

AUTHOR

Denzil Verardo, Ph.D.
California State Parks
1416 Ninth Street
Sacramento, CA 95814
Tel. 916.653.0528
Fax. 916.653.0015

Denzil Verardo is the Deputy
Director for Administration for
the California Department of
Parks and Recreation. He holds
a B.A. and M.A. in history and a
Ph.D. in management. He has
written seven books and over
200 articles on a variety of sub-
jects, including quality management implementation and
process improvement in government. He is regularly featured as
a trainer, presenter, and speaker
at conferences.

Editor
Cat Sharpe

Associate Editor
Patrick McHugh

Designer
Steven M. Blackwood

Copy Editor
Kay Larson

ASTD Internal Consultant
Dr. Walter Gray

Managing the Strategic Planning Process

Strategic Planning

Strategic planning allows organizations to make fundamental decisions that guide them to a developed vision of the future. The result of this effort, the strategic plan, serves as the basis for action—a road map that directs all resources toward an ideal future. Daily decisions are then made on the basis of this plan, which must be both practical—based on your organization's mission—and flexible, to allow for rapid change. Successful strategic plans are vital working documents that capture mission and lead to a predicted future state. They contain an internal dynamic and structure that captures, fosters, and promotes change.

Unlike linear planning, strategic planning assumes that your situation will change and encourages flexible plans that can adapt to today's fast-paced business environment. While it is impossible to predict *exactly* what will change and how, strategic planning positions organizations to respond quickly to opportunities or threats. For example, strategic planning at Microsoft allowed it to swiftly enter the market for Internet-related products while maintaining its lead in the software industry. Strategic planning requires serious, disciplined effort, whether in public, private, or nonprofit environments. To get it right, it is essential to devote the necessary resources.

Successful modern organizations such as Microsoft and Hewlett-Packard practice *strategic management,* which allows strategic plans to link future needs to annual plans based on current resources. As an example, strategic management promotes training that not only meets current needs, but also develops human potential and performance to meet future needs. Strategic planning is not a passive exercise, but a dynamic interaction of stakeholders that helps ensure the mission's success. Strategic planning professionals agree: Organizations that use strategic planning out-perform those that do not.

Effective strategic plans answer the following questions for an organization:

- What business are we really in?

- Who are our customers and stakeholders (that is, all individuals affected by the organization)?

- What factors are critical to our success?

- What are our strengths and weaknesses?

- What trends affect our environment?

- What values and principles must guide our decisions?

- What fundamental policy decisions must we make?

- What actions are required to implement them?

- What are our priorities; what resources will they need?

This *Info-line* will guide you to answering these questions as well as outline the steps to integrate your answers into an effective and flexible plan for success.

Devising a Strategic Plan

The components of strategic planning shown in the chart below and discussed in the pages that follow are presented in a systematic order. The process itself, however, is not truly linear. Steps may overlap or occur in a different order depending on the needs of your organization. Some activities, such as analysis and annual planning, are continuous once a plan has been developed. Each step, however, should be completed.

Components of a successful strategic plan include:

- define the organization's mission
- plan to plan strategically
- conduct environmental scans (analyses)
- develop a vision of the future
- set measurable goals and objectives (outcomes)
- integrate annual plans and contingency planning
- conduct continuous assessment

Defining the Mission Statement

The basic question to address in a mission statement is, "What is our business and who do we serve?" Whether private, public, or nonprofit, management must create a clear consensus statement that addresses your organization's role in society. An organization can survive (for now) without a strategic plan, but it may drift or maintain a status quo that leads to obsolescence. Virtually none can survive without a mission

A Seven-Step Strategic Planning Process Model

While this model illustrates the steps of strategic planning, you can rearrange steps to fit your needs.

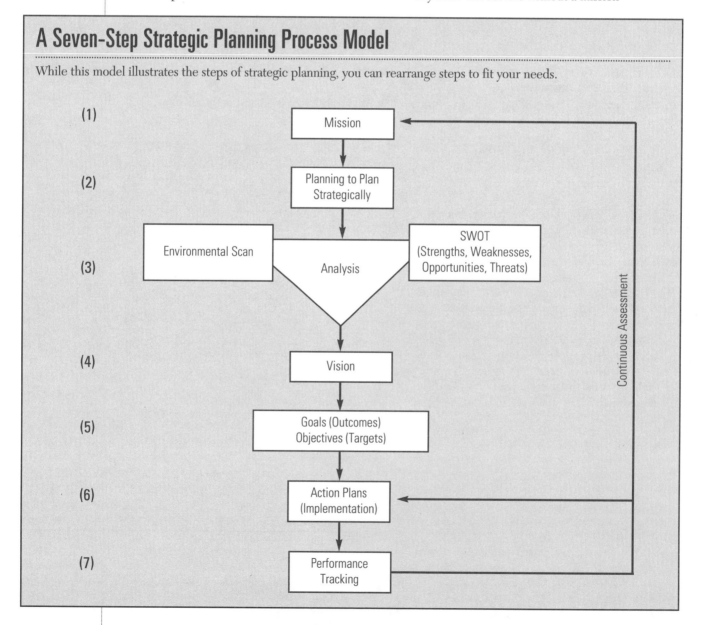

(1) Mission
(2) Planning to Plan Strategically
(3) Environmental Scan — Analysis — SWOT (Strengths, Weaknesses, Opportunities, Threats)
(4) Vision
(5) Goals (Outcomes) Objectives (Targets)
(6) Action Plans (Implementation)
(7) Performance Tracking

Continuous Assessment

An accurate description of your organization's purpose—the mission statement—drives the strategic plan. It embodies—in a few words or sentences—what your organization *is*. Why does it exist at all? What is its function? Who does it serve (customers, clients, or stakeholders)? The mission statement is the beginning of effective strategic planning. While formulating and reaching consensus on a mission statement can, and probably will, be time-consuming, every unit or department within your organization will take its lead and direction from it.

The mission statement is the foundation for all the strategies and plans in which your organization will invest its resources. That consideration alone warrants careful development of a statement embodying the soul of your organization, as the mission statements that appear in the box at right do for their organizations. Within the context of the strategic plan, many people—whether employee or customer—will not see the completed strategic plan. Every person with a stake in the organization, however, must see the mission statement. This visibility requires that the mission be developed or reevaluated methodically and with great care. You'll want to get it right.

Environmental scanning and SWOT (Strengths, Weaknesses, Opportunities, Threats) analyses, which are discussed later, can occur before mission formulation. Such analyses, however, skew a real-time look at the organization's current state. The mission may well be reevaluated after analyzing those influences that affect the organization, but should not necessarily be determined by those forces.

What Is Your Business?

Before putting pencil to paper, a discussion of the organization's history and development is imperative. The organization's *why* may have changed over time to cope with a fluid environment or for other reasons, but a review of its history should provide the answer to this fundamental question. The *why* also addresses the critical factor of public, customer, and client expectations from an organization. The organization certainly would not exist if it had not provided some meaningful product or service to those it has served. A historic review should answer these questions.

Sample Organization Mission Statements

The following is a selection of mission statements from businesses, nonprofit organizations, and government agencies.

■ ASTD
"We provide leadership to individuals, organizations, and society to achieve work-related competence, performance, and fulfillment."

■ AT&T Language Line Services
"To remove language as a barrier to effective communication over the telephone anytime, anywhere."

■ California Department of Parks and Recreation
"To provide for the health, inspiration, and education of the people of California by helping to preserve the state's extraordinary biological diversity, protecting its most valued natural and cultural resources, and creating opportunities for high-quality outdoor recreation."

■ The Graham Page
"The Graham Page develops and publishes technologically advanced management and organizational products, services, and systems and distributes them to individuals and organizations for their professional, personal, and organizational development."

■ Lincoln Electric Company
"To produce the best possible product at the lowest possible cost in order to sell to an ever-increasing number of customers."

■ Social Security Administration
"To administer National Social Security Programs as prescribed by legislation in an equitable, effective, efficient, and caring manner."

Whether a public service provider, a corporate manufacturer, or one of the myriad entities in between, knowing your "business" and expressing it in the mission statement is a critical part of strategic planning. No strategic management can occur without knowing what you do. Do not think this necessarily will be easy to define. Exercises at federal and state government levels have shown that there can be numerous internal disagreements over the mission statement specifically, and strategic planning in general. Nothing shows that it is any easier for nonprofit or corporate organizations.

Defining your business correctly can ultimately lead to resounding success or embarrassing corporate failure. In a now classic example, railroad companies had defined themselves as being in the railroad business rather than in the transportation business. Had they answered the question, "What is your business?" correctly, they may have emerged as an exploding growth industry rather than as a declining, or at best static, portion of the transportation industry. Again, *get it right* by identifying the following components in your business:

- principal services your organization provides
- product(s) you produce
- distribution of your product(s) or service(s)
- corporate philosophy toward distribution

Who Are Your Customers?

Once you define your business, you need to identify your customers. The entire public image of an organization rests with an appropriate description of who it serves. This may be as broad as "citizens of the United States," or as narrow as, "those who need emergency medical care." It may be implied or directly stated, market focused or legally directed. In every case, it is an organization's responsibility to define its customer(s).

After determining what you do and who you serve, it is time to express these facts in meaningful words that are as succinct and powerful as possible. While each sentence may be debated at length, the result must be an expression of the organization's reason for being.

Planning to Plan Strategically

The familiar questions of why, who, what, when, and where are the easiest way to remember the components that must be addressed prior to a strategic planning effort.

■ Why Plan at All?

Today's organizations cope with continual internal and external change. To survive, they must think and act strategically based on a sound plan. A strategic plan cannot be stagnant and the planning process must not be a passive activity. Organizations either plan well or fight the continual fires brought about by change.

■ Who Should Be Involved?

The effort must be a "top-down" plan involving the full commitment of the chief executive and the key executives who will "own" and drive the plan. Staff members familiar with the current organization and who are good communicators and information gatherers will also play a critical role in the effort.

As an organization gains maturity within the strategic planning process, it can and should increase "bottom up" involvement. Executive management must continue to be involved since it steers the course set by the plan. Broad-based participation from mid-management, supervisors, and rank-and-file employees can give true depth to environmental scanning (see the next page). They also provide the expectations of both internal and external stakeholders and customers. Information derived this way filters up through the organization. Viewed only through the eyes of a chief executive officer, strategic planning will have a narrow focus that is limited by that executive's experience.

■ What Process Will Yield Necessary Facts?

A thorough examination and discussion of the planning model must be shared with the executive team to achieve a true understanding of the planning process and the expected outcome(s) of the strategic plan. A review of the available and needed information at each stage of the planning process should take place in the *planning to plan* stage.

■ When Will the Effort Take Place?

It is critical to allow sufficient time for the planning effort and to develop deadlines for each stage. It can take weeks, often months, for an organization unfamiliar with strategic planning to go through the initial process. Once an organization's strategic initiatives have been implemented, the planning effort becomes cyclical. This involves a continual scanning of environmental factors that influence the organization.

■ Where Will the Effort Take Place?

Strategic plan preparation—planning for the plan—should take place off site. Concentrated and uninterrupted focus must be expended during various stages of the effort. This is as important for the planning team as for management. Ensure the chosen facility has adequate resources to facilitate the planning process.

Conducting the Analysis

The environmental scan and resulting SWOT determination are necessary to obtain a meaningful strategic plan. Too often, organizations prepare an unrealistic view of where they want to be in the future because they fail to accurately look at where the organization is within its current framework.

Environmental Scan

An environmental scan is an inventory of the political, technological, social, and economic forces that influence the way an organization functions. It involves analysis of the current environment and the trends that may affect it. An environmental scan also assesses customer needs and stakeholder expectations. Stakeholders can include allied agencies, employees, and suppliers—because each has a vested interest in the organization's future. There is no magic formula for conducting environmental scans. It is important, however, to get as much information as possible on relevant economic, political, social, and technological forces that could affect the direction of the organization.

Some examples of economic trends and forces to assess include:

- Who are your customers now? In the future?

- What are your major costs now? Which ones are likely to increase in the future? Can you estimate which will stay the same or decrease?

- Who is your competition? Who will be your competition in the future?

- What do your tax dollars now support that affects your organization? What will they support, or not support, in the future?

- What portion of your payroll is in benefits? How high are your workers' compensation costs? What will occur with these items in the next two to five years? Five to 10 years?

- What other economic factors influence your organization? How many of these will affect it in the future?

Some examples of trends and forces to assess in the political environment include:

- What will be the blend of similar services offered by the government, nonprofit, and corporate worlds? How will this blend change?

- Will there be more or less privatization of governmental services? What will be the role of nonprofits?

- What is the trend toward corporate mergers or breakups in your industry?

- What is the trend in your organization with respect to cooperation or competition with allied agencies or organizations, governmental, or non-governmental service providers?

- Will political trends affect your suppliers in the same way they affect your organization? Are there other trends that affect suppliers?

- What other political trends may affect your organization in the future?

Some examples of trends and forces to assess in the social environment include:

- Will a change in population diversity affect your organization? What are the relevant population trends for the next two to five years? Five to 10 years?

- How will a change in population density affect your organization?

- What is the age and make-up of your customer base? How could that change in the future?

- What social factors influence your workforce now (for example, family unit size, work flexibility for single parents, child care issues)? What trends in the social environment of the workforce affect your organization?

- What other social trends may affect your organization in the future?

Some examples of trends and forces to assess in the technological environment include:

SWOT Analysis

SWOT is a commonly used term in strategic planning referring to the identification of organizational strengths, weaknesses, opportunities, and threats.

Strengths

These might include:

- well-trained, top-performing employees
- a clear mission statement
- supportive constituency or customer base
- active volunteers
- a customer-oriented organizational culture

Weaknesses

These might include:

- outmoded technology
- high workers' compensation costs
- severe budget reductions
- loss of market share
- lack of cultural diversity in the workforce

Opportunities

Based on the organization's strengths and weaknesses, and analysis of the environmental scan, opportunities might include:

- low interest rates, which make infrastructure investments less costly

- an organization that responds rapidly to customer needs

Threats

Based on organizational strengths and weakness and analysis of the environmental scan, threats might include:

- a "bureaucratic" structure that inhibits rapid response to changes in customer needs

- a poor economy

- declining resources

- What changes in computer and communication technology are likely to affect your operation?

- What impact will energy saving devices have on your offices?

- How will transportation technology influence your operation and workforce?

- What other technological trends may affect your organization in the future?

SWOT Analysis

Executive staff must perform the SWOT analysis honestly and avoid the temptation to "paint a rosy picture." Organizational strengths should not be overemphasized nor should acknowledged weaknesses be omitted. To capitalize on the opportunities and threats that face your organization, it is essential to conduct an internal assessment of your current status. This assessment should not be limited to an executive perspective, but should include a representative cross section of many levels. See the box at the left for a sample SWOT analysis.

Employee surveys are excellent tools for acquiring knowledge regarding internal strengths and weaknesses. Since all staff have an opportunity to participate, surveys are an effective way to gain employee buy-in for the resulting strategic plan. Customer surveys also help chronicle major strengths and weaknesses. Assessments of what is done "well" and what is done "poorly" indicate the accuracy of executives' assessments.

The "culture" of an organization—the assumptions shared by employees about their work and their feelings toward your organization—cannot be ignored in the SWOT analysis. An assessment of the culture and the degree to which it helps or hinders deployment of a strategic plan is critical to the success of the plan.

Continual environmental scanning must be institutionalized to proactively assess the impact of change on your organization. A SWOT analysis, based on changes in environmental trends and forces—both current and future—should be performed as strengths and weaknesses shift and when new opportunities or threats are uncovered by the assessment.

Scenario Building

The final analysis stage is a look at the many possible developments and opportunities brought to light by the environmental scan and SWOT analysis. Scenarios should be built around the most likely developments. An example of a scenario could be as follows: *Should the economy suffer within the next five years, how would our organization react?* Your answer should be based on your current strengths and weaknesses and any opportunities that may present themselves along with the economic "threat." The most realistic scenarios, based on likely trends from the environmental scan, should be used to develop strategies that will lead your organization to its desired future (vision).

Strategies must be developed and enacted to nullify, as much as possible, any threats presented by each scenario. They also need to be created to amplify likely opportunities. Contingency strategies should be in place if a less-likely scenario materializes. Visioning, the act of developing a vision statement or organizational view of the future, overlaps the scenario-building phase of analysis.

Developing a Vision

A vision, quite simply, is a realistic look at where you want to be in the future. It needs to be a "stretch," but achievable within the current context of organizational resources. This stretch, when used properly, motivates and inspires staff and leads to meaningful goals.

Your vision must be consistent with your mission. Visioning is an important step in strategic planning, for it is a formative step in establishing goals and it is the blueprint for your organization's future. The more widely shared the vision, the greater the chance of success. For specific information on vision development see *Info-line* No. 9107, "How to Develop a Vision."

Setting Goals and Objectives

Where traditional strategic planning manages the objectives toward a result, performance managed strategic planning manages toward a desired ultimate outcome. Outcomes, much like goals, reflect an achievable result. Rather than managing objectives, however, performance managed strategic planning constantly focuses on the outcome. The difference between traditional strategic planning and performance managed strategic planning is managerial and organizational focus. In organizations where change is minimal, traditional strategic planning works well because the objectives lead to a result that allows sustained incremental deployment of objectives and accountability based on them.

Goals or outcomes in performance managed organizations allow you to accomplish the mission and advance to the vision. Goals and objectives manage the gap between the present and desired future by defining where you want to be and the steps you need to take to get there. Both traditional and performance managed strategic planning require that goals be:

■ *Reasonable*
A goal must be achievable within the resources available, or it serves no purpose other than to frustrate even the best efforts.

■ *Challenging*
While goals must be reasonable, they should require a degree of effort or "stretch" in order to achieve.

■ *Specific*
Goals must be specific enough to allow accurate measurement to take place. Vague or general goals lead to confusion.

■ *Measurable*
Strategic management requires hard data rather than intuition. Experience plays a role in the planning process, especially when discussing the mission of an organization. Measurable goals ensure proper progress.

Goal-setting is not a passive activity. It requires commitment and executive energy to properly construct meaningful, manageable components that lead to the organization's vision. In traditional strategic planning, goals are tied to the customer requirements that were elicited from the environmental scan and inherent in the organization's mission. Setting goals is a scientific activity, not one that relies on guesswork. The success and utility of a strategic plan depends on the degree to which goals are scientifically derived. Scientific goals are:

- based on current and projected customer requirements

- based on future quality requirements

- based on major suppliers' and competitors' performance data

- consistent with customer satisfaction goals

- consistent with quality improvement goals

- based on present and projected future technological capabilities

- based on realistic resource assessments—that the aggregate needs of all goals do not exceed the total resources of an organization

- initiated at the top and cascade down through all levels of an organization

Objectives are the clearly stated, incremental, agreed-upon steps to achieve a goal. They are often called "short-term goals" and normally use production output, production time, or both as indicators of success. To the degree that objectives are the incremental steps of goal attainment, they also serve as the basis for measuring progress. Objectives are defined in terms of desired output(s) and should have an owner who is responsible for and monitors the indicators of performance (output measures) relative to the objective.

Performance Managed Strategic Planning (PMSP)

Focusing on the objective provides a tool for increasing output and sustaining direction toward a goal. In PMSP, focus is on the ultimate outcome—the desired vision. Activities or processes are directed toward that outcome, and they are adapted in order to achieve it. PMSP works well in organizations that rapidly adjust to environmental changes (results of the environmental scan) and whose resources and energy require continual focus on the end result. Rather than a specific objective—a-step-by-step approach—a performance measured system is a continuum focused on the outcome. Planning and performance management terms are defined in the sidebar at left.

Outcomes are directly tied to the major activities of the organization. For example, cultural resource protection is a major program for some state, federal, and nonprofit organizations. A typical outcome might be, "significant cultural sites, features, structures, and collections are protected and preserved." For a municipality, an outcome could be

Planning and Performance Management Terms

Performance management and the supporting performance budgeting system use terminology similar to that used in traditional strategic planning. But there are also some unique definitions. The following list defines some of the terms used in this *Infoline*. Terms in *italics* are shared by both traditional and performance managed strategic plans. Underlined terms are primarily used in performance managed organizations.

Input: resources consumed by the system's organization.

Mission: the reason for an organization's existence. The mission statement succinctly identifies what it does, why, and for whom it does it.

Outcome: the results or impacts of activities designed to accomplish the organization's mission.

Outcome measure: the unit of measure used to evaluate the success of an outcome over time.

Output: a measure of what is actually produced—the amount of work accomplished.

Performance budgeting: a system of budgeting that links inputs and outputs to outcomes.

Program: the core responsibilities of an organization, which collectively represent its mission.

Strategic plan: the results of a structured effort to produce fundamental decisions and actions that shape and guide what an organization is, what it does, and why and how it does it.

Target: clear objectives for specific action that mark quantifiable interim steps toward achieving the organization's outcomes.

that new or redeveloped neighborhoods are, "convenient, affordable, accessible, and environmentally sensitive." A corporate outcome could be to ensure continuous profitability for shareholders. Outcomes should:

● be the ultimate result of a program area

● embrace the entire scope of the organization's primary influence

● contribute to the mission of the organization

Measuring Performance in PMSP

Performance measures are tools that measure and monitor work performed and the results achieved. They describe both what is to be measured and the methods of measurement. Like objective measurement in traditional strategic planning, PMSP uses output to measure performance, but outcome measures (indicators of the actual impact or effect of outcomes) are also used. These measures show movement from a stated condition toward solving a problem. These measures address whether, in the process of continual improvement, a service is delivered at its proposed level or if production is achieved at minimal defect levels.

Using safety as an example, because it spans all types of organizations, the listing that follows presents the execution of a hypothetical outcome:

■ *Outcome*
Our employees and customers interact in a safe, healthy environment.

■ *Outcome Measures*
Safety and health awareness by employees or customers (survey); number of accidents or workers' compensation claims (output measure); an index of how safe individuals "feel" in their work or customer-interaction environment (survey or other interactive data).

■ *Target*
During this year, reduce accidents by 5 percent (base this on predictable impacts of your programs, not arbitrarily); employees feel safer on an established survey measurement scale. The following year's target would either reduce accidents further and employees would feel "safer," or would maintain the level if the goal is met.

Performance measures are often difficult to determine or define—much like choosing the right objective—but it is imperative to choose the correct measure for the desired outcome. As a general rule, what gets measured gets accomplished. Goals that are not measured are not considered important.

Performance measurement characteristics may include:

● timeliness
● accuracy
● level of quality
● cost-effectiveness
● priority

Outcome measures should have the following characteristics:

● relevance
● reliability
● validity
● sufficient value
● ability to enable decisions

Outcome measures, unlike output measures, may report performance in terms of behavioral change. Societal, political, economic, and technological changes can affect the outcome. Forces outside the organization's control might necessitate routine environmental scanning to ensure that the outcome measures remain accurate. Output measures—again, the actual work performed—normally remain under control of the organization and are less affected by external environmental forces. It is clear then, that both output and outcome measurements are necessary to accurately assess achievement.

Targets ensure performance accountability. They are agreed-upon timelines for an established level of performance or achievement aimed toward an outcome. Targets utilize the data from outcome and output measures as indicators of performance. An example of an outcome measure and its targets begins on the following page.

Sample Program Deployment and Outcome Measurement

This sample, from the Performance Budget of the California Department of Parks and Recreation (DPR), illustrates program deployment and outcome measurement using performance managed strategic planning.

Core Program Area 4

Public Safety

OUTCOME 4.1
A safe environment within State Parks

Principle
Along with its role of resource protection, the department provides public safety services. The department deploys approximately 600 peace officers who provide law enforcement, resource patrol, and protection to the public in areas such as aquatic safety, protection from wildlife, and emergency services.

OUTCOME MEASURES

Measure 4.1A		Data Source
Ratio of accidents to park visitation		DPR Vital Statistics/ Public Safety Databases
Indicator of Success		
The department decreases or maintains a ratio of major accidents per 100,000 paying visitors.		

	Targets	
1997-1998	**1998-1999**	**3-5 Years**
The department will further refine its measurement process to determine appropriate response to the ration of accidents.	The department will continue its data refinement and target decreases or maintenance to the ratio of major accidents per 100,000 park visitors.	Continued targeted ratios based on analysis of data.

Year	# Acc.	# Per 100K
1993	1,070	1.63
1994	1,112	1.73
1995	1,298	2.02
1996	——	——

Used with permission of the California State Department of Parks and Recreation.

Annual Planning

Also called action plans, this is the implementation phase of strategic planning, which involves the entire organization. Using action plans, the strategic plan process is integrated into individual and departmental planning. Organizations without strategic plans often have multiple implementation strategies—business or annual plans that lead to conflicting goals and poor, if any, results. Action plans deployed from an all encompassing strategic plan allow goals and objectives to be integrated into each employee's performance goals. It is critical that employees know the direction of the organization and how they contribute to achieving its goals.

Depending on the structure of the corporation or agency, action plans can take the form of individual unit strategic plans, broader program plans, or individual business plans depending on the structure of the corporation or agency. No matter what

Measure 4.1B		Data Source
Ratio of crimes to park visitation		Public Safety Database

Indicator of Success		
Department decreases or maintains a ratio of crimes per 100,000 visitors.		

	Targets	
1997-1998	**1998-1999**	**3-5 Years**
The department will further refine its measurement process to determine appropriate response to the ratio of crimes.	The department will target decreases or maintenance to its ratio of crimes per 100,000 park visitors based on analysis of data.	Continued targeted ratios based on analysis of data.
Year # Crimes # Per 100K 1995 ——— ——— 1996 ——— ———		

Measure 4.1C		Data Source
Visitors' rating of their perception of parks as "safe zones."		Continuous Visitor Survey

Indicator of Success		
California state parks will receive an average score of 90 percent for the visiting public's perception of parks as "safe zones."		

	Targets	
1997-1998	**1998-1999**	**3-5 Years**
The department targets an average score for the visiting public's perception of safety.	The department will target a level of improved satisfaction.	Continued surveys and targeted improvements or maintenance of satisfaction level.
Average Satisfaction Scores (Summer Surveys) Visitors' Perception of Safety 1994 85.8 percent 1995 87.8 percent 1996 88.4 percent		

Used with permission of the California State Department of Parks and Recreation.

form action plans take, they possess several common characteristics. See *Info-line* No. 9206, "Strategic Planning for Human Resource Development" for an example of program planning.

While strategic plans have a multiyear outlook—leading to an organizational vision of the future—action plans are short-term efforts based on the strategic vision. They do, however, specify the level of resources provided to a program. Employee concerns, stakeholder issues, and action

plan results from the previous year must all be used as input. Then they become the strategies used to accomplish objectives and, ultimately, the goals of an organization.

Action plans may modify delivery processes, the delivery of services, or reengineer portions of an organization. They need to identify the training or skill development required as well as allocate or reallocate resources to accomplish the plan's vision. The art to formulating and implementing action plans is the ability to carefully prioritize issues and to focus limited resources on the most important element(s). Data collection tracks performance with regard to daily operations and serves as a measure for assessing results.

Continuous Assessment

Tracking performance is critical to the success of strategic plans because continual monitoring can keep plans on track. Systems to monitor progress and compile management information require data. What you measure and how you measure it produces the necessary tracking indices to assess results and track performance. While the quantity, type of data collected, collection methods, and measurement systems vary from organization to organization, some areas should be considered by all organizations. For example, data should be collected on:

- processes related to the performance of services or manufacture of goods

- internal and external customer satisfaction feedback

- the quality of supplier performance (goods or services)

- employee performance

- cost and financial performance

- health and safety issues

- quality indices such as cycle time, error rate, efficiency, and effectiveness

The breadth, scope, objectivity, validity, and number of sources of data to be collected, as well as the selection of *key* process measures are critical managerial decisions. Collecting information that is not needed or does not add value in gauging the true pulse of your organization is a frustrating exercise and wastes valuable resources. So think carefully about the kinds of data you need *before* starting to collect it.

Action plans and their inherent implementation strategies lead to results. By accurately tracking performance and continually assessing critical issues and objectives based on that performance, you are able to quickly make adjustments to meet goals. In short, action plans are normally formulated annually, but must be continually assessed. While the strategic plan takes a longer view (three to five years), it requires an annual reappraisal to ensure movement toward organizational goals and outcomes. It must also be relevant based on continuously changing environmental factors. Organizations must continuously and simultaneously create future plans while implementing current plans.

Strategic planning was virtually ignored during the 1980s as organizations struggled to cut every possible item from their budgets. Today, organizations of every size and type have realized that that was a mistake. Strategic planning encourages orderly growth—and organizations that fail to grow do not survive for long.

It doesn't matter if your company is as large as Microsoft or employs just a few people: The strategic planning process must become a normal part of organizational operations, not a separate activity. With a long-term planning process in place, fact-based, future-driven strategic decision making will become institutionalized within your organization and you will be poised for success in the future.

References & Resources

Articles

Bantel, K.A. "Strategic Planning Openness: The Role of Top Team Demography." *Group & Organizational Management,* December 1994, pp. 406-424.

———. "Top Team, Environment, and Performance Effects on Strategic Planning Formality." *Group & Organization Management,* December 1993, pp. 436-458.

Bechtell, M.L. "Navigating Organizational Waters With Hoshin Planning." *National Productivity Review,* Spring 1996, pp. 23-42.

Belohlav, J.A. "Quality, Strategy, and Competitiveness." *California Management Review,* February 1993, pp. 25-34.

Blakely, G.L., et al. "Management Development Programs: The Effects of Management Level and Corporate Strategy." *Human Resource Development Quarterly,* Spring 1994, pp. 5-19.

Byrne, J.A. "Strategic Planning." *Business Week,* August 26, 1996, pp. 46-52.

Camillus, J.C. "Reinventing Strategic Planning." *Strategy & Leadership,* May/June 1996, pp. 6-12.

Chakravarthy, B.S. "A New Strategy Framework for Coping With Turbulence." *Sloan Management Review,* Winter 1997, pp. 69-82.

———. "Flexible Commitment: A Key To Success." *Strategy & Leadership,* May/June 1996, pp. 14-20.

Corbett, C., and L. Van Wassenhove. "Trade-Offs? What Trade-Offs? Competence and Competitiveness in Manufacturing Strategy." *California Management Review,* Summer 1993, pp. 107-122.

Fuller, M. "Strategic Planning in an Era of Total Competition." *Strategy & Leadership,* May/June 1996, pp. 22-27.

Furey, T.R., and S.G. Diorio. "Making Reengineering Strategic." *Planning Review,* July/August 1994, pp. 6-11.

Galagan, P. "Strategic Planning Is Back." *Training & Development,* April 1997, pp. 32-37.

Garvin, D.A. "Manufacturing Strategic Planning." *California Management Review,* Summer 1993, pp. 85-106.

Gerwin, D. "Integrating Manufacturing Into the Strategic Phases of New Product Development." *California Management Review,* Summer 1993, pp. 123-136.

Grant, J.H., and D.R. Gnyawali. "Strategic Process Improvement Through Organizational Learning." *Strategy & Leadership,* May/June 1996, pp. 28-33.

Hamel, G. "Strategy as Revolution." *Harvard Business Review,* July/August 1996, pp. 69-82.

Hayes, R.H., and G.P. Pisano. "Beyond World-Class: The New Manufacturing Strategy." *Harvard Business Review,* January/February 1994, pp. 77-86.

Kaplan, R.S., and D.P. Norton. "Strategic Learning and the Balanced Scorecard." *Strategy & Leadership,* September/October 1996, pp. 18-24.

Kaufman, R. "Mega Planning: The Changed Realities—Part I." *Performance & Technology,* December 1995, pp. 8-15.

———. "Mega Planning: The Changed Realities—Part II." *Performance & Instruction,* January 1996, pp. 4-5.

———. "Mega Planning: The Changed Realities—Part III." *Performance & Instruction,* February 1996, pp. 4-7.

Keen, C.D. "Tips for Effective Strategic Planning." *HRMagazine,* August 1994, pp. 84-87.

Kiernan, M.J. "The New Strategic Architecture: Learning to Compete in the Twenty-First Century." *The Executive,* February 1993, pp. 7-21.

Lehn, K., and A.K. Makhija. "EVA and MVA as Performance Measures and Signals For Strategic Change." *Strategy & Leadership,* May/June 1996, pp. 34-38.

Long, C., and M. Vickers-Koch. "Using Core Capabilities to Create Competitive Advantage." *Organizational Dynamics,* Summer 1995, pp. 7-22.

Lorange, P. "Strategic Planning For Rapid and Profitable Growth." *Strategy & Leadership,* May/June 1996, pp. 42-48.

References & Resources

Marshall, B., and L. Kelleher. "A Test of Restructuring Success." *HRMagazine,* August 1993, pp. 82-85.

Mintzberg, H. "The Fall and Rise of Strategic Planning." *Harvard Business Review,* January/February 1994, pp. 107-114.

———. "Managing Government, Governing Management." *Harvard Business Review,* May/June 1996, pp. 75-83.

———. "The Pitfalls of Strategic Planning." *California Management Review,* Fall 1993, pp. 32-47.

Murray, D. "The Future of Eugene, Oregon." *At Work: Stories of Tomorrow's Workplace,* July/August 1995, pp. 5-6.

Nanus, B. "Leading the Vision Team." *Futurist,* May/June 1996, pp. 20-23.

Nutt, P.C. "Transforming Public Organizations With Strategic Management and Strategic Leadership." *Journal of Management,* Summer 1993, pp. 299-347.

Perrottet, C.M. "Scenarios for the Future." *Management Review,* January 1996, pp. 43-46.

Plevel, M.J., et al. "AT&T Global Business Communications Systems: Linking HR With Business Strategy." *Organizational Dynamics,* Winter 1994, pp. 59-72.

Rajagopalan, N., et al. "Strategic Decision Processes: Critical Review and Future Directions." *Journal of Management,* Summer 1993, pp. 349-384.

Schoemaker, P. "Scenario Planning: A Tool for Strategic Thinking." *Sloan Management Review,* Winter 1996, pp. 25-40.

Stadler, A. "A Transformational Learning Cycle." *At Work: Stories of Tomorrow's Workplace,* July/August 1995, pp. 9-11.

Teng, J.T.C., et al. "Business Process Engineering: Charting a Strategic Path for the Information Age." *California Management Review,* Spring 1994, pp. 9-31.

Verardo, D. "To the Seventh Generation." *Journal for Quality and Participation,* September 1994, pp. 46-50.

Veliquette, M., and T. Ward. "Performance Budgeting." *Public Sector Network News,* Summer 1997.

Wall, S.J. "Creating Strategists." *Training & Development,* May 1997, pp. 75-79.

Wall, S.J., and S.R. Wall. "The Evolution (Not the Death) of Strategy." *Organizational Dynamics,* Autumn 1995, pp. 6-19.

Books

Abrahams, J. *The Mission Statement Book: 301 Corporate Mission Statements From America's Top Companies.* Berkeley: Ten Speed Press, 1995.

Albrecht, K. *The Northbound Train: Finding the Purpose, Setting the Direction, Shaping the Destiny of Your Organization.* New York: American Management Association, 1994.

Barry, T.J. *Excellence Is a Habit: How to Avoid Quality Burnout.* Milwaukee: American Society for Quality Control, 1994.

Black, R. *Strategic Planning.* Loomis, CA: Meta Dynamics, 1995.

Bryson, J.M. *Strategic Planning for Public and Nonprofit Organizations: A Guide to Strengthening and Sustaining Organizational Achievement.* San Francisco: Jossey-Bass, 1995.

Goodwin, B.T. *Write On the Wall: A How-To Guide For Effective Planning in Groups.* Alexandria, VA: ASTD, 1994.

Haines, S., and K. McCoy. *Sustaining High Performance: The Strategic Transformation to a Customer-Focused Learning Organization.* Delray Beach, FL: St. Lucie Press, 1995.

Imparato, N., and O. Harari. *Jumping the Curve: Innovation and Strategic Choice in an Age of Transition.* San Francisco: Jossey-Bass, 1994.

References & Resources

Info-lines

Jacobs, R.W. *Real Time Strategic Change: How to Improve an Entire Organization in Fast and Far-Reaching Change.* San Francisco: Berrett-Koehler, 1994.

Jones, P., and L. Kahaner. *Say It and Live It: 50 Corporate Mission Statements That Hit the Mark.* New York: Double-day, 1995.

Kaufman, R. *Strategic Thinking: A Guide to Identifying and Solving Problems.* Alexandria, VA: ASTD and International Society for Performance Improvement, 1996.

Nanus, B. *Visionary Leadership.* San Francisco: Jossey-Bass, 1992.

The Paradox Principles: How High-Performance Companies Manage Chaos, Complexity, and Contradiction to Achieve Superior Results. Chicago: Irwin, 1996.

Pfeiffer, W.J., ed. *Strategic Planning: Selected Readings.* San Diego: Pfeiffer, 1991.

Phillips, N. *From Vision to Beyond Teamwork: 10 Ways to Wake Up and Shake Up Your Company.* Chicago: Irwin, 1995.

Ross, J.E. *Total Quality Management: Text, Cases, Readings.* Delray Beach, FL: St. Lucie Press, 1995.

Rowe, I., et al. *Strategic Management and Business Policy.* Reading, MA: Addison-Wesley, 1985.

Austin, M. "Needs Assessment by Focus Group." No. 9401 (revised 1998).

Chang R.Y. "Continuous Process Improvement." No. 9210 (revised 2000).

Cowan, S.L. "Change Management." No. 9904.

Gilley, J.W. "Strategic Planning for Human Resource Development." No. 9206 (revised 1998).

Patterson, J.G. "Fundamentals of Leadership." No. 9402.

Sparhawk, S., and M. Schickling. "Strategic Needs Analysis." No. 9408 (revised 1998).

Younger, S.M. "How to Develop a Vision." No. 9107 (revised 1999).

Job Aid

The 30-Minute Strategic Plan

By answering the following questions, you will accomplish the steps required to complete a strategic plan. Answers should be from your personal point of view.

I. Mission

A. What is your organization's "business?"

_____

B. Who does your organization serve? (What is your customer base or what group of individuals does your agency serve?)

_____

II. Planning

Scan the remainder of the questions and remember, you only have 30 minutes for the entire exercise!

III. Analysis

Environmental Scan

A. Name one trend in the economy you are pleased or concerned about.

_____

B. Name one political trend you are pleased or concerned about.

_____

C. Name one social trend you think could affect you five years from now.

_____

D. Name one technological trend which could affect you.

_____

SWOT

A. Name one positive attribute (strength) of the organization you work for.

_____

B. Name one negative feature (weakness) of the organization you work for.

_____

Analytical Determination

A. How would you enhance, or contribute to, the strength listed above?

_____

B. How could you mitigate the weakness listed above?

_____

IV. Vision

What one thing would you like to see your organization doing five to 10 years from now?

_____

V. Goals/Objectives

Name one thing that could be done to help your organization meet what you listed in No. IV?

_____

VI. Action Plans

What one step would you take now, if within your ability to do so, to begin No. V?

_____

VII. Performance Tracking

A. Did you finish this task in 30 minutes or less?

☐ Yes ☐ No

B. If yes, how long did it take? _____

C. If no, why did it take you longer?

_____

Congratulations! You have just gone through the thought process required for strategic planning.

212